Fodor's
Sweden

Reprinted from *Fodor's Scandinavia*

Fodor's Travel Publications, Inc.
New York • Toronto • London • Sydney • Auckland

Copyright © 1994
by Fodor's Travel Publications, Inc.

Fodor's is a registered trademark of Fodor's Travel Publications, Inc.

All rights reserved under International and Pan-American Copyright Conventions. Published in the United States by Fodor's Travel Publications, Inc., a subsidiary of Random House, Inc., New York, and simultaneously in Canada by Random House of Canada Limited, Toronto. Distributed by Random House, Inc., New York.

No maps, illustrations, or other portions of this book may be reproduced in any form without written permission from the publishers.

ISBN 0–679–02590–1

Interview with Astrid Lindgren, by Chris Mosey. Reprinted by permission of Chris Mosey. Copyright © by Chris Mosey.

"The Stagestruck King," by Dan Hofstadter. Reprinted by permission of Curtis Brown, Ltd. Copyright © 1989 by Curtis Brown, Ltd.

Fodor's Sweden

Editor: Nancy van Itallie
Contributors: Susan M. Bain, Andrew Collins, Dan Hofstadter, Margaret Hunter, Hilary Jacobs, Laura M. Kidder, Chris Mosey, Brian Owens, Marcy Pritchard, Melanie Roth
Creative Director: Fabrizio La Rocca
Cartographer: David Lindroth
Illustrator: Karl Tanner
Cover Photograph: Bernd Kappelmeyer/FPG International

Design: Vignelli Associates

Special Sales

Fodor's Travel Publications are available at special discounts for bulk purchases for sales promotions or premiums. Special editions, including personalized covers, excerpts of existing guides, and corporate imprints, can be created in large quantities for special needs. For more information contact your local bookseller or write to Special Markets, Fodor's Travel Publications, 201 East 50th Street, New York, NY 10022. Inquiries from Canada should be directed to your local bookseller or sent to Random House of Canada, Ltd., Marketing Department, 1265 Aerowood Drive, Mississauga, Ontario L4W 1B9. Inquiries from the United Kingdom should be sent to Fodor's Travel Publications, 20 Vauxhall Bridge Road, London, England SW1V 2SA.

MANUFACTURED IN THE UNITED STATES OF AMERICA
10 9 8 7 6 5 4 3 2 1

Contents

Maps

Foreword

We would like to express our gratitude to Viveca Nordström of the Swedish Tourist Board in New York City for her valuable assistance during the preparation of this new edition of Fodor's *Sweden*.

While every care has been taken to ensure the accuracy of the information in this guide, the passage of time will always bring change, and consequently the publisher cannot accept responsibility for errors that may occur.

All prices and opening times quoted here are based on information supplied to us at press time. Hours and admission fees may change, however, and the prudent traveler will avoid inconvenience by calling ahead.

Fodor's wants to hear about your travel experiences, both pleasant and unpleasant. When a hotel or restaurant fails to live up to its billing, let us know and we will investigate the complaint and revise our entries where the facts warrant it. Send your letters to the editors of Fodor's Travel Publications, 201 E. 50th Street, New York, NY 10022.

Highlights and Fodor's Choice

Highlights

The 1993 recovery of the dollar in relation to Scandinavian currencies means less expensive travel here for Americans. The dramatic changes in Eastern Europe, the Baltic, and the Commonwealth of Independent States have also brought shifts in prices, new opportunities to combine visits to the two regions, and a greater need to reserve ahead, as travel to and from these countries has become easy and rapid.

Sweden, anticipating increased trade with and travel to and from the continent in the wake of its application for EC membership, started construction in 1993 on an 18-kilometer (13-mile) rail and road bridge across the Öresund, linking the country with Denmark. Good news for travelers in 1993 was the reduction of the value-added tax on accommodations and transportation from 25% to 12% and on food from 25% to 21%. Most hotels and restaurants have responded by keeping their prices down in order to attract budget-minded visitors.

The hotel industry is placing new emphasis on the beauties of the Swedish countryside and historic houses. Two recently formed hotel groups focus on these assets: Scandinavian Mountain Hotels in chalet resorts and CS CountrySide Sweden Hotels in scenic locations around the country.

Skiing, long a major sport for Swedes, has recently become a magnet for visitors as well. Spring downhill skiing at areas such as Åre and Storlien in north central Sweden and summer midnight-sun cross-country treks at Riksgränsen above the Arctic Circle offer distinctively Swedish experiences.

Fodor's Choice

No two people will agree on what makes a perfect vacation, but it can be fun and helpful to know what others think. We hope you'll have a chance to experience some of Fodor's Choices yourself while visiting Sweden. For detailed information on individual entries, see the relevant sections of this guidebook.

Dining

Den Gyldene Freden, Stockholm (*Expensive*)

Kokska Krogen, Malmö (*Expensive*)

Nils Emil, Stockholm (*Moderate*)

Jukkasjärvis Wärdshus och Hembyggdsgård, Jukkasjärvi (*Inexpensive*)

Lodging

Grand Hotel, Stockholm (*Very Expensive*)

Clas på Hörnet, Stockholm (*Expensive*)

Mäster Johan Hotel, Malmö (*Expensive*)

Castles and Churches

Drottningholm Palace, Stockholm

Glimmingehus, Skåne

Läckö Slott, Läckö

Royal Palace, Stockholm

Towns and Villages

Rättvik

Sigtuna

Simrishamn

Visby

Parks and Gardens

Djurgården, Stockholm

Muddus National Park, Norrland

Trädgårdsföreningen, Göteborg

Museums

Millesgården, Stockholm

Vasa Museum, Stockholm

Zorn Museum, Mora

Lakes, Fjords, and Islands

Siljan and Sollerön

Mälaren and Björkö

Special Moments

Dogsledding in Norrland

Eating a Shrove Tuesday bun during Lent

Sailing in the Stockholm archipelago

Scandinavia

KEY

- - - - Ferry

0 ___ 500 miles
0 ___ 750 km

Barents Sea

North Cape
TO SVALBARD

Vardø
Vadsø
Vard
Vadsø
Kirkenes
Hammerfest
Ulsjok
Inari
Ivalo
Alta
Karasjok
Kautokeino
Enontekiö
Kilpisjärvi
Muonio
Kittilä

COMMONWEALTH OF
INDEPENDENT STATES
(RUSSIA)

Ioutsijärvi
Posio
Kuusamo
Suomussalmi
Sodankylä
Kemijärvi
Pudasjärvi
Rovaniemi
Oulu
Raahe
Pulkkila
Oulunjärvi
Kajaani
Nurmes
Pielinen
Otanmäki
Iisalmi
Kärsämäki
Kolari
Kokkola
Kyyjärvi
Nivala
Haapajärvi

Tromsø
Harstad
Narvik
Vestfjorden
LOFOTEN
VESTERÅLEN
Bodø
Fauske

Kiruna
Torniojoki
Torneälv
Tornio
Kemi
Torneå
Kalix
Gällivare
Jokkmokk
SUOMI
(FINLAND)

Gulf of Bothnia

Arctic Circle
Mo i Rana
Arjeplog
Arvidsjaur
Piteå
Skellefteå
Umeå
Sandnessjøen
Mosjøen
Tärnaby
Sorsele
Storuman
Lycksele
Vilhelmina
Ångermanälven
Brønnøysund
Åsele
SVERIGE
(SWEDEN)
Rørvik
Namsos
Steinkjer
Strömsund
Meråker
Trondheim
Kristiansund

Norwegian Sea

ATLANTIC OCEAN

ISLAND (ICELAND)

Arctic Circle
TO ICELAND

Þingeyri
Ísafjörður
Skjálfandi
Siglufjörður
Húnaflói
Raufarhöfn
Bakkaflói
Vesfirðir
Dalvík
Húsavík
Vopnafjörður
Bolafjörður
Blönduós
Tjörnes
Akureyri
Egilsstaðir
Héraðsflói
Stykkishólmur
Búðardalur
Neskaupstaður
Breiðifjörður
Breiðdalsvík
Búðir
Langjökull
Reykholt
Hofsjökull
Vatnajökull
Djúpivogur
Faxaflói
Hveragerði
Mýdals-
jökull
Höfn
Hornafjarðarós
Reykjavik
Hafnarfjörður
Hella
Hvolsvöllur
Fagurhólsmýri
Kirkjubæjarklaustur
Vík
Westmann Islands

TO ICELAND

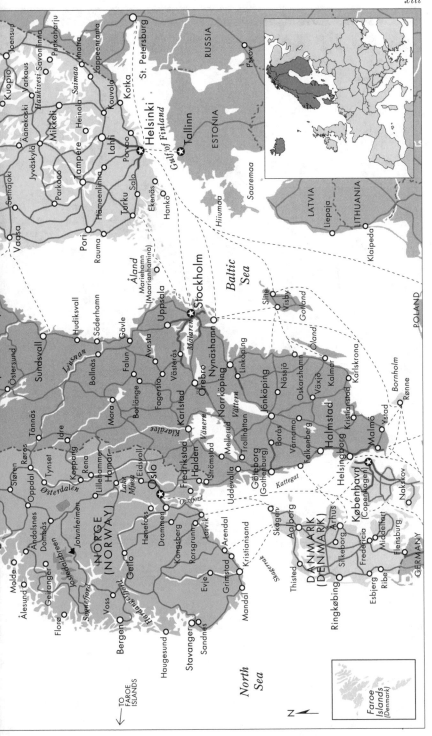

World Time Zones

Numbers below vertical bands relate each zone to Greenwich Mean Time (0 hrs.).
Local times frequently differ from these general indications,
as indicated by light-face numbers on map.

Algiers, **29**	Berlin, **34**	Delhi, **48**	Istanbul, **40**
Anchorage, **3**	Bogotá, **19**	Denver, **8**	Jerusalem, **42**
Athens, **41**	Budapest, **37**	Djakarta, **53**	Johannesburg, **44**
Auckland, **1**	Buenos Aires, **24**	Dublin, **26**	Lima, **20**
Baghdad, **46**	Caracas, **22**	Edmonton, **7**	Lisbon, **28**
Bangkok, **50**	Chicago, **9**	Hong Kong, **56**	London (Greenwich), **27**
Beijing, **54**	Copenhagen, **33**	Honolulu, **2**	Los Angeles, **6**
	Dallas, **10**		Madrid, **38**
			Manila, **57**

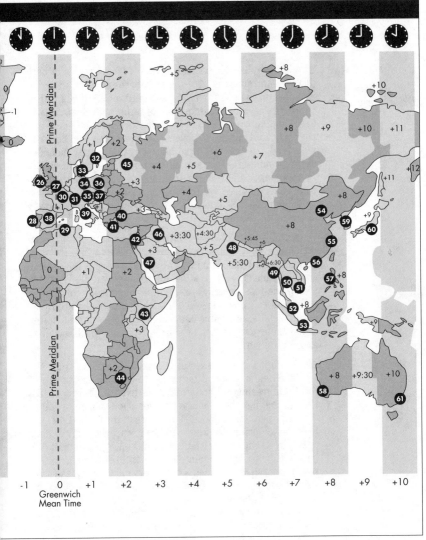

Introduction

By Chris Mosey

*Updated by
Brian Owens*

Sweden requires the visitor to travel far, in terms of both distance and attitude. Approximately the size of California, Sweden reaches as far north as the Arctic fringes of Europe, where glacier-topped mountains and thousands of acres of pine, spruce, and birch forests are broken here and there by wild rivers, countless pristine lakes, and desolate moorland. In the more populated south, roads meander through mile after mile of softly undulating countryside, skirting lakes and passing small villages with their ubiquitous sharp-pointed church spires. Here, the lush forests, which dominate Sweden's northern landscape, have largely fallen to the plow.

Once the dominant power of the region, Sweden has traditionally looked mostly inward, seeking to find its own, Nordic solutions. During the cold war, it tried with considerable success to steer its famous "Middle Way" between the two superpowers, both economically and politically. Its citizens were in effect benignly subjected to a giant social experiment aimed at creating a perfectly just society, one that adopted the best aspects of both socialism and capitalism.

As it slipped into the worst economic recession since the 1930s, Sweden made adjustments that lessened the role of its all-embracing welfare state in the lives of its citizens. Although fragile, the conservative coalition, which defeated the long-incumbent Social Democrats in the fall of 1991, has been attempting to make further cutbacks in welfare spending as the country faces one of the largest budget deficits in Europe. At the same time, an influx of immigrants is reshaping what was once a homogeneous society. As a result, the mostly blond, blue-eyed Swedes may now be more open to the outside world than at any other time in their history. Indeed, another indication of change is Sweden's formal application to join the European Community (EC), a move that represents a radical break with its traditional go-it-alone policies in defense and many other areas of life.

The country possesses stunning natural assets. In the forests, moose, deer, bear, and lynx roam, coexisting with the whine of power saws and the rumble of automatic logging machines as mankind exploits a natural resource that remains the country's economic backbone. Fish abound in sparkling lakes and tumbling rivers, sea eagles and ospreys soar over myriad pine-clad islands in the archipelagoes off the east and west coasts.

The population is thinly spread, with 8.5 million people inhabiting a country 173,731 square miles in area, Europe's fourth largest. If, like Greta Garbo, one of its most famous exports, you want to be alone, you've come to the right place. A law called *Allemansrätt* guarantees public access to the countryside; you'll seldom encounter signs warning NO TRESPASSING.

Sweden stretches 977 miles from the barren, Arctic north to the fertile plains of the south. Contrasts abound, but they are neatly tied together by a superbly efficient infrastructure, embracing air, road, and rail. You can catch salmon in the far north and, thanks to the excellent domestic air network, have it cooked by the chef of your luxury hotel in Stockholm later the same day.

The seasons contrast savagely: Sweden is usually warm and exceedingly light in the summer, then cold and dark in the winter. The sea may freeze, and in the north, iron railway lines may snap.

Sweden is also an arresting mixture of ancient and modern. The countryside is dotted with rune stones recalling its Viking past: trade beginning in the 8th century eastward to Kiev and as far south as Constantinople and the Mediterranean, expansion to the British Isles in the 9th through the 11th century, and settlement in Normandy in the 10th century. Small timbered farmhouses and maypoles around which villagers still dance at Midsummer in their traditional costumes evoke both the pagan early history and the more recent agrarian culture.

Many of the country's cities are sci-fi modern, their shop windows filled with the latest in consumer goods and fashions, but Swedes are reluctant urbanites: Their hearts and souls are in the forests and the archipelagoes, and there they faithfully retreat in the summer and on weekends to take their holidays, pick berries, or just listen to the silence. The skills of the wood-carver, the weaver, the leatherworker, and the glassblower are all highly prized. Similarly, Swedish humor is earthy and slapstick. Despite the praise lavished abroad on introspective dramatic artists such as August Strindberg and Ingmar Bergman, it is the simple trouser-dropping farce that will fill Stockholm's theaters, the scatological joke that will get the most laughs.

Again, despite the international musical success of two Swedish rock groups, Roxette and Abba, the domestic penchant is more often for the good old-fashioned dance band. Gray-haired men in pastel-shaded sweaters playing saxophones are more common on TV than heavy-metal rockers. Strangely, in ultramodern concert halls and discos, it is possible to step back in time to the 1950s, if not the 1940s.

Despite the much-publicized sexual liberation of Swedes, the joys of hearth and home are most prized in what remains in many ways an extremely conservative society. Conformity, not liberty, is the real key to the Swedish character: The good of the collective has always come before that of the individual, and this is why socialism had such a strong appeal here.

At the same time, Swedes remain devoted royalists and patriots, avidly following the fortunes of King Carl XVI Gustaf, Queen Silvia, and their children in the media and raising the blue-and-yellow national flag each morning on the flag poles of their country cottages. Few nations, in fact, take as much effort to preserve and defend their natural heritage. It is sometimes difficult in cities such as Stockholm, Göteborg, or Malmö to realize that you are in an urban area. Right in the center of Stockholm, thanks to a cleanup program in the 1970s, you can fish for salmon or go for a swim. In Göteborg's busy harbor, you can sit aboard a ship bound for the archipelago and watch fish jump out of the water; in Malmö hares hop around in the downtown parks. It is this pristine quality to life that can make a visit to Sweden a step out of time, a relaxing break from the modern world.

Money-Saving Tips

As one of Europe's most expensive and highly taxed countries (Sweden has a 25% value-added tax on consumer products), Sweden does not offer the same bargains and money-saving opportunities that are more typically available in other countries. Nevertheless, with patience, foresight, and a little research, they can be found.

Sweden's three major cities—Stockholm, Göteborg, and Malmö—offer a "key to the city" card that provides not only discounted or unlimited travel on city subways, buses, and rail services, but also free admission to museums, sightseeing trips, and discounted prices at restaurants and shops. For example, the Stockholmskort (Key to Stockholm) costs SKr150 for 24 hours, SKr300 for two days, and SKr450 for three days and entitles you to free transportation and museum entrance. Contact the tourist office in the city you are visiting to find out how to purchase this card.

Transportation

The VAT on transportation has been reduced to 12%. Statens Järnvägar (SJ, the Swedish state railway company) offers the Reslutskort (Desire-to-travel card) which costs SKr150 and entitles the holder to 50% discounts on "red" day fares (less frequently traveled days) and 25% discount on regular fares (Tues.–Thurs. and Sat., tel. 020/757575). SJ has introduced the Nordturistkort, a pass that gives the holder unlimited travel by train throughout Denmark, Finland, Norway, and Sweden for 21 days. It costs SKr1,980 for adults over 25, SKr1,480 for young people ages 12 to 25, and SKr1,000 for children ages 4 to 11. Children under 4 travel free.

Communications

Purchase a Telefonkort (telephone card) from any Telebutik, pressbyrå, or hospital for SKr45 or SKr80, depending on the number of calls you wish to make. The cost per call is much cheaper if you make numerous domestic calls.

Shopping

More than 13,000 shops are part of a tax-free shopping service for visitors. When you buy goods, you are given a voucher for the value-added tax paid on them for which you can obtain a 14%–18% refund when you leave the country. Look for the blue and yellow TAX FREE sign. Cotton-made children's clothes at Hennes & Mauritz, a Swedish department store chain, are priced at a level that is at least on a par with the least expensive U.S. stores, where 100% cotton clothes can be difficult to find.

Dining

The restaurant VAT is 21%, but even the fanciest restaurants have what is called *dagens rätt* (today's special) for lunch, which typically costs SKr60–80 and includes a main dish, a salad, a drink, and a cup of coffee. One of the most common eateries is the Konditori, a cross between a bakery and a café that offers coffee, soft drinks, and sandwiches at reasonable prices. They exist on practically every other street in the cities, towns, and villages of Sweden. *Korv* (sausage), which tastes better than its U.S. counterpart, costs SKr10 at the ubiquitous city hot-dog stands. Ice cream is also a good deal in Sweden, costing as little as SKr10 for a standard yogurt ice-cream cone if you buy it from a kiosk.

Accommodations

The VAT on hotel accommodations has been reduced to 12%. All hotels in Sweden offer as much as 50% off the regular rate on weekends and during the summer. In addition, most of the major hotels provide some kind of discount program. Ask for Reso's Piccolo Card, which costs SKr150 and entitles the holder to a 20% discount on summer rates (June 1–Aug. 31), which are already reduced by 50%. The Scandic Hotel summer check plan enables you to pay for your accommodations in advance, with a weekend check costing SKr550 and a supplement of SKr150 for inner-city hotels. Sweden Hotels offers the Scandinavian Bonus Pass which costs SKr160 and gives discounts of between 15% and 50% during May 15–Oct. 1. Biltur-Logi (Go-as-you-please) is a hotel pass that offers discount rates to some 200 hotels and bed-and-breakfasts through Sweden. With an SKr65 pass, you have a choice of rooms ranging from SKr158 per person for a modest room to SKr198 per person for a room with a bathroom and shower. Contact Biltur-Logi, S-793 Tällberg, Sweden, tel. 0247/509 25, fax 0247/509 25.

1 Essential Information

Before You Go

Government Information Offices

Tourist Information In the United States
Scandinavian Tourist Board, 655 3rd Ave., New York, NY 10017, tel. 212/949–2333, fax 212/983–5260. This is the umbrella organization that includes the **Danish Tourist Board,** the **Finnish Tourist Board,** the **Iceland Tourist Board,** the **Norwegian Tourist Board,** and the **Swedish Travel and Tourism Council.**

In Canada
For information on Sweden, contact the Scandinavian Tourist Board (*see above*).

In the United Kingdom
Swedish Travel and Tourism Council, 73 Welbeck St., London W1M 8AN, tel. 071/487–3135, fax 071/935–5833.

U.S. Government Travel Briefings
The U.S. Department of State's **Citizens Emergency Center** issues Consular Information Sheets, which cover crime, security, and health risks as well as embassy locations, entry requirements, currency regulations, and other routine matters. For the latest information, stop in at any U.S. passport office, consulate, or embassy; call the interactive hotline (tel. 202/647–5225); or, with your PC's modem, tap into the Bureau of Consular Affairs' computer bulletin board (tel. 202/647–9225).

Tours and Packages

Should you buy your travel arrangements to Sweden packaged or do it yourself? There are advantages either way. Buying packaged arrangements saves you money, particularly if you can find a program that includes exactly the features you want. You also get a pretty good idea of what your trip will cost from the outset. Generally, you have two options: fully escorted tours and independent packages. Escorted tours are most often via motorcoach, with a tour director in charge. They're ideal if you don't mind having limited free time and traveling with strangers. Your baggage is handled, your time rigorously scheduled, and most meals planned. Such tours are therefore the most hassle-free way to see a destination, as well as generally the least expensive. Independent packages allow plenty of flexibility. They generally include airline travel and hotels, with certain options available, such as sightseeing, car rental, and excursions. Such packages are usually more expensive than escorted tours, but your time is your own.

While you can book directly through tour operators, you will pay no more to go through a travel agent, who will be able to tell you about tours and packages from a number of operators. Whatever program you ultimately choose, be sure to find out exactly what is included: taxes, tips, transfers, meals, baggage handling, ground transportation, entertainment, excursions, sports or recreation (and rental equipment if necessary). Ask about the level of hotel used, its location, the size of its rooms, the kind of beds, and its amenities, such as pool, room service, or programs for children, if they're important to you. Find out the operator's cancellation penalties. Nearly everyone charges them, and the only way to avoid them is to buy trip-cancellation insurance (*see* Trip Insurance, *below*). Also ask about the single supplement, a surcharge assessed to solo travelers. Some operators do not make you pay it if you agree to be matched up with a roommate of the same sex, even if one is not found by departure time. Remember that a program that has features you won't use, whether for rental sporting equipment or discounted museum admissions, may not be the most cost-wise choice for you.

Fully Escorted Tours   Escorted tours are usually sold in three categories: deluxe, first-class, and tourist or budget class. The most important differences are the price, of course, and the level of accommodations. Some operators specialize in one category, while others offer a range.

For tours in Scandinavia that include Sweden, contact **Maupintour** (Box 807, Lawrence, KS 66044, tel. 800/255–4266 or 913/843–1211), **Tauck Tours** (11 Wilton Rd., Westport, CT 06881, tel. 203/226–6911), and **Abercrombie & Kent** (1520 Kensington Rd., Oak Brook, IL 60521, tel. 800/325–7308 or 708/954–2944) in the deluxe category; **American Airlines Fly AAway Vacations** (tel. 800/321–2121), **Bennett Tours** (270 Madison Ave., New York, NY 10016, tel. 800/221–2420 or 212/532–5060), **British Airways** (tel. 800/247–9297), **Caravan Tours** (401 N. Michigan Ave., Chicago, IL 60611, tel. 800/227–2826 or 312/321–9800), **Continental Airlines' Grand Destinations** (tel. 800/634–5555), **Delta Dream Vacations** (tel. 800/872–7786), **Gadabout Tours** (700 E. Tahquitz Way, Palm Springs, CA 92262, tel. 800/952–5068 or 619/325–5556), **Globus** (95–25 Queens Blvd., Rego Park, NY 11374, tel. 800/221–0090), **SAS** (tel. 800/221–2350, press "3" for tour desk), and **Trafalgar Tours** (21 E. 26th St., New York, NY 10010, tel. 800/854–0103 or 212/689–8977) in the first-class category; and **Cosmos,** a sister company of Globus (*see above*), in the budget category.

Contact **Bennett Tours** (*see above*; winter only) and **Scantours** (1535 6th St., Suite 205, Santa Monica, CA 90401, tel. 310/451–0911 or 800/223–7226) for escorted tour packages to Sweden only.

Most itineraries are jam-packed with sightseeing, so you see a lot in a short amount of time (usually one place per day). To judge just how fast-paced the tour is, review the itinerary carefully. If you are in a different hotel each night, you will be getting up early each day to head out, travel to your next destination, do some sightseeing, have dinner, and go to bed; then you'll start all over again. If you want some free time, make sure it's mentioned in the tour brochure; if you want to be escorted to every meal, confirm that any tour you consider does that. Also, when comparing programs, be sure to find out if the motorcoach is air-conditioned and has a restroom on board. Make your selection based on price and stops on the itinerary.

Independent Packages   Independent packages, which travel agents call FITs (for foreign independent travel), are offered by airlines, tour operators who may also do escorted programs, and any number of other companies from large, established firms to small, new entrepreneurs.

All the airlines listed above (**American, Delta, Continental, British Airways,** and **SAS**) offer independent packages. Other operators include **Bennett Tours** (*see above*), **Gadabout Tours** (*see above*), and **Travel Bound** (599 Broadway, Penthouse, New York, NY 10012, tel. 800/456–8656 or 212/334–1350).

For independent packages to Sweden only, contact **KITT Holidays/Kirstensen International** (2 Apple Tree Sq., Suite 150, Minneapolis, MN 55425, tel. 612/854–8005 or 800/262–8728), **Scanam World Tours** (933 Highway 23, Pompton Plains, NJ 07444, tel. 800/545–2204), **Scantours** (*see above*), and **Scan Travel Center** (66 Edgewood Ave., Larchmont, NY 10538, tel. 914/834–3944 or 800/759–7226).

Their programs come in a wide range of prices based on levels of luxury and options—in addition to hotel and airfare, sightseeing, car rental, transfers, admission to local attractions, and other extras. Note that when pricing different packages, it sometimes pays to purchase the same arrangements separately, as when a rock-bottom promotional airfare is being offered, for example. Again, base your choice on what's available at your budget for the destinations you want to visit.

Special-Interest Travel Special-interest programs may be fully escorted or independent. Some require a certain amount of expertise, but most are for the average traveler with an interest and are usually hosted by experts in the subject matter. When the program is escorted, it enjoys the advantages and disadvantages of all escorted programs; because your fellow travelers are apt to be passionate or knowledgeable about the subject, they can prove as enjoyable a part of your travel experience as the destination itself. The price range is wide, but the cost is usually higher—sometimes a lot higher—than for ordinary escorted tours and packages, because of the expert guiding and special activities.

Outdoor Adventure **Borton Overseas** (5516 Lyndale Ave. S, Minneapolis, MN 55419, tel. 612/824–4415 or 800/843–0602) and **Scanam World Tours** (*see above*) can arrange hiking, skiing, and other outdoor adventure tours in Sweden.

Heritage **KITT Holidays, Scanam World Tours,** and **Scan Travel Center** (*see above*) all handle tours for people who want to trace their roots in Sweden.

When to Go

The best time to visit Sweden is in summer, from mid-May through August, when temperatures are usually high and the days exceptionally long. However, remember to pack some warm and rainproof clothing, just in case. The winters are usually long, dark, and hard, the country covered with snow and ice. January is too dark for skiing, but in February the days start to lengthen and the trails are in prime condition. A word of warning: Temperatures will be far lower than those of central Europe. The following are average daily maximum and minimum temperatures for Stockholm.

Jan.	30F	−1C	May	57F	14C	Sept.	59F	15C
	23	−5		43	6		48	9
Feb.	30F	−1C	June	66F	19C	Oct.	48F	9C
	23	−5		52	11		41	5
Mar.	37F	3C	July	72F	22C	Nov.	41F	5C
	25	−4		57	14		34	1
Apr.	46F	8C	Aug.	68F	20C	Dec.	36F	2C
	34	1		55	13		28	− 2

Climate
Information Sources For current weather conditions for cities in the United States and abroad, plus the local time and helpful travel tips, call the

Weather Channel Connection (tel. 900/932–8437; 95¢ per minute) from a touch-tone phone.

Festivals and Seasonal Events

January 13: Knut signals the end of Christmas festivities and "plundering" of the Christmas tree: Trinkets are removed from the tree, edible ornaments eaten, and the tree itself thrown out.

February (first Thursday, Friday, and Saturday): A **market** held in the small town of Jokkmokk, above the Arctic Circle, features both traditional Lapp artifacts and plenty of reindeer.

Shrove Tuesday: Special buns called *semlor* are eaten; lightly flavored with cardamom, filled with almond paste and whipped cream, they are traditionally placed in a dish of warm milk and topped with cinnamon.

March (first Sunday): The **Vasaloppet 55-mile ski race** from Sälen to Mora in Dalarna attracts entrants from all over the world.

Maunday Thursday: Small girls dress up as witches and hand out "Easter letters" for small change. *Päskris,* twigs tipped with brightly colored chicken feathers, decorate homes.

April 30: For the **Feast of Valborg,** bonfires are lit to celebrate the end of winter. The liveliest celebrations involve the students of the university city of Uppsala, 60 kilometers (37 miles) north of Stockholm.

May 1: Labor Day marches and rallies are held nationwide.

June 6: National Day is celebrated, with parades, speeches, and band concerts nationwide.

June: Midsummer's Day celebrations are held on the Saturday that falls between June 20 and 26. Swedes decorate their homes with flower garlands, raise maypoles, and dance around them to folk music.

August 5–13: Stockholm Water Festival celebrates the city's clean water environment with water-sports performances, a crayfish party, a fireworks competition, and 1,500 other events next to the Royal Palace.

August (second Wednesday): Crayfish are considered a delicacy in Sweden, and on this day, the **Crayfish premiere,** friends gather to eat them at outdoor parties.

November 11: St. Martin's Day is celebrated primarily in the southern province of Skåne. Roast goose is served, accompanied by *svartsoppa,* a bisque made of goose blood and spices.

December: For each of the four weeks of **Advent,** leading up to Christmas, a candle is lit in a four-pronged candelabra.

December 10: Nobel Day sees the presentation of the Nobel prizes by King Carl XVI Gustaf at a glittering banquet held in the Stockholm City Hall.

December 13: On **Santa Lucia Day** young girls (preferably blondes) are selected to be "Lucias," and wear candles (today usually electric substitutes) in their hair and sing hymns along with their handmaidens and "stablelads" at ceremonies around the country.

December 24: Christmas Eve is the principal day of Christmas celebration. Traditional Christmas dishes include ham, rice porridge, and *lutfisk* (ling that is dried and then boiled).

What to Pack

Pack light, then take half of what you thought you needed and leave it at home as well. A light suitcase with wheels is a real joy, as porters are usually difficult to find and baggage restrictions are tight on international flights. Be sure to check your airline's policy before you pack. Make sure, too, to leave room for the bulky sweaters, furs, and crystal that you may bring home from Scandinavian shops.

Clothing Don't forget to bring a bathing suit even in winter, as many hotels have pools and in Iceland, the volcanic springs are particularly delightful then. Also bring a warm sweater, socks, and slacks during summer. Fresh summer days become cool evenings, and the wind is often brisk, particularly on the water, if you plan to travel by boat.

Take a folding umbrella, but be prepared for gusty winds that can destroy even the sturdiest. Take a lightweight raincoat too as it can double as a windbreaker. You will probably find yourself taking them with you every day, everywhere you go, as it is common for the sky to be clear at 9 AM, rainy at 11 AM, and clear again in time for lunch. Don't forget that your feet get wet, as well: an extra pair of walking shoes that dry quickly will come in handy. Except in summer, you'll be glad to have waterproof boots to keep you cozy.

Perhaps because of the climate, Scandinavians tend to be practical and resilient, and fashion follows suit. Slacks and comfortable shoes are almost always acceptable attire, but don't forget to bring one nice outfit for your visit to a fancy Stockholm restaurant.

Miscellaneous If you can't sleep when it is light and you are traveling during summer, bring a comfortable eye-mask, so you won't wake up automatically at the 4 AM sunrise.

Bug repellent is a good idea if you plan to venture away from the capital cities. Large mosquitoes can be a real nuisance on summer evenings in the far northern reaches of Sweden.

Because of the far northern latitude, the sun slants at angles unseen elsewhere on the globe, and a pair of dark sunglasses can prevent eyestrain if, for example, you're unlucky enough to drive westward at sundown. Sunscreen is less a requirement here than in most places but can nonetheless be a good idea during summer and for winter skiing.

Bring an extra pair of eyeglasses or contact lenses. If you have a health problem that may require you to purchase a prescription drug, pack enough to last the duration of the trip, or have your doctor write a prescription using the drug's generic name, since brand names vary from country to country. And don't forget to pack a list of the addresses of offices that supply refunds for lost or stolen traveler's checks.

Electricity The electrical current in Scandinavia is 220 volts, 50 cycles alternating current (AC); the United States runs on 110-volt, 60-cycle AC current. Unlike wall outlets in the United States, which accept plugs with two flat prongs, outlets in Scandinavia take plugs with two round prongs.

Adapters, To plug in U.S.-made appliances abroad, you'll need an adapter
Converters, plug. To reduce the voltage entering the appliance from 220 to
Transformers 110 volts, you'll also need a converter, unless it is a dual-voltage
appliance, made for travel. There are converters for high-watt-
age appliances (such as hair dryers), low-wattage items (such
as electric toothbrushes and razors), and combination models.
Hotels sometimes have outlets marked "For Shavers Only"
near the sink; these are 110-volt outlets for low-wattage appliances; don't use them for a high-wattage appliance. If you're
traveling with a laptop computer, especially an older one, you
may need a transformer—a type of converter used with
electronic-circuitry products. Newer laptop computers are
auto-sensing, operating equally well on 110 and 220 volts (so
you need only the appropriate adapter plug). When in doubt,
consult your appliance's owner's manual or the manufacturer.
Or get a copy of the free brochure "Foreign Electricity is No
Deep Dark Secret," published by adapter-converter manufacturer Franzus (Murtha Industrial Park, Box 142, Beacon Falls,
CT 06403, tel. 203/723–6664; send a stamped, self-addressed
envelope when ordering).

Luggage Free baggage allowances on an airline depend on the airline,
Regulations the route, and the class of your ticket. In general, on domestic
flights and on international flights to or from the United States,
you are entitled to check two bags—neither exceeding 62
inches, or 158 centimeters (length + width + height), or weigh-
ing more than 70 pounds (32 kilograms). A third piece may be
brought aboard as a carryon; its total dimensions are generally
limited to less than 45 inches (114 centimeters), so it will fit easily under the seat in front of you or in the overhead compartment. There are variations, so ask in advance. The single rule,
a Federal Aviation Administration safety regulation that per-
tains to carry-on baggage on U.S. airlines, requires that
carryons be properly stowed and allows the airline to limit allowances and tailor them to different aircraft and operational
conditions. Charges for excess, oversize, or overweight pieces
vary, so inquire before you pack.

If you are flying between two foreign destinations, note that
baggage allowances may be determined not by piece but by
weight, which generally allows 88 pounds (40 kilograms) of luggage in first class, 66 pounds (30 kilograms) in business class,
and 44 pounds (20 kilograms) in economy. If your flight between two cities abroad *connects* with your transatlantic or
transpacific flight, the piece method still applies.

Safeguarding Your Before leaving home, itemize your bags' contents and their
Luggage worth; this list will help you estimate the extent of your loss if
your bags go astray. To minimize that risk, tag them inside and
out with your name, address, and phone number. (If you use
your home address, cover it so that potential thieves can't see
it.) At check-in, make sure that the tag attached by baggage
handlers bears the correct three-letter code for your destination. If your bags do not arrive with you, or if you detect damage, do not leave the airport until you've filed a written report
with the airline.

Taking Money Abroad

Traveler's Checks Although you will want plenty of cash when visiting small cities
or rural areas, traveler's checks are usually preferable. The

most widely recognized are **American Express, Barclay's, Thomas Cook,** and those issued by major commercial banks such as **Citibank** and **Bank of America.** American Express also issues *Traveler's Cheques for Two*, which can be counter-signed and used by you or your traveling companion. Some checks are free; usually the issuing company or the bank at which you make your purchase charges 1% of the checks' face value as a fee. Be sure to buy a few checks in small denominations to cash toward the end of your trip, when you don't want to be left with more foreign currency than you can spend. Always record the numbers of checks as you spend them, and keep this list separate from the checks.

Currency Exchange Banks and bank-operated exchange booths at airports and railroad stations are usually the best places to change money. Hotels, stores, and privately run exchange firms typically offer less favorable rates.

Before your trip, pay attention to how the dollar is doing vis-à-vis Swedish currency. If the dollar is losing strength, try to pay as many travel bills as possible in advance, especially the big ones. If it is getting stronger, pay for costly items overseas, and use your credit card whenever possible—you'll come out ahead, whether the exchange rate at which your purchase is calculated is the one in effect the day the vendor's bank abroad processes the charge, or the one prevailing on the day the charge company's service center processes it at home.

To avoid lines at airport currency-exchange booths, arrive in Sweden with a small amount of the local currency already in your pocket—a so-called tip pack. **Thomas Cook Currency Services** (630 5th Ave., New York, NY 10111, tel. 212/757–6915) supplies foreign currency by mail.

Getting Money from Home

Cash Machines Automated-teller machines (ATMs) are proliferating; many are tied to international networks such as **Cirrus** and **Plus.** You can use your bank card at ATMs away from home to withdraw money from an account and get cash advances on a credit-card account (providing your card has been programmed with a personal identification number, or PIN). Check in advance on limits on withdrawals and cash advances within specified periods. Ask whether your bank-card or credit-card PIN number will need to be reprogrammed for use in the area you'll be visiting—a possibility if the number has more than four digits. Remember that on cash advances you are charged interest from the day you get the money from ATMs as well as from tellers. And note that, although transaction fees for ATM withdrawals abroad will probably be higher than fees for withdrawals at home, Cirrus and Plus exchange rates tend to be good.

Be sure to plan ahead: Obtain ATM locations and the names of affiliated cash-machine networks before departure. For specific foreign Cirrus locations, call 800/424–7787; for foreign Plus locations, consult the Plus directory at your local bank.

American Express Cardholder Services The company's **Express Cash** system lets you withdraw cash and/or traveler's checks from a worldwide network of 57,000 American Express dispensers and participating bank ATMs. You must *enroll first* (call 800/227–4669 for a form and allow two weeks for processing). Withdrawals are charged not to your card but to a designated bank account. You can withdraw up to $1,000 per seven-day period on the basic card, more if your card is gold or platinum. There is a 2% fee (minimum $2.50, maximum $10) for each cash transaction, and a 1% fee for traveler's checks (except for the platinum card), which are available only from American Express dispensers.

At AmEx offices, cardholders can also cash personal checks for up to $1,000 in any seven-day period (21 days abroad); of this $200 can be in cash, more if available, with the balance paid in traveler's checks, for which all but platinum cardholders pay a 1% fee. Higher limits apply to the gold and platinum cards.

Wiring Money You don't have to be a cardholder to send or receive an **American Express MoneyGram** for up to $10,000. To send one, go to an American Express MoneyGram agent, pay up to $1,000 with a credit card and anything over that in cash, and phone a transaction reference number to your intended recipient, who needs only present identification and the reference number to the nearest MoneyGram agent to pick up the cash. There are MoneyGram agents in more than 60 countries (call 800/543–4080 for locations). Fees range from 5% to 10%, depending on the amount and how you pay. You can't use American Express, which is really a convenience card—only Discover, MasterCard, and Visa credit cards.

You can also use **Western Union.** To wire money, take either cash or a check to the nearest office. (Or you can call and use a credit card.) Fees are roughly 5%–10%. Money sent from the United States or Canada will be available for pick up at agent locations in Scandinavia within minutes. (Note that once the money is in the system it can be picked up at *any* location. You don't have to miss your train waiting for it to arrive in City A, because if there's an agent in City B, where you're headed, you can pick it up there, too.) There are approximately 20,000 agents worldwide (call 800/325–6000 for locations).

Swedish Currency

The unit of currency is the krona (plural kronor), which is divided into 100 öre and is written as SKr. There are 50-öre, SKr1, and SKr10 coins. Bank notes are at present: SKr20, 50, 100, 500, and 1,000. At press time (fall 1993), the exchange rate was 7.75 to the dollar, 12.15 to the pound, and 5.70 to the Canadian dollar.

Bank Cards

There is an American Express cash and traveler's check dispenser at Arlanda, Stockholm's international airport, and outside the American Express office at Birger Jarlsgatan 1, Stockholm. The 1,000 or so blue Bankomat cash dispensers nationwide have been adapted to take some foreign cards. For more information, contact Bankomat Centralen, tel. 08/7257240.

What It Will Cost

The short answer is a lot! Special tourist rates usually apply in the summer and most of the major hotel chains give discounts. For details, contact any of the Swedish hotel chains or your travel agent. Some sample prices: cup of coffee, SKr16; strong beer, SKr38–SKr55; mineral water, SKr10–SKr17; cheese roll, SKr16; pepper steak, à la carte, SKr120–SKr160; cheeseburger, SKr30; pizza, starting at SKr32.

Passports and Visas

If your passport is lost or stolen abroad, report it immediately to the nearest embassy or consulate and to the local police. If you can provide the consular officer with the information contained in the passport, he or she will usually be able to issue you a new passport. For this reason, it is a good idea to keep a copy of the data page of your passport in a separate place, or to leave the passport number, date, and place of issuance with a relative or friend at home.

U.S. Citizens All U.S. citizens, even infants, need a valid passport to enter Sweden for stays of up to three months. Note that this three-month period is calculated from the time you enter *any* Scandinavian country. You can pick up new and renewal application forms at any of the 13 U.S. Passport Agency offices and at some post offices and courthouses. Although passports are usually mailed within two weeks of your application's receipt, it's best to allow three weeks for delivery in low season, five weeks or more from April through summer. Call the Department of State Office of Passport Services' information line (1425 K St. NW, Washington, DC 20522, tel. 202/647–0518) for fees, documentation requirements, and other details.

Canadian Citizens Canadian citizens need a valid passport to enter Sweden for stays of up to three months. Note that this three-month period is calculated from the time you enter *any* Scandinavian country. Application forms are available at 23 regional passport offices as well as post offices and travel agencies. Whether applying for a first or subsequent passport, you must apply in person. Children under 16 may be included on a parent's passport but must have their own passport to travel alone. Passports are valid for five years and are usually mailed within two weeks of an application's receipt. For fees, documentation requirements, and other information in English or French, call the passport office (tel. 514/283–2152).

U.K. Citizens Citizens of the United Kingdom need a valid passport to enter Sweden for stays of up to three months. Applications for new and renewal passports are available from main post offices as well as at the six passport offices, located in Belfast, Glasgow, Liverpool, London, Newport, and Peterborough. You may apply in person at all passport offices, or by mail to all except the London office. Children under 16 may travel on a parent's passport when accompanying them. All passports are valid for 10 years. Allow a month for processing.

A British Visitor's Passport is valid for holidays and some business trips of up to three months to Scandinavia. It can include both partners of a married couple. Valid for one year, it will be issued on the same day that you apply. You must apply in person at a main post office.

Customs and Duties

On Arrival Tourists entering Sweden are allowed to bring with them duty-free one liter of spirits, one liter of wine (includes aperitifs), and two liters of strong beer (exceeding 2.8% alcohol by weight). Travelers from Europe may bring in 200 cigarettes or 250 grams of other tobacco products. Other travelers are allowed to bring in 400 cigarettes or 500 grams of other tobacco products duty-free.

Returning Home   Provided you've been out of the country for at least 48 hours
U.S. Customs   and haven't already used the exemption, or any part of it, in the past 30 days, you may bring home $400 worth of foreign goods duty-free. So can each member of your family, regardless of age; and your exemptions may be pooled, so one of you can bring in more if another brings in less. A flat 10% duty applies to the next $1,000 worth of goods; above $1,400, the rate varies with the merchandise. (If the 48-hour or 30-day limits apply, your duty-free allowance drops to $25, which may not be pooled.)

Travelers 21 or older may bring back 1 liter of alcohol duty-free, provided the beverage laws of the state through which they reenter the United States allow it. In addition, 100 non-Cuban cigars and 200 cigarettes are allowed, regardless of your age. Antiques and works of art more than 100 years old are duty-free.

Gifts valued at less than $50 may be mailed duty-free to stateside friends and relatives, with a limit of one package per day per addressee (do not send alcohol or tobacco products, nor perfume valued at more than $5). These gifts do not count as part of your exemption, unless you bring them home with you. Mark the package "Unsolicited Gift" and include the nature of the gift and its retail value.

For a copy of "Know Before You Go," a free brochure detailing what you may and may not bring back to the United States, rates of duty, and other pointers, contact the **U.S. Customs Service** (Box 7407, Washington, DC 20044, tel. 202/927–6724).

Canadian Customs   Once per calendar year, when you've been out of Canada for at least seven days, you may bring in $300 worth of goods duty-free. If you've been away less than seven days but more than 48 hours, the duty-free exemption drops to $100 but can be claimed any number of times (as can a $20 duty-free exemption for absences of 24 hours or more). You cannot combine the yearly and 48-hour exemptions, use the $300 exemption only partially (to save the balance for a later trip), or pool exemptions with family members. Goods claimed under the $300 exemption may follow you by mail; those claimed under the lesser exemptions must accompany you on your return.

Alcohol and tobacco products may be included in the yearly and 48-hour exemptions but not in the 24-hour exemption. If you meet the age requirements of the province through which you reenter Canada, you may bring in, duty-free, 1.14 liters (40 imperial ounces) of wine or liquor *or* two dozen 12-ounce cans or bottles of beer or ale. If you are 16 or older, you may bring in, duty-free, 200 cigarettes, 50 cigars or cigarillos, and 400 tobacco sticks or 400 grams of manufactured tobacco. Alcohol and tobacco must accompany you on your return.

Gifts may be mailed to friends in Canada duty-free. These do not count as part of your exemption. Each gift may be worth up to $60—label the package "Unsolicited Gift—Value under $60." There are no limits on the number of gifts that may be sent per day or per addressee, but you can't mail alcohol or tobacco.

For more information, including details of duties on items that exceed your duty-free limit, ask the Revenue Canada Customs and Excise Department (Connaught Bldg., MacKenzie Ave., Ottawa, Ont., K1A OL5, tel. 613/957–0275) for a copy of the free brochure "I Declare/Je Déclare."

U.K. Customs If your journey was wholly within EC countries, you no longer need to pass through customs when you return to the United Kingdom. According to EC guidelines, you may bring in 800 cigarettes, 400 cigarillos, 200 cigars, and 1 kilogram of smoking tobacco, plus 10 liters of spirits, 20 liters of fortified wine, 90 liters of wine, and 110 liters of beer. If you exceed these limits, you may be required to prove that the goods are for your personal use or are gifts.

From countries outside the EC, you may import duty-free 200 cigarettes, 100 cigarillos, 50 cigars or 250 grams of tobacco; 1 liter of spirits or 2 liters of fortified or sparkling wine; 2 liters of still table wine; 60 millileters of perfume; 250 millileters of toilet water; plus £36 worth of other goods, including gifts and souvenirs.

For further information or a copy of "A Guide for Travellers," which details standard customs procedures as well as what you may bring into the United Kingdom from abroad, contact HM Customs and Excise (New King's Beam House, 22 Upper Ground, London SE1 9PJ, tel. 071/620–1313).

Traveling with Cameras, Camcorders, and Laptops

Film and Cameras If your camera is new or if you haven't used it for a while, shoot and develop a few rolls of film before leaving home. Pack some lens tissue and an extra battery for your built-in light meter, and invest in an inexpensive skylight filter, to both protect your lens and provide some definition in hazy shots. Store film in a cool, dry place—never in the car's glove compartment or on the shelf under the rear window.

Films above ISO 400 are more sensitive to damage from airport security X-rays than others; very high speed films, ISO 1,000 and above, are exceedingly vulnerable. To protect your film, don't put it in checked luggage; carry it with you in a plastic bag and ask for a hand inspection. Such requests are honored at American airports, up to the inspector abroad. Don't depend on a lead-lined bag to protect film in checked luggage—the airline may very well turn up the dosage of radiation to see what you've got in there. Airport metal detectors do not harm film, although you'll set off the alarm if you walk through one with a roll in your pocket. Call the Kodak Information Center (tel. 800/242–2424) for details.

Camcorders Before your trip, put new or long-unused camcorders through their paces, and practice panning and zooming. Invest in a skylight filter to protect the lens, and check the lithium battery that lights up the LCD (liquid crystal display) modes. As for the rechargeable nickel-cadmium batteries that are the camera's power source, take along an extra pair, so while you're using your camcorder you'll have one battery ready and another recharging. Most newer camcorders are equipped with the battery (which generally slides or clicks onto the camera body) and, to recharge it, with what's known as a universal or world-wide AC adapter charger (or multivoltage converter) that can be used whether the voltage is 110 or 220. All that's needed is the appropriate plug.

Videotape Unlike still-camera film, videotape is not damaged by X-rays. However, it may well be harmed by the magnetic field of a walk-through metal detector. Airport security personnel may want you to turn the camcorder on to prove that that's what it is, so make sure the battery is charged when you get to the airport. Note that although the United States, Canada, Japan, Korea, Taiwan, and other countries operate on the National Television System Committee video standard (NTSC), Scandinavia uses PAL technology. So you will not be able to view your tapes through the local TV set or view movies bought there in your home VCR. Blank tapes bought in Scandinavia can be used for NTSC camcorder taping, however—although you'll probably find they cost more abroad and wish you'd brought an adequate supply along.

Laptops Security X-rays do not harm hard-disk or floppy-disk storage. Most airlines allow you to use your laptop aloft but request that you turn it off during takeoff and landing so as not to interfere with navigation equipment. Make sure the battery is charged when you arrive at the airport, because you may be asked to turn on the computer at security checkpoints to prove that it is what it appears to be. If you're a heavy computer user, consider traveling with a backup battery. For international travel, register your laptop with U.S. Customs as you leave the country, providing it's manufactured abroad (U.S.-origin items cannot be registered at U.S. Customs); when you do so, you'll get a certificate, good for as long as you own the item, containing your name and address, a description of the laptop, and its serial number, that will quash any questions that may arise on your return. If your laptop is U.S.-made, call the consulate of the country you'll be visiting to find out whether it should be registered with customs in that country upon arrival. Some travelers do this as a matter of course and ask customs officers to sign a document that specifies the total configuration of the system, computer and peripherals, and its value. In addition, before leaving home, find out about repair facilities at your destination, and don't forget any transformer or adapter plug you may need (*see* Electricity, *above*).

Language

Swedish derives primarily from German. After "z," the Swedish alphabet has three extra letters: the Swedish "ö," pronounced somewhat like the "oo" in "goop," but with a bit more r-sound to it; "ä," which sounds like the "a" in "cat"; and the "å," which sounds like the "o" in "ghost." The important thing about these characters isn't that you pronounce them correctly—foreigners usually can't—but that you know to find them in the phone book at the very end. Mr. Sören Åstrup, for example, will be found after "Z." Ä and Ö follow. Most Swedes speak English.

Staying Healthy

If necessary, many clinics in Sweden will write a prescription for you free of charge, which you can pick up at a nearby *apotek* (drug store), often at subsidized prices.

Finding a Doctor The **International Association for Medical Assistance to Travellers** (IAMAT, 417 Center St., Lewiston, NY 14092, tel. 716/ 754–4883; 40 Regal Rd., Guelph, Ontario N1K 1B5; 57 Voirets, 1212 Grand-Lancy, Geneva, Switzerland) publishes a worldwide directory of English-speaking physicians whose qualifications meet IAMAT standards and who have agreed to treat members for a set fee. Membership is free.

Assistance Companies Pretrip medical referrals, emergency evacuation or repatriation, 24-hour telephone hot lines for medical consultation, dispatch of medical personnel, relay of medical records, up-front cash for emergencies, and other personal and legal assistance are among the services provided by several membership organizations specializing in medical assistance to travelers. Among them are **International SOS Assistance** (Box 11568, Philadelphia, PA 19116, tel. 215/244–1500 or 800/523–8930; Box 466, Pl. Bonaventure, Montréal, Qué. H5A 1C1, tel. 514/874– 7674 or 800/363–0263), **Near Services** (450 Prairie Ave., Suite 101, Calumet City, IL 60409, tel. 708/868–6700 or 800/654– 6700), and **Travel Assistance International** (1133 15th St. NW, Suite 400, Washington, DC 20005, tel. 202/331–1609 or 800/ 821–2828), part of Europ Assistance Worldwide Services, Inc. Because these companies will also sell you death-and-dismemberment, trip-cancellation, and other insurance coverage, there is some overlap with the travel-insurance policies discussed below, which may include the services of an assistance company among the insurance options or reimburse travelers for such services without providing them.

Insurance

For U.S. Residents Most tour operators, travel agents, and insurance agents sell specialized health-and-accident, flight, trip-cancellation, and luggage insurance as well as comprehensive policies with some or all of these features. But before you make any purchase, review your existing health and homeowner policies to find out whether they cover expenses incurred while travelling.

Health-and-Accident Insurance Supplemental health-and-accident insurance for travelers is usually a part of comprehensive policies. Specific policy provisions vary, but they tend to address three general areas, beginning with reimbursement for medical expenses caused by illness or an accident during a trip. Such policies may reimburse anywhere from $1,000 to $150,000 worth of medical expenses; dental benefits may also be included. A second common feature is the personal-accident, or death-and-dismemberment, provision, which pays a lump sum to your beneficiaries if your die or to you if you lose one or both limbs or your eyesight. This is similar to the flight insurance described below, although it is not necessarily limited to accidents involving airplanes or even other "common carriers" (buses, trains, and ships) and can be in effect 24 hours a day. The lump sum awarded can range from $15,000 to $500,000. A third area generally addressed by these policies is medical assistance (referrals, evacuation, or repatriation and other services). Some policies reimburse travelers for the cost of such services; others may automatically enroll you as a member of a particular medical-assistance company.

Flight Insurance This insurance, often bought as a last-minute impulse at the airport, pays a lump sum to a beneficiary when a plane crashes and the insured dies (and sometimes to a surviving passenger who loses eyesight or a limb); thus it supplements the airlines' own coverage as described in the limits-of-liability paragraphs on your ticket (up to $75,000 on international flights, $20,000 on domestic ones—and that is generally subject to litigation). Charging an airline ticket to a major credit card often automatically signs you up for flight insurance; in this case, the coverage may also embrace travel by bus, train, and ship.

Baggage Insurance In the event of loss, damage, or theft on international flights, airlines limit their liability to $20 per kilogram for checked baggage (roughly about $640 per 70-pound bag) and $400 per passenger for unchecked baggage. On domestic flights, the ceiling is $1,250 per passenger. Excess-valuation insurance can be bought directly from the airline at check-in but leaves your bags vulnerable on the ground.

Trip Insurance There are two sides to this coin. **Trip-cancellation-and-interruption insurance** protects you in the event you are unable to undertake or finish your trip. **Default** or **bankruptcy insurance** protects you against a supplier's failure to deliver. Consider the former if your airline ticket, cruise, or package tour does not allow changes or cancellations. The amount of coverage to buy should equal the cost of your trip should you, a traveling companion, or a family member get sick, forcing you to stay home, plus the nondiscounted one-way airline ticket you would need to buy if you had to return home early. Read the fine print carefully; pay attention to sections defining "family member" and "preexisting medical conditions." A characteristic quirk of default policies is that they often do not cover default by travel agencies or default by a tour operator, airline, or cruise line if you bought your tour and the coverage directly from the firm in question. To reduce your need for default insurance, give preference to tours packaged by members of the United States Tour Operators Association (USTOA), which maintains a fund to reimburse clients in the event of member defaults. Even better, pay for travel arrangements with a major credit card, so that you can refuse to pay the bill if services have not been rendered—and let the card company fight your battles.

Comprehensive Policies Companies supplying comprehensive policies with some or all of the above features include **Access America, Inc.,** underwritten by BCS Insurance Company (Box 11188, Richmond, VA 23230, tel. 800/284–8300); **Carefree Travel Insurance,** underwritten by The Hartford (Box 310, 120 Mineola Blvd., Mineola, NY 11501, tel. 516/294–0220 or 800/323–3149); **Tele-Trip** (Mutual of Omaha Plaza, Box 31762, Omaha, NE 68131, tel. 800/228–9792), a subsidiary of Mutual of Omaha; **The Travelers Companies** (1 Tower Sq., Hartford, CT 06183, tel. 203/277–0111 or 800/243–3174); **Travel Guard International,** underwritten by Transamerica Occidental Life Companies (1145 Clark St., Stevens Point, WI 54481, tel. 715/345–0505 or 800/782–5151); and **Wallach and Company, Inc.** (107 W. Federal St., Box 480, Middleburg, VA 22117, tel. 703/687–3166 or 800/237–6615), underwritten by Lloyds, London. These companies may also offer the above types of insurance separately.

For U.K. Residents Most tour operators, travel agents, and insurance agents sell specialized policies covering accident, medical expenses, personal liability, trip cancellation, and loss or theft of personal property. Some policies include coverage for delayed departure and legal expenses, winter-sports, motoring abroad, or their accidents. You can also purchase an annual travel-insurance policy valid for every trip you make during the year in which it's purchased (usually only trips of less than 90 days). Before you leave, make sure you will be covered if you have a preexisting medical condition or are pregnant; your insurers may not pay for routine or continuing treatment, or may require a note from your doctor certifying your fitness to travel.

For advice by phone or a free booklet, "Holiday Insurance," that sets out what to expect from a holiday-insurance policy and gives price guidelines, contact the **Association of British Insurers** (51 Gresham St., London EC2V 7HQ, tel. 071/600–3333; 30 Gordon St., Glasgow G1 3PU, tel. 041/226–3905; Scottish Provincial Bldg., Donegall Sq. W, Belfast BT1 6JE, tel. 0232/249176; call for other locations).

Car Rentals

Driving through Scandinavia is delightful. You'll notice that drivers keep their headlights on even during the day—it is required by law in most of Scandinavia. Take a good pair of sunglasses—the slanting sunlight creates a lot of glare. Drivers' licenses from Britain, Canada, and the United States are valid in Scandinavia. Several countries require drivers to be over 20 years old, but some car-rental companies require that drivers be at least 25, so it is wise to ask.

Most major car-rental companies are represented in Scandinavia, including **Avis** (tel. 800/331–1084, 800/879–2847 in Canada); **Budget** (tel. 800/527–0700); **Dollar** (tel. 800/800–6000); **Hertz** (tel. 800/654–3001, 800/263-0600 in Canada); **National** (tel. 800/227–3876), known internationally as InterRent and Europcar. In cities, unlimited-mileage rates range from about $55–$75 per day for an economy car and $70–$103 for a large car; weekly unlimited-mileage rates range from $235–$315 to $330–$425. Prices vary according to country as well as exchange rates; these prices do not include VAT tax, which in Scandinavia ranges from 22%–25%.

Requirements Your own U.S., Canadian, or U.K. driver's license is acceptable. An International Driver's Permit, available from the American or Canadian Automobile Association, is a good idea.

Extra Charges Picking up the car in one city or country and leaving it in another may entail drop-off charges or one-way service fees, which can be substantial. The cost of a collision or loss-damage waiver (*see below*) can be high, also. Automatic transmissions and air-conditioning are not universally available abroad; ask for them when you book if you want them, and check the cost before you commit yourself to the rental.

Cutting Costs If you know you will want a car for more than a day or two, you can save by planning ahead. Major international companies have programs that discount their standard rates by 15%–30% if you make the reservation before departure (anywhere from two to 14 days), rent for a minimum number of days (typically three or four), and prepay the rental. Ask about these advance-purchase schemes when you call for information. More economical rentals are those that come as part of fly/drive or other packages, even those as bare-bones as the rental plus an airline ticket (*see* Tours and Packages, *above*).

Other sources of savings are the several companies that operate as wholesalers—companies that do not own their own fleets but rent in bulk from those that do and offer advantageous rates to their customers. Rentals through such companies must be arranged and paid for before you leave the United States. Among them are **Auto Europe** (Box 1097, Camden, ME 04843, tel. 207/236–8235 or 800/223–5555, 800/458–9503 in Canada), **Europe by Car** (mailing address, 1 Rockefeller Plaza, New York, NY 10020; walk-in address, 14 W. 49th St, New York, NY 10020, tel. 212/581–3040 or 212/245–1713; 9000 Sunset Blvd., Los Angeles, CA 90069, tel. 213/252–9401 or 800/223–1516 in CA), and **Kemwel** (106 Calvert St., Harrison, NY 10528, tel. 914/835–5555 or 800/678–0678). You won't see these wholesalers' deals advertised; they're even better in summer, when business travel is down. Always ask whether the prices are guaranteed in U.S. dollars or foreign currency and if unlimited mileage is available. Find out about any required deposits, cancellation penalties, and drop-off charges, and confirm the cost of the collision damage waiver (CDW).

One last tip: Remember to fill the tank when you turn in the vehicle, to avoid being charged for refueling at what you'll swear is the most expensive pump in town.

Insurance and Collision Damage Waiver The standard rental contract includes liability coverage (for damage to public property, injury to pedestrians, etc.) and coverage for the car against fire, theft (not included in certain countries), and collision damage with a deductible—most commonly $2,000–$3,000, occasionally more. In the case of an accident, you are responsible for the deductible amount unless you've purchased the CDW, which costs an average $12 a day, although this varies depending on what you've rented, where, and from whom.

Because this adds up quickly, you may be inclined to say "no thanks"—and that's certainly your option, although the rental agent may not tell you so. Note before you decline that deductibles are occasionally high enough that totaling a car would make you responsible for its full value. Planning ahead will help you make the right decision. By all means, find out if your own insurance covers damage to a rental car while traveling (not simply a car to drive when yours is in for repairs). And check whether charging car rentals to any of your credit cards will get you a CDW at no charge.

Personal accident insurance covers medical injuries. One expense not generally covered by rental-car personal accident insurance policies is emergency transportation home (*see* Insurance, *above*).

Rail Passes

The **EurailPass,** valid for unlimited first-class train travel through 17 countries, including Denmark, Finland, Norway, and Sweden, is an excellent value if you plan to travel around the Continent.

The ticket is available for periods of 15 days ($460), 21 days ($598), one month ($728), two months ($998), and three months ($1,260). For two or more people traveling together, a 15-day rail pass costs $390 each. Between April 1 and September 30, you need a minimum of three in your group to get this discount. For those younger than 26, there is the **Eurail Youthpass,** for one or two months of unlimited second-class train travel at $508 and $698.

If you like to spread out your train journey, you can use the **Eurail Flexipass.** With a Flexipass you can choose between 5, 10, or 15 days unlimited first-class train travel within a period of two months. You pay $298, $496, and $676 for the **Eurail Flexipass,** sold for first-class travel; and $220, $348, $474 for the **Eurail Youth Flexipass,** available to those under 26 on their first travel day, sold for second-class travel.

Ask also about the **EurailDrive** Pass, which lets you combine four days of train travel with three days of car rental (through Hertz or Avis) at any time within a two-month period. Charges vary according to size of car, but two people traveling together can get the basic package for $289 per person.

The **EurailPass** is available only if you live outside Europe and North Africa. You can apply through an authorized travel agent or through **Rail Europe** (226–230 Westchester Ave., White Plains, NY 10604, tel. 914/682–5172 or 800/848–7245 from the East and 800/438-7245 from the West).

The **Scanrail Pass** is valid for unlimited rail travel in Scandinavia, and offers free and discounted crossings on several ferry lines. A second-class pass costs $155 for four travel days within a period of 15 days, $265 for nine days travel within 21 days, and $369 for 14 travel days within one month. The first-class rates are $189, $325, and $475, respectively. If you want the flexibility of a car combined with the speed and comfort of the train, try **Scanrail 'n Drive** (from $289 per person, based on two adults sharing an economy car). This pass gives you a four- or nine-day Scanrail pass, plus three days of car rental to use within a 14- or 21-day period. Both of these passes can be purchased from Rail Europe (*see above*) or from the **NSB** (Norweigian State Railways) travel agency in London (tel. 071/930–6666).

Don't make the mistake of assuming that your rail pass guarantees you seats on the trains you want to ride. Seat reservations are required on some trains, particularly high-speed trains, and are a good idea on trains that may be crowded. You will also need reservations for overnight sleeping accommodations. Rail Europe can help you determine if you need reservations and can make them for you (about $10 each, less if you purchase them in Europe at the time of travel). (*See also* Staying in Sweden: Getting Around by Train, *below*).

Student and Youth Travel

Most major cities in Scandinavia (including Stockholm) offer special **City Cards,** which entitle the holder to unlimited, reduced-rate travel on public transportation as well as free or discounted admission to museums, theaters, and other attractions. The cards can be purchased at tourist offices and major rail stations. Additional information is available from the **Scandinavian Tourist Board** (*see* Tourist Information, *above*).

Travel Agencies The foremost U.S. student travel agency is **Council Travel,** a subsidiary of the nonprofit Council on International Educational Exchange. It specializes in low-cost travel arrangements, is the exclusive U.S. agent for several discount cards, and, with its sister CIEE subsidiary, **Council Charter,** is a source of airfare bargains. The Council Charter brochure and CIEE's twice-yearly *Student Travels* magazine, which details its programs, are available at the Council Travel office at CIEE headquarters (205 E. 42nd Street, New York, NY 10017, tel. 212/661–1450) and at 37 branches in college towns nationwide (free in person, $1 by mail). The **Educational Travel Center** (ETC, 438 N. Francis St., Madison, WI 53703, tel. 608/256–5551) also offers low-cost rail passes, domestic and international airline tickets (mostly for flights departing from Chicago), and other budgetwise travel arrangements. Other travel agencies catering to students include **Travel Management International** (TMI, 18 Prescott St., Suite 4, Cambridge, MA 02138, tel. 617/661–8187) and **Travel Cuts** (187 College St., Toronto, Ont. M5T 1P7, tel. 416/979–2406).

Discount Cards For discounts on transportation and on museum and attractions admissions, buy the **International Student Identity Card** (ISIC) if you're a bona fide student, or the **International Youth Card** (IYC) if you're under 26. In the United States the ISIC and IYC cards cost $15 each and include basic travel accident and sickness coverage. Apply to **CIEE** (*see* address *above*, tel. 212/661–1414; the application is in *Student Travels*). In Canada the cards are available for $15 each from **Travel Cuts** (*see above*). In the United Kingdom they cost £5 and £4 respectively at student unions and student travel companies, including Council Travel's London office (28A Poland St., London W1V 3DB, tel. 071/437–7767).

Hosteling An **International Youth Hostel Federation** (IYHF) membership card is the key to more than 5,300 hostel locations in 59 countries; the sex-segregated, dormitory-style sleeping quarters, including some for families, go for $7–$20 a night per person. Membership is available in the United States through **American Youth Hostels** (733 15th St. NW, Washington, DC 20005, tel. 202/783–6161), the American link in the worldwide chain, and costs $25 for adults 18–54, $10 for those under 18, $15 for those 55 and over, and $35 for families. Volume 1 of the two-volume *Guide to Budget Accommodation* lists hostels in Europe and the Mediterranean ($13.95, including postage). IYHF membership is available in Canada through the **Canadian Hostelling Association** (1600 James Naismith Dr., Suite 608, Gloucester, Ont. K1B 5N4, tel. 613/748–5638) for $26.75, and in the United Kingdom through the **Youth Hostel Association of England and Wales** (8 St. Stephen's Hill, St. Albans, Herts. AL1 2DY, tel. 0727/55215) for £9.

Traveling with Children

In Scandinavia children are to be seen AND heard and are genuinely welcome in most public places. Even so, on some occasions hiring a babysitter may be warranted.

On Swedish trains, up to two children under 12 years of age can travel with an adult free, except for a small fee to make a reservation. Each additional child under the age of 12 receives a 50% discount. In summer, families traveling with at least one child under

16 can receive a 50% discount for trips over 140 kilometers (87 miles) in second-class seats. Tickets can be bought only in Sweden. There are special family cars equipped with toys for children on the Stockholm–Malmö and Stockholm–Göteborg lines. Ask for this service when you are making reservations.

Publications *Family Travel Times*, published 10 times a year by Travel With
Newsletter Your Children (TWYCH, 45 W. 18th St., 7th Floor Tower, New York, NY 10011, tel. 212/206–0688; annual subscription $55), covers destinations, types of vacations, and modes of travel.

Books *Great Vacations with Your Kids*, by Dorothy Jordon and Marjorie Cohen ($13; Penguin USA, 120 Woodbine St., Bergenfield, NJ 07621, tel. 800/253–6476) and *Traveling with Children—And Enjoying It*, by Arlene K. Butler ($11.95 plus $3 shipping per book; Globe Pequot Press, Box 833, Old Saybrook, CT 06475, tel. 800/243–0495, or 800/962–0973 in CT) help plan your trip with children, from toddlers to teens. *Innocents Abroad: Traveling with Kids in Europe*, by Valerie Wolf Deutsch and Laura Sutherland ($15.95 or $4.95 paperback, Penguin USA, *see above*), covers child- and teen-friendly activities, food, and transportation.

Tour Operators **GrandTravel** (6900 Wisconsin Ave., Suite 706, Chevy Chase, MD 20815, tel. 301/986–0790 or 800/247–7651) offers international and domestic tours for grandparents traveling with their grandchildren. The catalogue, as charmingly written and illustrated as a children's book, positively invites armchair traveling with lap-sitters aboard. **Families Welcome!** (21 W. Colony Pl., Suite 140, Durham, NC 27705, tel. 919/489–2555 or 800/326–0724) packages and sells family tours to Europe. **Rascals in Paradise** (650 5th St., Suite 505, San Francisco, CA 94107, tel. 415/978–9800, or 800/872–7225) specializes in programs for families.

Getting There On international flights, the fare for infants under 2 not occupy-
Air Fares ing a seat is generally 10% of the accompanying adult's fare; children ages 2–11 usually pay half to two-thirds of the adult fare. On domestic flights, children under 2 not occupying a seat travel free, and older children currently travel on the "lowest applicable" adult fare.

Baggage In general, infants paying 10% of the adult fare are allowed one carry-on bag, not to exceed 70 pounds or 45 inches (length + width + height). The adult baggage allowance applies for children paying half or more of the adult fare. Check with the airline for particulars, especially regarding flights between two foreign destinations, where allowances for infants may be less generous than those above.

Safety Seats The FAA recommends the use of safety seats aloft and details approved models in the free leaflet "Child/Infant Safety Seats Recommended for Use in Aircraft" (available from the Federal Aviation Administration, APA–200, 800 Independence Ave. SW, Washington, DC 20591, tel. 202/267–3479). Airline policy varies. U.S. carriers must allow FAA-approved models, but because these seats are strapped into a regular passenger seat, they may require that parents buy a ticket even for an infant under 2 who would otherwise ride free. Foreign carriers may not allow infant seats, may charge the child's rather than the infant's fare for their use, or may require you to hold your baby during takeoff and landing, thus defeating the seat's purpose.

Facilities Aloft Airlines do provide other facilities and services for children, such as children's meals and freestanding bassinets (to those sitting in seats on the bulkhead, where there's enough legroom to accommodate them). Make your request when reserving. The annual February/March issue of *Family Travel Times* gives details of the children's services of dozens of airlines ($10; *see above*). "Kids and Teens in Flight" (free from the U.S. Department of Transportation, tel. 202/366–2220) offers tips for children flying alone.

Getting Around Children are entitled to discount tickets (often as much as 50% off) on buses, trains, and ferries throughout Scandinavia, as well as reductions on special City Cards. During summer months children under 12 pay half price and children under two fly free or pay maximum 10% on SAS and Linjeflyg roundtrips. The only restriction on this discount is that the family travel together and return to the originating city in Scandinavia at least two days later. With the Nordturist Pass—good for rail journeys throughout Scandinavia for 21 days—children under four travel free and children four to 11 pay half-fare.

Lodging In most Scandinavian hotels children stay free or at reduced rates when sharing their parents' rooms; there is a nominal charge for an extra bed.

Many youth hostels offer special facilities (including multiple-bed rooms and separate kitchens) for families with children. Family hostels also provide an excellent opportunity for children to meet youngsters from other countries. Contact the **AYH** (*see* Student and Youth Travel, *above*) for information.

Baby-Sitting Services For information on local baby-sitting agencies, contact the tourist office in the city or region you are visiting.

Hints for Travelers with Disabilities

Sweden has made great efforts to make life as easy as possible for disabled travelers. There are lifts and ramps for wheelchairs, specially adapted public toilets, and a host of other aids. Special taxi and bus services, help for disabled travelers to board trains, and a list of camp sites, youth hostels, and hotels with special facilities for the disabled are also available. One annual guide, "Hotels in Sweden," lists hotels with rooms adapted for disabled visitors. **Swiss Chalets** (28 Hillcrest Rd., Orpington, Kent BR69AW, England) offers holidays in Sweden designed for the disabled.

Organizations Several organizations provide travel information for people with disabilities, usually for a membership fee, and some publish newsletters and bulletins. Among them are the **Information Center for Individuals with Disabilities** (Fort Point Pl., 27–43 Wormwood St., Boston, MA 02210, tel. 617/727–5540 or 800/462–5015 in MA between 11 and 4, or leave message; TDD/TTY tel. 617/345–9743); **Mobility International USA** (Box 3551, Eugene, OR 97403, voice and TDD tel. 503/343–1284), the U.S. branch of an international organization based in Britain (*see below*) and present in 30 countries; **MossRehab Hospital Travel Information Service** (1200 W. Tabor Rd., Philadelphia, PA 19141, tel. 215/456–9603, TDD tel. 215/456–9602); the **Society for the Advancement of Travel for the Handicapped** (SATH, 347 5th Ave., Suite 610, New York, NY 10016, tel. 212/447–7284, fax 212/725–8253); the **Travel Industry and Disabled Exchange**

(TIDE, 5435 Donna Ave., Tarzana, CA 91356, tel. 818/368–5648); and **Travelin' Talk** (Box 3534, Clarksville, TN 37043, tel. 615/552–6670).

In the United Kingdom Main information sources include the **Royal Association for Disability and Rehabilitation** (RADAR, 25 Mortimer St., London W1N 8AB, tel. 071/637–5400), which publishes travel information for the disabled in Britain, and **Mobility International** (228 Borough High St., London SE1 1JX, tel. 071/403–5688), the headquarters of an international membership organization that serves as a clearinghouse of travel information for people with disabilities.

Travel Agencies and Tour Operators **Directions Unlimited** (720 N. Bedford Rd., Bedford Hills, NY 10507, tel. 914/241–1700), a travel agency, has expertise in tours and cruises for the disabled. **Evergreen Travel Service** (4114 198th St. SW, Suite 13, Lynnwood, WA 98036, tel. 206/776–1184 or 800/435–2288) operates Wings on Wheels Tours for those in wheelchairs, White Cane Tours for the blind, and tours for the deaf and makes group and independent arrangements for travelers with any disability. **Flying Wheels Travel** (143 W. Bridge St., Box 382, Owatonna, MN 55060, tel. 800/535–6790 or 800/722–9351 in MN), a tour operator and travel agency, arranges international tours, cruises, and independent travel itineraries for people with mobility disabilities. **Nautilus,** at the same address as TIDE (*see above*), packages tours for the disabled internationally.

Publications In addition to the fact sheets, newsletters, and books mentioned above are several free publications available from the Consumer Information Center (Pueblo, CO 81009): "New Horizons for the Air Traveler with a Disability," a U.S. Department of Transportation booklet describing changes resulting from the 1986 Air Carrier Access Act and those still to come from the 1990 Americans with Disabilities Act (include Department 608Y in the address), and the Airport Operators Council's *Access Travel: Airports* (Dept. 5804), which describes facilities and services for the disabled at more than 500 airports worldwide.

Twin Peaks Press (Box 129, Vancouver, WA 98666, tel. 206/694–2462 or 800/637–2256) publishes the *Directory of Travel Agencies for the Disabled* ($19.95), listing more than 370 agencies worldwide; *Travel for the Disabled* ($19.95), listing some 500 access guides and accessible places worldwide; the *Directory of Accessible Van Rentals* ($9.95) for campers and RV travelers worldwide; and *Wheelchair Vagabond* ($14.95), a collection of personal travel tips. Add $2 per book for shipping.

Lodging Some hotels are suitable for unaccompanied travelers, but, in many others, individuals will require the assistance of an able-bodied companion. Contact the organizations listed above for further information.

The **Best Western** chain (tel. 800/528–1234) offers properties with wheelchair-accessible rooms in Stockholm. If wheelchair rooms are not available, ground-floor rooms are provided.

Hints for Older Travelers

A **Senior Rail Card** can be bought for about $25 in Scandinavia that gives a year's worth of 30% to 50% discounts on train travel in 19 European countries for travelers over 60.

Organizations The **American Association of Retired Persons** (AARP, 601 E St. NW, Washington, DC 20049, tel. 202/434–2277) provides independent travelers the Purchase Privilege Program, which offers discounts on hotels, car rentals, and sightseeing, and arranges group tours, cruises, and apartment living through AARP Travel Experience from American Express (400 Pinnacle Way, Suite 450, Norcross, GA 30071, tel. 800/927–0111); these can be booked through travel agents, except for the cruises, which must be booked directly (tel. 800/745–4567). AARP membership is open to those 50 and over; annual dues are $8 per person or couple.

Two other membership organizations offer discounts on lodgings, car rentals, and other travel products, along with such nontravel perks as magazines and newsletters. The **National Council of Senior Citizens** (1331 F St. NW, Washington, DC 20004, tel. 202/347–8800) is a nonprofit advocacy group with some 5,000 local clubs across the United States; membership costs $12 per person or couple annually. **Mature Outlook** (6001 N. Clark St., Chicago, IL 60660, tel. 800/336–6330), a Sears Roebuck & Co. subsidiary with 800,000 members, charges $9.95 for an annual membership.

Note: When using any senior-citizen identification card for reduced hotel rates, mention it when booking, not when checking out. At restaurants, show your card before you're seated; discounts may be limited to certain menus, days, or hours. If you are renting a car, ask about promotional rates that might improve on your senior-citizen discount.

Educational Travel **Elderhostel** (75 Federal St., 3rd floor, Boston, MA 02110, tel. 617/426–7788) is a nonprofit organization that has offered inexpensive study programs for people 60 and older since 1975. Programs take place at more than 1,800 educational institutions in the United States, Canada, and 45 other countries; courses cover everything from marine science to Greek myths and cowboy poetry. Participants generally attend lectures in the morning and spend the afternoon sightseeing or on field trips; they live in dorms on the host campuses. Fees for two- to three-week international trips—including room, board, and transportation from the United States—range from $1,800 to $4,500.

Interhostel (University of New Hampshire, 6 Garrison Ave., Durham, NH 03824, tel. 800/733–9753), a slightly younger enterprise than Elderhostel, caters to a slightly younger clientele—that is, 50 and over—and runs programs in some 25 countries. But the idea is similar: Lectures and field trips mix with sightseeing, and participants stay in dormitories at cooperating educational institutions or in modest hotels. Programs are usually two weeks in length and cost $1,500–$2,100, not including airfare from the United States.

Tour Operators **Saga International Holidays** (222 Berkeley St., Boston, MA 02116, tel. 800/343–0273), which specializes in group travel for people over 60, offers a selection of variously priced tours and cruises covering five continents. If you want to take your grandchildren, look into **GrandTravel** (*see* Traveling with Children, *above*).

Further Reading

One of the easiest and certainly most entertaining ways of finding out about modern Swedish society is to read the Martin Beck detective series of thrillers by Maj Sjöwall and Per Wahlöö, all of which have been translated into English. One of these, *The Terrorists*, was even prophetic, containing a scene in which a Swedish prime minister was shot, a precursor to the murder of Olof Palme in 1986.

Similarly, an entertaining, insight into how life was in the bad old days when Sweden was one of the most backward agrarian countries in Europe may be obtained from Vilhelm Moberg's series of novels on poor Swedes who emigrated to America: *The Emigrants*, *Unto a Good Land*, and *The Last Letter Home*.

One Swedish writer of genius was August Strindberg (1849–1912), whose plays greatly influenced modern European and American drama. Perhaps the most enduringly fascinating of these, *Miss Julie*, mixes the explosive elements of sex and class to stunning effect.

Another major talent was the novelist Selma Lagerlöf, the first Swedish writer to win the Nobel Prize in literature, whose works are rooted in local legend and saga. Best for providing insights on things specifically Swedish are the collection *Tales of a Manor* (1899) and the children's book *The Wonderful Adventures of Nils* (1906).

One of the most exhaustive and comprehensive studies in English of the country published in recent years is *Sweden: The Nation's History*, by Franklin D. Scott (University of Minnesota Press). Chris Mosey's *Cruel Awakening, Sweden and the Killing of Olof Palme* (C. Hurst, London 1991) seeks to provide an overview of the country and its recent history seen through the life and assassination of its best-known politician of recent times and the farcical hunt for his killer.

Arriving and Departing

From North America by Plane

Flights are either nonstop, direct, or connecting. A **nonstop** flight requires no change of plane and makes no stops. A **direct** flight stops at least once and can involve a change of plane, although the flight number remains the same; if the first leg is late, the second waits. This is not the case with a **connecting** flight, which involves a different plane and a different flight number.

Airlines Stockholm's **Arlanda** airport and Göteborg's **Landvetter** Airport are served by **SAS** (tel. 800/251–2350), **British Airways** (tel. 800/247–9297), **Delta** (tel. 800/241–4141), and other major international airlines.

Cutting Flight Costs The Sunday travel section of most newspapers is a good source of deals. When booking, particularly through an unfamiliar company, call the Better Business Bureau to find out whether any complaints have been registered against the company, pay with a credit card if you can, and consider trip-cancellation and default insurance (*see* Insurance, *above*).

Promotional All the less expensive fares, called promotional or discount
Airfares fares, are round-trip and involve restrictions. The exact nature
of the restrictions depends on the airline, the route, and the
season and on whether travel is domestic or international, but
you must usually buy the ticket—commonly called an APEX
(advance purchase excursion) when it's for international travel—in advance (seven, 14, or 21 days are usual). You must also
respect certain minimum- and maximum-stay requirements
(for instance, over a Saturday night or at least seven and no
more than 30, 45, or 90 days), and you must be willing to pay
penalties for changes. Airlines generally allow some changes
for a fee. But the cheaper the fare, the more likely the ticket is
to be nonrefundable; it would take a death in the family for the
airline to give you any of your money back if you had to cancel.
The lowest fares are also subject to availability; because only a
certain percentage of the plane's total seats will be sold at that
price, they may go quickly.

Consolidators Consolidators or bulk-fare operators—also known as bucket
shops—buy blocks of seats on scheduled flights that airlines
anticipate they won't be able to sell. They pay wholesale prices,
add a markup, and resell the seats to travel agents or directly
to the public at prices that still undercut the airline's promotional or discount fares. You pay more than on a charter but or-
dinarily less than for an APEX ticket, and, even when there is
not much of a price difference, the ticket usually comes without
the advance-purchase restriction. Moreover, although tickets
are marked nonrefundable so you can't turn them in to the airline for a full-fare refund, some consolidators sometimes give
you your money back. Carefully read the fine print detailing
penalties for changes and cancellations. If you doubt the relia-
bility of a company, call the airline once you've made your booking and confirm that you do, indeed, have a reservation on the
flight.

The biggest U.S. consolidator, C.L. Thomson Express, sells
only to travel agents. Well-established consolidators selling
to the public include **UniTravel** (Box 12485, St. Louis, MO 63132,
tel. 314/569–0900 or 800/325–2222); **Council Charter** (205 E.
42nd St., New York, NY 10017, tel. 212/661–0311 or 800/800–
8222), a division of the Council on International Educational
Exchange and a longtime charter operator now functioning
more as a consolidator; and **Travac** (989 6th Ave., New York,
NY 10018, tel. 212/563–3303 or 800/872–8800), also a former
charterer.

Charter Flights Charters usually have the lowest fares and the most restrictions. Departures are limited and seldom on time, and you can
lose all or most of your money if you cancel. (Generally, the closer to departure you cancel, the more you lose, although sometimes you will be charged only a small fee if you supply a
substitute passenger.) The charterer, on the other hand, may
legally cancel the flight for any reason up to 10 days before departure; within 10 days of departure, the flight may be can-
celed only if it becomes physically impossible to operate it. The
charterer may also revise the itinerary or increase the price after you have bought the ticket, but if the new arrangement con-
stitutes a "major change," you have the right to a refund.
Before buying a charter ticket, read the fine print for the
company's refund policy and details on major changes. Money
for charter flights is usually paid into a bank escrow account,

the name of which should be on the contract. If you don't pay by credit card, make your check payable to the escrow account (unless you're dealing with a travel agent, in which case, his or her check should be payable to the escrow account). The Department of Transportation's Consumer Affairs Office (I–25, Washington, DC 20590, tel. 202/366–2220) can answer questions on charters and send you its "Plane Talk: Public Charter Flights" information sheet.

Charter operators may offer flights alone or with ground arrangements that constitute a charter package. Well-established charter operators include **Council Charter** (205 E. 42nd St., New York, NY 10017, tel. 212/661–0311 or 800/800–8222), now largely a consolidator, despite its name, and **Travel Charter** (1120 E. Long Lake Rd., Troy, MI 48098, tel. 313/528–3500 or 800/521–5267), with Midwestern departures. **DER Tours** (Box 1606, Des Plains, IL 60017, tel. 800/782–2424), a charterer and consolidator, sells through travel agents.

Discount Travel Travel clubs offer their members unsold space on airplanes,
Clubs cruise ships, and package tours at nearly the last minute and at well below the original cost. Suppliers thus receive some revenue for their "leftovers," and members get a bargain. Membership generally includes a regular bulletin or access to a toll-free telephone hot line giving details of available trips departing anywhere from three or four days to several months in the future. Packages tend to be more common than flights alone, so if airfares are your only interest, read the literature before joining. Reductions on hotels are also available. Clubs include **Discount Travel International** (114 Forrest Ave., Suite 203, Narberth, PA 19072, tel. 215/668–7184; $45 annually, single or family), **Moment's Notice** (425 Madison Ave., New York, NY 10017, tel. 212/486–0503; $45 annually, single or family), **Travelers Advantage** (CUC Travel Service, 49 Music Sq. W, Nashville, TN 37203, tel. 800/548–1116; $49 annually, single or family), and **Worldwide Discount Travel Club** (1674 Meridian Ave., Miami Beach, FL 33139, tel. 305/534–2082; $50 annually for family, $40 single).

Enjoying the Almost all flights to Scandinavia are night flights, unless you
Flight prefer to take a morning flight to London or Reykjavík and stay overnight before continuing on. Because the air aloft is dry, drink plenty of beverages while on board; remember that drinking alcohol contributes to jet lag, as do heavy meals. Sleepers usually prefer window seats to curl up against; restless passengers ask to be on the aisle. Bulkhead seats, in the front row of each cabin, have more legroom, but since there's no seat ahead, trays attach awkwardly to the arms of your seat, and you must stow all possessions overhead. Bulkhead seats are usually reserved for the disabled, the elderly, and people traveling with babies.

Smoking Since February 1990, smoking has been banned on all domestic flights of less than six hours' duration; the ban also applies to domestic segments of international flights aboard U.S. and foreign carriers. On U.S. carriers flying to Scandinavia and other destinations abroad, a seat in a no-smoking section must be provided for every passenger who requests one, and the section must be enlarged to accommodate such passengers if necessary as long as they have complied with the airline's deadline for check-in and seat assignment. If smoking bothers you, request a seat far from the smoking section.

Foreign airlines are exempt from these rules but do provide no-smoking sections, and some nations, including Canada as of July 1, 1993, have gone as far as to ban smoking on all domestic flights; other countries may ban smoking on flights of less than a specified duration. The International Civil Aviation Organization has set July 1, 1996, as the date to ban smoking aboard airlines worldwide, but the body has no power to enforce its decisions.

From the United Kingdom by Plane

Many of the airlines listed above make stops in London en route to Scandinavia. The list below includes other major carriers from Great Britain.

SAS (in London, tel. 071/734–6777; fax 071/465–0125) offers nonstop flights connecting London to Århus, Bergen, Copenhagen, Göteborg, Malmö, Oslo, Stavanger, and Stockholm. **British Airways** (tel. 081/897–4000) flies from Heathrow to Bergen, Copenhagen, Gothenburg, Helsinki, Oslo, Stavanger, and Stockholm. **Air Europe** (tel. 0345/444737), **Aer Lingus** (in London, tel. 081/569–555; in Dublin, 0001/377–777), **Cimber Air** (tel. 0652/688491), and **Icelandair** (tel. 071/388–5599) all have flights between Great Britain or Ireland and major Scandinavian cities.

Flying Time

The following are typical in-air times between major airports in North America, London, and Scandinavia. Add extra time for stopovers and connections.

From New York to Stockholm, 8 hours.

From London to Stockholm, 2 hours 25 minutes.

From Helsinki to Stockholm, 55 minutes.

From Copenhagen to Stockholm, 1 hour 10 minutes.

From North America by Ship

Only one firm now offers trans-Atlantic crossings: **Cunard** (tel. 800/221–4770; in the United Kingdom, through British Airways, tel. 081/897–4000), sailing the famed *Queen Elizabeth 2* between New York and Southampton. The trip takes five days. Those arriving at Southampton wishing to sail on to Scandinavia should be aware that the Scandinavian ferries leave from Harwich, on the other side of London from Southampton.

From the United Kingdom by Car, Ferry, Train, and Bus

By Car and Ferry There are excellent links between Harwich and Göteborg and Newcastle and Göteborg aboard **Scandinavian Seaways** ferries (Scandinavian Seaways, DFDS Ltd., Scandinavia House, Parkeston Quay, Harwich, Essex, CO12 4QG, England, tel. 0255/240–240). An alternate approach is through Denmark using ferry crossings to Malmö or Helsingborg.

By Train From London, the **British Rail European Travel Center** (Victoria Station, London, tel. 071/834–2345) can be helpful in arranging connections through to Sweden's **SJ** (Statens Jarnvagar).

By Bus Bus travel is the least expensive alternative, but it is a slower and less comfortable.

Staying in Sweden

Getting Around

By Plane All major cities and towns are linked with regular flights by **Scandinavian Airlines System** (SAS), which recently merged with Linjeflyg to form one airline network under the SAS name. Most Swedish airports are located a long way from city centers but are linked to them by fast and efficient bus services. SAS also operates a limousine service at leading airports. For more information, contact SAS, Inrikes (Flygcity, Klarabergsviaducten 72, 111 64 Stockholm, tel. 020/550550).

By Train **SJ**, the state railway company, has a highly efficient network of comfortable, electrified trains. On nearly all long-distance routes there are buffet cars, and, on overnight trips, sleeping cars and couchettes in both first and second class. A high-speed train, which takes just less than three hours, runs the Stockholm–Göteborg route. Look for so-called *röda avgångar* (red departures), which offer 50% reductions. Children under 16 travel at half fare. Up to two children under 12 may travel free if accompanied by an adult. For more information, contact **SJ** (Vasagatan 22, 105 51 Stockholm, tel. 020/757575).

By Bus There is excellent bus service between all major towns and cities. Consult the yellow pages under *Bussresearrangörer* for telephone numbers of the companies concerned. Recommended are the services offered to different parts of Sweden from Stockholm by **Swebus** (Cityterminalen, Klarabergsviadukten 72, tel. 020/640640).

By Car There are few expressways, but roads are well maintained and relatively traffic-free. Major car-rental companies such as **Avis, Hertz, Europcar, Bonus, Budget, OK,** and **InterRent** have facilities in all major towns and cities and at airports. It is worth shopping around for special rates. See the yellow pages under *Biluthyrning* for telephone numbers and addresses.

By Boat An excellent way of seeing Sweden is from its many ferry boats, which ply the archipelagoes and main lakes. In Stockholm, visitors should buy a special *båtluffarkort*. This gives unlimited travel on the white archipelago ferry boats for a 16-day period and is available at the ferry ticket offices. Highly popular four-day cruises are available on the Göta Canal, which makes use of rivers, lakes, and, on its last lap, the Baltic Sea. This lovely waterway, which links Göteborg on the west coast with Stockholm on the east, has a total of 65 locks, and you travel on fine old steamers, some of which date almost from the canal's opening in 1832. The oldest and most desirable is the *Juno*, built in 1874. Prices start at SKr5,400 for a bed in a double cabin. For more information, contact the **Göta Canal Steamship Company** (Box 272, S–401 24 Göteborg, tel. 031/806315).

Telephones

Post offices do not have telephone facilities, but there are plenty of pay phones, and long-distance calls can be made from special telegraph offices called *Telebutik*, or marked "Tele." You can also purchase a **Telefonkort** (Telephone card) from the Telebutik, pressbyrå, or hospitals for SKr45 or SKr80, which works out to be cheaper if you're making numerous domestic calls.

Local Calls The new orange pay phones, which are rapidly replacing the old green models, take 50-öre, SKr1, and SKr5 coins. A local call costs a minimum of SKr2. For calls outside the locality, dial the area code.

International Calls The foreign dialing code is 009 followed by the country code, then the number you require. Sweden's country code is 46. The AT&T USA direct-access code is 020–795–611. The MCI call-USA access code is 020–795–922.

Operators and Information For directory inquiries, dial 07975 for information concerning Sweden, 0013 for the Nordic area, and 0019 for other foreign inquiries. For operator-assisted foreign calls, dial 0018 on green pay phones.

Mail

Postal Rates Letters up to 20 grams and postcards cost SKr3.50 to send inside the Nordic Area, SKr5 to elsewhere in Europe, and SKr6 to the United States and the rest of the world by air. Surface mail costs SKr5.

Tipping

In addition to the 12% value-added tax, most hotels usually include a service charge of 15%; it is not necessary to tip unless you have received extra services. Similarly, a service charge of 13% is usually included in restaurant bills. It is a custom, however, to leave small change when buying drinks. Taxi drivers and hairdressers expect a tip of around 10%.

Opening and Closing Times

Banks Banks are open from 9:30 to 3. In the larger cities some stay open until 5:30. All banks are closed on Saturday and Sunday. The bank at Arlanda Airport, Stockholm, is open daily between 7 AM and 10 PM. There is also a bank at Landvetter Airport, Göteborg, which is open daily from 8 to 8. There are "Forex" **currency exchange** offices at Central Station in Stockholm City Terminal (9 AM–6 PM), Göteborg Central Station (8 AM–9 PM), and at the Malmö tourist office (Hamngatan 1; 8 AM–9 PM).

Museums Most **museums** are open Tuesday through Sunday 10–5, though some have other hours. A free guide called "Stockholm This Week" is available from stores, hotels, and tourist offices.

Stores Shopping hours vary, but most businesses are open 10–6 on weekdays and 9–1 (and sometimes 4) on Saturday. Some grocery shops are open until 9 PM, sometimes even 11 PM, and these are almost exclusively Swedish franchises of 7-Eleven stores.

Shopping

Sweden produces expensive, high-quality handicraft goods that are available at special *Hemslöjd* shops and in leading department stores such as **NK, Åhléns,** and **Pub.** Swedish crystal is a traditional favorite, the leading brands being Orrefors and Kosta Boda. At the glass factories themselves in the south, "seconds" shops provide bargain buys; otherwise expect to pay heavily for the craftsmanship, design, and reputation.

One way to beat the prices is to take advantage of tax-free shopping. You can make major purchases free of tax if you have a foreign passport. Ask about tax-free shopping when you make a purchase for $50 (about £32) or more. When your purchases exceed a specified limit, you receive a special export receipt. Keep the parcels intact and take them out of the country within 30 days of purchase. When you leave, you can obtain a refund of the tax in cash at the airport, or, upon arriving home, you can send your receipts to an office in the country of purchase to receive your refund by mail. Be aware that limits for EC tourists are higher than for those coming from outside the EC. In Sweden, for non-EC tourists, the refund is about 14%.

Sports and Outdoor Activities

Bicycling As there are separate bicycle tracks through most cities, and Swedish roads are usually not congested, bicycling is a popular way of getting around. Rental costs average around SKr80 per day. Tourist offices and Sveriges Turist förening (STF; the Swedish Touring Association) in Stockholm (tel. 08/790–3100) have information about cycling package holidays that include bike rentals, overnight accommodations, and meals. The bicycling organization, **Cykelfrämjandet** (tel. 08/321680), publishes an English-language guide to cycling trips.

Boating and STF, in cooperation with Televerket (Sweden's PTT—Postal, Sailing Telephone, and Telegraph authority), publishes an annual guide in Swedish to all the country's marinas with telephone numbers. It is available from STF (tel. 08/790–3250) or in your nearest PTT "Telebutik." The **Swedish Canoeing Association** (Svenksa Kanotföfbundet, Skeppsbron 11, 611 35 Nyköping, tel. 0155/69508) publishes a similar booklet for canoers.

Camping There are 760 registered campsites nationwide, many located close to uncrowded bathing places and with fishing, boating, or canoeing; they may also offer bicycle rentals. Prices range from SKr60 to SKr110 per 24-hour period. Many camping places also offer accommodations in log cabins at various prices, depending on the facilities offered, and some have special facilities for the disabled. Most are open between June and September, but about 200 remain open in winter for skiing and skating enthusiasts. An annual catalogue in English is available from tourist bureaus. For additional information, contact **Sveriges Campingvärdarnas Riksförbund** (Kålgårdsbergsgatan 1, Box 255, S–45 117 Uddevalla, tel. 0522/38345).

Golf Sweden has 283 golf clubs; you can even play by the light of the midnight sun at Boden in the far north. The **Swedish Golfing Association** (Svenska Golfförbundet, Box 84, 182 11 Danderyd, tel. 08/622–1500) publishes an annual guide in Swedish with current information; it costs around SKr55, plus postage.

Hiking There are countless trails nationwide, but **Kungsleden** (The King's Trail) through the mountains of Lappland, including Kebnekaise, at 7,000 feet the country's highest peak, is especially rewarding. Information on walking routes and overnight accommodations is available from **STF** (Box 25, S–101 20 Stockholm, tel. 08/790–3100).

Skiing There are plenty of both downhill and cross-country facilities. The best-known resorts are in the country's western mountains: **Åre** in the north, with 29 lifts; **Idre Fjäll,** to the south of Åre, offering accommodation for 10,000; and **Sälen** in the folklore region of Dalarna. You can ski in summer at **Riksgränsen** in the far north. A new center called the **Discover Sweden Shop,** now located in the Sweden House (Kungsträdgården, Stockholm, tel. 08/789–2000), has information on skiing and other sport and leisure activities, and will advise on equipment needed.

Tennis Since the time Björn Borg began to win Wimbledon with almost monotonous regularity, Sweden has been a force in world tennis. There are indoor and outdoor courts throughout the country. The **Swedish Tennis Association** (Svenska Tennisförbundet, Lidingövägen 75, Box 27915, S–115 94 Stockholm, tel. 08/667–9770) can supply more information.

Water Sports Windsurfing and waterskiing are extremely popular in Sweden. One can learn the basics and rent equipment at many locations nationwide.

Beaches

There are relatively few sand beaches but thousands of unspoiled *bad,* or "bathing places." These are more likely to be grassy or rocky areas by the lakeside than sandy beaches, though these, too, can be found along both the east and west coasts and on the Baltic resort islands of Gotland and Öland. It is possible to swim in clear, clean waters close to most urban centers.

Dining

In August look for *kräftor* (crayfish), which are boiled with dill, salt, and sugar, then cooled overnight. Swedes eat them with hot buttered toast, caraway seeds, and schnapps or beer. Later comes an exotic assortment of mushrooms and wild berries.

Regional specialties include *spettekaka,* a cake of eggs and sugar made in Skåne, and *Gotlandsflundror,* a smoked flat fish from the island of Gotland. *Husmanskost* (home-cooking) recipes are often served in restaurants as a *dagens rätt* (the daily special). Examples are *pytt i panna* (literally, "put in the pan"—beef and potato hash topped with a fried egg), or pea soup with pancakes, a traditional meal on Thursday.

Sweden is known for its coffee. Jealous Danes theorized that foreigners like their coffee weak and therefore prefer Swedish varieties; Swedes just say it tastes better.

Local liquor laws arouse almost obsessional interest among Scandinavians. In Sweden, liquor and strong beer (over 3% alcohol) can be purchased only in state-owned shops, at very high prices, during weekday business hours, usually 9:30 to 6. A 70 or 75 centiliter bottle of whiskey, for example, can easily cost SKr230 to SKr260, or about $40.

The nation's standard home-cooked meal is basically peasant fare—sausages, potatoes, and other hearty foods to ward off the winter cold. However, it has also produced the *smörgåsbord*, a generous and artfully arranged buffet featuring both hot and cold dishes. You start with the herring, then eat your way through salads, vegetable dishes, meats, cheeses, and breads, winding up with a slice of *tårta* (cake) or some fruit. Fish—fresh, smoked, or pickled—is a Swedish specialty; herring and salmon both come in myriad traditional and new preparations.

The hotel breakfast is often a well-stocked smörgåsbord-style buffet. Lunches are markedly less expensive than dinner. Even in Stockholm, it is still possible to eat the *dagens rätt* (dish of the day) between 11:30 AM and 2 PM for less than SKr60, with bread, salad, and either a light beer or cup of coffee.

Dinner is a different matter entirely. An indifferent steak and potatoes can set you back SKr160, and a bottle of mediocre wine with the meal will cost at least that much again. Dinner for two with wine in one of the better Stockholm restaurants could easily cost SKr600 or more.

Category	Cost*
Very Expensive	Over SKr500
Expensive	SKr250–SKr500
Moderate	SKr120–SKr250
Inexpensive	under SKr120

*per person, for a two-course meal, including service charge and tax but not wine.

Lodging

Though they are usually extremely clean and efficient, hotels are very expensive all over the country. In mid-1993 the government reduced the tax on hotels and domestic travel services from 21% to 12%, a welcome change for visitors. However, in summer many discounts, special passes, and summer packages are available. Your travel agent or the Swedish Travel and Tourism Council (in New York) will have full details, but some of the better buys are as follows: The **Reso** hotel chain offers the **Piccolo Card,** which costs SKr150 and entitles the holder to a 20% discount on summer rates (June 1–Aug. 31), which are reduced by as much as 50%. The **Scandic Hotel** summer check plan enables you to pay for your accommodation in advance, with a weekend check costing SKr550, and a supplement of SKr150 at city-center hotels. **Sweden Hotels** offer a **Scandinavian Bonus Pass** costing SKr160 that gives between 15% and 50% discounts from May 15 to October 1.

Manor houses are less expensive than city hotels and offer quaint, countryside locations and distinctive Swedish character. Tour operators in the United States (*see* Tours and Packages, *above*), Sweden House in Stockholm, or tourist offices in each town can provide you with information on these and on hotel groups that specialize in rural or sports resort accommodations.

Vandrarhem (youth hostels), also scrupulously clean and well run, are more expensive than elsewhere in Europe. **Sveriges Turistförening** (STF; the Swedish Touring Association, Box 25, S–101 20 Stockholm, tel. 08/790–3100) has 280 nationwide, most with 4- to 6-bed family rooms and 80 with running hot and cold water in the rooms. They are open to anyone irrespective of age. Prices are from SKr60 to SKr90 per night for members of STF or organizations affiliated with the International Youth Hostel Federation. Nonmembers are charged SKr35 extra per night. A hostel handbook is published annually by STF.

Two things about hotels usually surprise North Americans: the relatively limited dimensions of beds and the generous size of the breakfasts. Scandinavian double beds are often around 60″ wide or slightly less, close in size to the U.S. queen size. King-size beds (72″ wide) are difficult to find and, if available, require special reservations.

Older hotels may have some rooms described as "double," which in fact have one double bed plus one fold-out sofa big enough for two people. This arrangement is occasionally called a "combi-room" but is being phased out.

Many older hotels, particularly the country inns and independently run smaller hotels in the cities, do not have private bathrooms. Ask ahead if this is important to you.

Scandinavian breakfasts resemble what many people would call lunch, usually including breads, cheeses, marmalade, hams, lunch meats, eggs, juice, cereal, milk, and coffee. In contrast, the typical Continental breakfast served in other parts of Europe is just a roll and coffee. Breakfast is often included in the price of the hotel.

Sweden offers **Inn Checks,** or prepaid hotel vouchers, for accommodations ranging from first-class hotels to country cottages. These vouchers, which must be purchased from travel agents or from the Scandinavian Tourist Board (*see* Tourist Information, *above*) before departure, are sold individually and in packets for as many nights as needed and offer savings of up to 50%. For further information about Scandinavian hotel vouchers, contact the Scandinavian Tourist Board.

Reservations The need for reservations depends on where you want to stay and when. In general, reservations are a good idea. It is virtually impossible to get a room on a weekday in Stockholm in the late spring because large conventions soak up all available space. Countryside inns usually have space, but not always: Norwegians and Danes call vacationing Germans *vandhunde* (water-dogs) because waterside areas attract them in large numbers. With eastern Germans suddenly more mobile, some coast-side inns have recently been filling their summer vacancies by January.

Home Exchange This is obviously an inexpensive solution to the lodging problem, because house-swapping means living rent-free. You find a house, apartment, or other vacation property to exchange for your own by becoming a member of a home-exchange organization, which then sends you its annual directories listing available exchanges and includes your own listing in at least one of them. Arrangements for the actual exchange are made by the two parties to it, not by the organization. Principal clearinghouses include **Intervac U.S./International Home Exchange** (Box 590504, San Francisco, CA 94159, tel. 415/435–3497), the oldest, with thousands of foreign and domestic homes for exchange in its three annual directories; membership is $62, or $72 if you want to receive the directories but remain unlisted. The **Vacation Exchange Club** (Box 650, Key West, FL 33041, tel. 800/638–3841), also affiliated with HomeLink International, has thousands of foreign and domestic listings and publishes four annual directories plus updates; the $50 membership includes your listing in one book. **Loan-a-Home** (2 Park La., Apt. 6E, Mount Vernon, NY 10552, tel. 914/664–7640) specializes in long-term exchanges; there is no charge to list your home, but the directories cost $35 or $45 depending on the number you receive.

Apartment and Villa Rentals If you want a home base that's roomy enough for a family and comes with cooking facilities, a furnished rental may be the solution. It's generally cost-wise, too, although not always—some rentals are luxury properties (economical only when your party is large). Home-exchange directories do list rentals—often second homes owned by prospective house swappers— and there are services that can not only look for a house or apartment for you (even a castle if that's your fancy) but also handle the paperwork. Some send an illustrated catalogue and others send photographs of specific properties, sometimes at a charge; up-front registration fees may apply.

Among the companies is **Rent a Home International** (7200 34th Ave. NW, Seattle, WA 98117, tel. 206/789–9377 or 800/488–7368), with properties in Denmark, Finland, and Sweden. **Hideaways International** (767 Islington St., Box 4433, Portsmouth, NH 03802, tel. 603/430–4433 or 800/843–4433) functions as a travel club. Membership ($79 yearly per person or family at the same address) includes two annual guides plus quarterly newsletters; rentals are arranged directly between members, not by the club staff.

Ratings Each of the national tourist offices distributes lists of hotels with information about opening times, pricing, accommodations for disabled travelers, and discounts for children and senior citizens.

Category	Cost*
Very Expensive	over SKr1,500
Expensive	SKr1,200–SKr1,500
Moderate	SKr800–SKr1,200
Inexpensive	under SKr800

All prices are for a standard double room, including tax.

Credit Cards

The following credit card abbreviations are used in this book: AE, American Express; D, Discover; DC, Diners Club; MC, MasterCard; V, Visa. It's a good idea to call ahead to check current credit card policies.

2 Portraits of Sweden

Sweden at a Glance: A Chronology

c 12,000 BC The first migrations into Sweden.

2,000 BC Southern European tribes migrate toward Denmark. The majority of early settlers in Scandinavia were Germanic.

---

c 770 The Viking Age begins. For the next 250 years, Scandinavians set sail on expeditions stretching from the Baltic to the Irish seas and to the Mediterranean as far as Sicily, employing superior ships and weapons and efficient military organization.

c 800–c 1000 Swedes control river trade routes between the Baltic and Black seas; establish Novgorod, Kiev, and other cities.

830 Frankish monk Ansgar makes one of the first attempts to Christianize Sweden and builds the first church in Slesvig, Denmark. Sweden is not successfully Christianized until the end of the 11th century, when the temple at Uppsala, a center for pagan resistance, is destroyed.

1248 Erik Eriksson appoints Birger as Jarl, in charge of military affairs and expeditions abroad. Birger improves women's rights, makes laws establishing peace in the home and church, and begins building Stockholm.

1250 Stockholm, Sweden, is officially founded.

1319 Sweden and Norway form a union that lasts until 1335.

1370 The Treaty of Stralsund gives the north German trading centers of the Hanseatic League free passage through Danish waters. German power increases throughout Scandinavia.

1397 The Kalmar Union is formed as a result of the dynastic ties between Sweden, Denmark, and Norway, the geographical position of the Scandinavian states, and the growing influence of Germans in the Baltic. Erik of Pomerania is crowned king of the Kalmar Union.

1477 University of Uppsala, Sweden's oldest university, is founded.

1520 Christian II, ruler of the Kalmar Union, executes 82 people who oppose the Scandinavian union, an event known as the "Stockholm blood bath." Sweden secedes from the Union three years later.

1523 Gustav Ericsson founds Swedish Vasa dynasty as King Gustav I Vasa.

1611–1613 The Kalmar War: Denmark wages war against Sweden in hope of restoring the Kalmar Union.

1611–1660 Gustav II Adolphus reigns in Sweden. Sweden defeats Denmark in the Thirty Years War and becomes the greatest power in Scandinavia as well as Northern and Central Europe.

1660 Peace of Copenhagen establishes modern boundaries of Denmark, Sweden, and Norway.

1668 Bank of Sweden, the world's oldest central bank, is founded.

1700–1721 Sweden, led by Karl XII, first broadens then loses its position to Russia as Northern Europe's greatest power in the Great Northern War.

1807 During the Napoleonic wars, Gustav III joins the coalition against France and accepts war with France and Russia.

1809 Sweden surrenders the Åland Islands and Finland to Russia, Finland becomes a Grand Duchy of the Russian Empire, and the Instrument of Government, Sweden's constitution, is adopted.

1813 Sweden takes a Frenchman as king: Karl XIV Johann estalishes the Bernadotte dynasty.

1814 Sweden, after Napoleon's defeat at the Battle of Leipzig, attacks Denmark and forces the Danish surrender of Norway. The Treaty of Kiel, in 1814, calls for a union between Norway and Sweden despite Norway's desire for independence.

c 1850 The building of railroads begins in Scandinavia.

1889 The Swedish Social Democratic Party is founded.

1901 Alfred Nobel, the Swedish millionaire chemist and industrialist, initiates the Nobel prizes.

1905 Norway's union with Sweden is dissolved.

1914 At the outbreak of World War I, Sweden declares neutrality but is effectively blockaded.

1918 Women gain the right to vote.

1920 Scandinavian countries join the League of Nations.

1929–1937 The first social democratic government takes office in Sweden.

1939 Sweden declares neutrality in World War II.

1949 Sweden declines membership in NATO.

1952 The Nordic Council, which promotes cooperation among the Nordic parliaments, is founded.

1975 Sweden's Instrument of Government of 1809 is revised and replaced with a new Instrument of Government. This constitution reduces the voting age to eighteen and removes many of the king's powers and responsibilities.

1980 Fifty-eight percent of Sweden's voters advocate minimizing the use of nuclear reactors at Sweden's four power plants.

1986 Sweden's prime minister, Olof Palme, is assassinated for unknown reasons. Ingvar Carlsson succeeds him.

1991 The Social Democrats are voted out of office and a conservative coalition government takes over.

1992 Sweden's Riksbank (National Bank) raises overnight interest rates to a world record of 500% in an effort to defend the Swedish krona against speculation.

The Stagestruck King

by Dan
Hofstadter

Dan Hofstadter,
who spent a
number of years
in Sweden, now
lives in Italy. He
writes frequently
for the New
Yorker and is the
author of the
recent book
Temperaments:
Artists Facing
Their Work. This
essay first
appeared in the
February 1989
issue of Condé
Nast Traveler.

The SS *Mariefred*, built in 1903, is the only passenger vessel that still plies the length of the waters of Lake Mälaren. The little steamship has two decks, a tall single funnel, and plenty of gleaming brass and wood. At the turn of the century there were fifty or so boats of comparable size that steamed about on the lake, and to passengers who board her today, the *Mariefred* feels distinctly Edwardian—or "Oscarian," as the Swedes would say. There is a hint of wistfulness, too—of melancholy antiquity—about the tiny town of Mariefred, which you reach after four and a half hours of hugging Lake Mälaren's southern shore. From a distance, to the traveler out of Stockholm, the place seems a marzipan town bedecked with paper flags. Closer inspection reveals a copper church spire, some board-and-batten houses, a narrow-gauge railway, and a dusty station trimmed with the sort of gingerbread the Swedes call "carpenter merriment." In the park there's a charming gazebo with a café.

A leisurely outing to Mariefred is a typical way for a Stockholm family to spend a summer's day. On the other side of the park rises the castle of Gripsholm, the only one of Sweden's royal estates to measure up to a child's notion of what a castle ought to be. It is an affair of keeps and cupolas, in red brick and terra-cotta tile; you approach it through a meadow full of clover, pass over a moat, and enter a labyrinth of courtyards, winding passages, and dizzying spiral stairs.

From this lofty fortress you can look down through ancient, wavering panes of glass at the village below and the toylike steamer waiting by the jetty. Often in the older towns in Scandinavia you get this feeling of playful miniaturization: It is as if the great creations of the Continent were being reproduced in a scale model. Even the castle itself does not quite escape this feeling of diminution, for if you wander about its top floor you eventually find yourself in a round turret room outfitted as a tiny playhouse. This is the Mirror Theater, designed by Erik Palmstedt in the late eighteenth century as a sort of dainty echo of Palladio's grandiose Olympic Theater in Vicenza. It has five ascending rows of benches, a semicircular Ionic colonnade surmounted by masks and garlands, and a trompe l'oeil–coffered ceiling. Between the columns there are mirrors that reflect some of the movement onstage and thus surround the audience with dramatic action. During performances the whole hall glitters and dissolves.

Lovely in itself, the Mirror Theater is also a perfect emblem of the strange reign of Gustav III, who mounted the Swed-

ish throne in 1771 and died in 1792. It was Gustav who
dreamed up this theater and played the first major roles
upon its boards; a talented and innovative dramatist, he
also wrote many of the lines he delivered. He was, in sum,
one of those extraordinary eighteenth-century people who
seem to belong to fantasy rather than to history. Deeply
uncomfortable in his own skin, he rewrote his royal role and
made himself into something resembling a dramatic character. The parallel with Hamlet is obvious, especially since
Gustav had an utterly weird mother and was nasty to his
wife. Yet the Swedish prince was in one crucial respect
more remarkable than the Danish one: Unlike Hamlet, he
actually ruled a kingdom.

The Swedes in some ways resemble a family, and like
any family they tend to be unforgiving of members
who affect extravagant ways. From the first,
Gustav's performance as king drew dubious notices from
his fellow countrymen. They found him foppish, fretful, and
prey to foreign ideas; the courtiers complained about his
horrible breath and his habit of plastering himself with
medals, which he even wore over his dressing gown. He had
no affection for his queen, Sofia Magdalena of Denmark—
"Prenez-vous garde, madame," were his first words to
her—and it was rumored that he was actually a homosexu-
al. His real crime, one suspects, was simply having too
much power and too much imagination at the same time.
Like his uncle, Frederick of Prussia, Gustav regarded himself as an enlightened despot: a posture that necessarily of-
fended many people.

Posthumous critics have regarded Gustav with an equally
skeptical eye. August Strindberg wrote an unsympathetic
play about him, and a nineteenth-century biographer of
stern moral fiber characterized him as dreamy and effemi-
nate. A more recent authority has suggested a drift toward
schizophrenia. The one view in which all critics concur,
however, is that his mother, the temperamental Lovisa
Ulrika, sister to Frederick the Great, caused him constant
agitation and grief.

Gustav's birth had been difficult. He was wrenched from
his mother's womb with such violence that his forehead was
permanently dented and one hip deformed; when he
learned to walk, he limped. The queen's concern for his welfare did not, unhappily, take the form of tenderness. She
alternately smothered and bullied him, and she spoke of his
future in high-flown terms that scarcely concealed her mis-
givings. Fortunately, her influence was counteracted by
that of his tutor, Carl Gustav Tessin. Tessin set out to teach
little Gustav all that he could, and he arranged the crown
prince's schedule so that lessons started at daybreak and
ended at bedtime. One of the talents he noticed in Gustav
was that of playacting, and this he encouraged by compos-
ing for his pupil little dramas that were packed with useful

facts and precepts. At seven Gustav was observed mount-
ing his writing table to declaim soliloquies until he col-
lapsed. Soon he was writing his own plays. Gustav's
memory was such that he could recite all the major speeches
of a well-written play after a single performance; with
alarm one courtier noticed that the prince preferred the fe-
male roles, especially if the actress in question had been
splendidly costumed.

His mother tacitly encouraged these histrionic inclinations.
She herself was fond of flattery and ceremony, and besides,
her passion for him was so exigent that he had to playact
merely to survive her fits of jealousy. He learned to address
her in unctuous tones, which in time became his usual man-
ner of speaking. "There was not an honest hair on his head,"
wrote one memoirist. "He was pliant and weak and wildly
vain. He was slinky and sly and elusive, and clever at strik-
ing the right sort of pose. To achieve his ends he used a
thousand slippery shifts and devices. He loved pomp and
circumstance, and always put appearance before truth."

It was at a theater in Paris, in March of 1771, that Gustav
learned of the death of his father, King Adolf Fredrik.
By the following year he had already started building a
court theater for Gripsholm. Soon the fortnight around
Christmas became the castle's theatrical season; in 1775–
76, for instance, Racine's *Athalie*, Corneille's *Cinna*, and
four other full-length plays were all performed within a few
weeks of each other, with the king in each of the leading
roles. He had memorized 3,784 alexandrines—it was stu-
pendous—but much of the court recoiled in horror. "When
the King got up in the morning," one nobleman later remembered, "he went straight to the theater to rehearse
with his actors the plays to be performed that evening.
There His Majesty often dined as well, and after the performance the King, still in costume, would join the entire
Court for supper. So it was that we saw him tricked up as
Rhadamiste, as Cinna, and as the High Priest of the Temple
of Jerusalem, offering himself as an object of derision at his
own table." Despite his love of finery, though, Gustav was a
notoriously sloppy dresser. He seemed unaware that his
naked knees often poked out from under his breeches, or
that his costumes and makeup suggested an obscene trav-
esty of the very notion of kingship. But only the French am-
bassador had the nerve to tell him the truth: "It is unworthy
for Your Majesty to appear in the guise of a *comédien*." The
king took the point and reluctantly retired from the stage.
From then on he would devote himself to theatrical writing,
producing, and designing.

The theater at Gripsholm is not the only one that calls to
mind the life of Sweden's enigmatic player-king. There are
two other court theaters outside Stockholm, both erected
by Gustav's mother during his childhood. One is at the man-
or of Ulriksdal, near Bergshamra; the other is at the royal

summer residence of Drottningholm. Of the two, Drottningholm is by far the more interesting. It was built in
1764–66 by the court architect Carl Frederick Adelcrantz
and decorated by the French painter Adrien Masreliez. An
Italian theater mechanic named Donato Stopani was en-
listed to provide the necessary technical arrangements.
This man had been trained as a shipbuilding engineer, and
today as you stand beneath the stage amid the still-func-
tioning machinery you feel distinctly at sea: You are
claustrophobically encaged by hand-hewn beams, huge
windlasses, elaborate dispositions of block and tackle, and
cables leading every which way. It is like being trapped inside one of the more bamboozling plates of Diderot's *Ency-
clopaedia.*

About a year after the celebrated Christmas season
at Gripsholm, Gustav bought Drottingholm and its
playhouse from his mother. One of his first moves
was to summon to Sweden the gifted French decorative
painter Jean-Louis Desprez. Over the next decade or so,
Desprez and his associates painted an extraordinary series
of stage sets—including wings, borders, and backdrops—
that have survived until today. Exact copies of these are
still used in the summer productions at Drottningholm; the
thirty or so originals have been carefully stored away. They
constitute the only major collection of eighteenth-century
stage sets in Europe. To see wing after wing pulled out on
their runners, as I did on a visit to the theater's storage
shed, is to witness the whole world of eighteenth-century
scenography come alive. A city street appears, then melts
into a grotto; pergolas and parlors and piazzas succeed each
other with dizzying splendor.

Gustav did have his moments of greatness. He made war on
Catherine of Russia and founded the Swedish Academy and
the Royal Dramatic Theater and did a hundred other unusual things, many of them beneficial. For all that, he seems a
little king—a royal provincial. As his theatrical imaginings
swelled, his actual power shrank, for Sweden was fast losing her great-power status. The war with Catherine de-
pleted the state treasury, alarming the governing classes;
adding insult to injury, the king mounted a coup d'état in
1789 and assumed total power. For decades Sweden had
been a parliamentary and constitutional monarchy, so this
autocratic stoke enraged large segments of the nobility and
the wealthy bourgeoisie.

On the ides of March in 1792, a masquerade ball was given in
Gustav's new opera house in Stockholm. The king looked on
from his box, clad in a black silk disguise with a white mask;
a little before midnight he went down into the orchestra,
the Order of Seraphim flashing on his chest. Easily recognized, he was suddenly surrounded by a throng of men in
identical masks. A shot rang out and the king fell, mortally
wounded; the most disaffected clique of the aristocratic

party had exacted its revenge. Much later, Giuseppe Verdi and Antonio Somma would base their opera, *Un Ballo in Maschera*, on this strange incident.

Gustav played to many audiences in many ways, but always he played to the mirror. You feel this today when you stand in the enchanted, kaleidoscopic space of the Mirror Theater. The life of the player-king reminds us that in some respects the narcissism of art is very like the narcissism of autocracy. When the lights are dimmed and the leading man delivers his soliloquy, he finds that he is alone with himself. Many fine actors have made their stage into a realm; only Gustav made his realm into a stage.

Astrid Lindgren

by Chris Mosey

Appropriately, the career of Astrid Lindgren, Sweden's best-known children's writer, author of the *Pippi Longstocking* books and many others, had a fairy-tale beginning. Once upon a time, Karin, her seven-year-old daughter, ill in bed with pneumonia, begged her: "Tell me a story . . . tell me the story of Pippi Longstocking."

"Neither she nor I know where on earth she got that name from," says Lindgren. "That was the first time I ever heard it. I made up the character right there and then, told her a story, and only wrote it down much later."

Thus was born one of the most memorable characters in children's fiction, her adventures translated from Lindgren's native Swedish into more than 50 languages.

"A few years later, I was awarded a prize for the stories and offered to share it with Karin," recalls Lindgren, "but by then she decided that she was too old. She said she was bored with Pippi."

With younger children all over the world, however, Pippi continues to strike a responsive chord: a little girl of indeterminate age with a gap-toothed smile, freckle face, and a wild mop of ginger hair from which a braid juts lopsidedly out over each ear.

Phenomenally strong, irrepressibly cheeky, she lives, independent of adults, with a horse and monkey in a tumbledown house, supporting herself from a hoard of gold coins. She has no table manners and doesn't go to school. She does just what she likes, when she feels like doing it.

"Bertrand Russell once said that children dream of power the way that adults dream of sex," says Lindgren. "I was very impressed with that at the time, and I think I must have had it in mind when I created Pippi."

Despite vociferous protests from educationalists and child psychologists, Pippi won immediate favor with kids. Lindgren has since created several other memorable characters, but Pippi remains the basis of her enormous popularity in her home country.

It would be well-nigh impossible to find a Swede who has not heard of Lindgren. She is *Tant Astrid*, Aunty Astrid, a gray-haired, short-sighted little old lady who is a symbol of hearth and home, of faith in traditional values and love of rural Sweden, with its deep, dark pine forests, wide blue lakes and meadows dotted with red-painted wood houses.

The independent spirit that created such an unconventional character as Pippi Longstocking still exists within this grandmother, however, and, using her awesome popularity, Lindgren has been partly responsible for the fall of one Swedish government and for forcing a second one in 1989 to draft radical new legislation protecting the rights of pets and farm animals, about which she has a bee in her bonnet.

She remains refreshingly unspoiled by all the adulation and attention she receives.

"When I go out, people come up to me in the street and tell me how much they've enjoyed my books, and children will hug and kiss me," she says. "Of course, that's very nice, but you know somehow I always feel it's not happening to *me*.

"It's as though someone else had all that celebrity and I am standing alongside her."

The mere suggestion that she wields power brings a steely glint to her blue eyes. "Power? I have only the power of the word," she says. "I wouldn't want power in the real sense. That's the worst thing I know. People always abuse it."

Yet there is more than a suspicion that, Pippilike, she revels in the influence she, an ordinary (or perhaps one should say, extraordinary) citizen can use to inject rebellious ideas into the heads of her youthful public and bend Sweden's rulers to her will.

One of her characters is *The World's Best Karlson*. Lovable figment of a little boy's imagination, Karlson is a jovial type who laughs at reality and flies around the house aided by a propeller set in the middle of his back. The Karlson books have become particularly popular in Russia, where *Literaturnaja Gaseta*, a literary review, has described the character as "the symbol of innocent, uncorrupted childhood, the childhood we as adults find so difficult to remember and accept."

The Satirical Theater in Moscow staged a play based on the character in the 1960s, and Lindgren says that when she visits Russia, taxi drivers always talk to her about Karlson.

When former Swedish Prime Minister Ingvar Carlsson visited Moscow, she was delighted to hear that many Russians were disappointed because he wasn't the *real* Karlson.

However, says Lindgren, it is the stories of the Bullerby children that most closely approximate her own childhood. These feature the adventures of children from three families in a little village somewhere in Sweden and eulogize rural life set against a fondly painted picture of seasonal contrast. The Bullerby children are Lindgren's *nicest* characters: playful but, unlike Pippi, unwilling to overstep the line.

Bullerby is based on the little village of Sevedstorp, set amid the dense pine-and-spruce forests that cover the

MCI brings Europe and America closer together.

Call the U.S. for less with MCI CALL USA®

It's easy and affordable to call home when you use MCI CALL USA!

- Less expensive than calling through hotel operators
- Available from over 80 countries and locations worldwide
- You're connected to English-speaking MCI® Operators
- Even call 800 numbers in the U.S.†

†Regular MCI CALL USA rates apply to 800 number calls.

Call the U.S. for less from these European locations.

Dial the toll-free access number for the country you're calling from. Give the U.S. MCI Operator the number you're calling and the method of payment: MCI Card, U.S. local phone company card or collect. Your call will be completed!

Austria	022-903-012	Hungary	00*-800-01411	Poland	0*-01-04-800-222
Belgium	078-11-00-12	Ireland	1-800-551-001	Portugal	05-017-1234
Czech/Slovak	00-42-000112	Italy	172-1022	San Marino	172-1022
Denmark	8001-0022	Liechtenstein	155-0222	Spain	900-99-0014
Finland	9800-102-80	Luxembourg	0800-0112	Sweden	020-795-922
France	19*-00-19	Monaco	19*-00-19	Switzerland	155-0222
Germany	0130-0012	Netherlands	06*-022-91-22	United Kingdom	0800-89-0222
Greece	00-800-1211	Norway	050-12912	Vatican City	172-1022

* Wait for 2nd dial tone.
Collect calls not accepted on MCI CALL USA calls to 800 numbers.
Some public phones may require deposit of coin or phone card for dial tone.

MCI®

Call 1-800-444-3333 in the U.S. to apply for your MCI Card® now!

© MCI International Inc. 1993

6/93

Spend your
vacation
touring
castles.
Not train
stations.

© 1993 Budget Rent a Car Corporation

Vacation Cars. Vacation Prices. Wherever your destination
in Europe, there is sure to be one of more than 1,000 Budget locations nearby.
Budget offers considerable values on a wide variety of quality cars, and if
you book before you leave the U.S., you'll save even more with a special
rate package from the Budget World Travel Plan.℠ For information and
reservations, contact your travel consultant or call Budget in the U.S. at
800-472-3325. Or, while traveling abroad, call a Budget reservation center.

THE SMART MONEY IS ON BUDGET.®

We feature Ford and other fine cars.   *A system of corporate and licensee owned locations.*

southern Swedish province of Småland, birthplace of her father, Samuel August Ericsson, who by the time Astrid was born, in 1907, had moved to the nearby town of Vimmerby.

Home was a simple clapboard house, painted red and with a glassed-in porch, surrounded by well-tended flower beds, daisy-strewn lawns, and apple trees. Her father had started life as a hired hand but wound up running his own farm. The family was reasonably well off, though there was rarely money left over for luxuries. Samuel Ericsson was an excellent storyteller, and many of the anecdotes he told his children surfaced later in Lindgren's books. Her mother, Hanna, wrote poetry in her youth and at one time dreamed of becoming a schoolteacher.

Lindgren was one of four children. She had an elder brother, Gunnar (born 1906), and two younger sisters, Stina (born 1911) and Ingegerd (born 1916). All displayed literary talents of some kind or another: Gunnar became a member of parliament renowned for his political satires; Stina a translator; and Ingegerd a journalist.

The innocent childhood fun and games described in the Bullerby books are, by and large, those of Astrid herself and her brothers and sisters. "We played the whole time from morning to night, just like the children in the Bullerby stories," she says.

She enjoyed a warm relationship with Samuel August, a fact that is reflected time and again in her books, peopled in the main with warm, understanding, though often gruff fathers. She describes her mother, on the other hand, as a rather distant person, recalling that as a child Hanna hugged her only once. It was from her that she inherited her willpower, energy, and stubbornness, she says.

The creator of Pippi Longstocking rebelled against Hanna's authority just once as a child: "I was quite young—perhaps three or four—and one day I thought she was stupid so I decided to run away and hide in the outside toilet. I wasn't there for too long, and when I came back in my brother and sisters had been given sweets. I thought this was so unfair that I kicked out in mother's direction. I was taken into the front room and beaten."

When she started at the local school at the age of seven, in 1914, she was overcome with shyness (a traditional Swedish handicap) when the teacher called out her name and, instead of answering "yes," burst into tears.

The priest in charge of registering the new arrivals told her she could go and sit down instead of standing with the other children. "I wanted to be with the others," she says. "I absolutely didn't want to go and sit down." The tears subsided, and she now sees the incident as the day she broke through her "wall of shyness."

She was a conscientious pupil, remembered by classmate Anne-Marie Fries, the model for Madicken, another of her characters, as "unbelievably nimble. I remember her in the gym; she could climb from floor to ceiling like a monkey."

Astrid also began to show evidence of literary talents. Her essays were frequently read to the rest of the class, and, when she was 13, one of them was even published in *Wimmerby Tidning*, Vimmerby's local newspaper. This was titled "Life in Our Backyard" and described two small girls and the games they played. "They joked and called me Vimmerby's answer to Selma Lagerlöf, and I decided that if there was one thing I would never be it was an author."

She recalls her teens as a melancholy episode. "Like most teenagers, I thought I was ugly," she says, "and I just *never* fell in love. Everyone else was in love."

She left school at 16 and was given a job on *Wimmerby Tidning*, reading proofs and even covering some local events such as weddings and funerals as a reporter.

I n 1926 Astrid's blissful childhood came to a very definite end, when, at the age of 18, she had an affair with a man and became pregnant. In recent years Sweden has developed a reputation for liberality in such matters, but in those days, pregnant and unmarried, she created a huge scandal in Vimmerby, a small town steeped in traditional Lutheran values.

Astrid left home and traveled to the capital, Stockholm. "Of course, my parents weren't pleased, but I wasn't thrown out or anything like that," she explains; "wild horses wouldn't have kept me there."

She knew nobody in Stockholm. "I was terribly alone at first," she says. "I had left behind all my friends. I was very unhappy. Childhood is one thing," she says philosophically; "youth is something else."

She took solace in reading the works of Norwegian author Knut Hamsun. Hamsun's book *Hunger* made a deep impression on her. She still names it as her principal literary influence. Lonely and poor herself, she identified strongly with Hamsun's graphic descriptions of the life of a starving young writer in Norway.

In an essay for the mass-circulation Stockholm evening newspaper *Expressen* in 1974, she recalled sitting under a bird-cherry tree outside a church, reading *Hunger*. "That was the greatest literary experience I've ever had," she said.

She gave birth to a son, Lars, whom she handed over to foster parents in Copenhagen, returning to Stockholm to study shorthand and typing and to land a job at a local firm working for the father of Viveca Lindfors, the Swedish actress.

"I soon started to make friends in Stockholm, and I went to Copenhagen as often as I could to see Lars. There was never any question of his being adopted. He was my son and I loved him deeply," she says.

On one occasion she left her job during working hours to take the train to Copenhagen, only to be spotted by her boss. She was sacked.

However, her luck seemed to have turned. Astrid found an editorial job with KAK, the Swedish automobile association. There she met Sture Lindgren, whom she married in the spring of 1931. Her son came to live with them, and in 1934 she gave birth to her daughter, Karin.

The family lived in the part of Stockholm known as Vasastan, at first in a small apartment close to the main railway line to the north of Sweden, later in a spacious, light apartment overlooking a park. Lindgren still lives there today, surrounded by her books and memorabilia of her lifetime as an author.

It was in the winter of 1941 that Karin asked her to tell the story of Pippi Longstocking. "Much later I was out walking in the park when I slipped and sprained my ankle," she recalls. "I was forced to lie in bed, so I began to write down the stories I had told to Karin."

She typed a manuscript and sent it to Bonniers, one of Sweden's leading publishing houses. It was refused. Undaunted, she wrote a girl's story, *The Confidences of Britt-Mari*, which she entered for a contest organized by another, much smaller, publishing house, Rabén and Sjögren. She won second prize, and in 1944 the story was published. Lindgren also began working for the company as an editor.

The following year Rabén and Sjögren published her follow-up, titled *Kerstin and I*. Then in 1945 the company announced a new contest for books aimed at children age 6–10.

Lindgren revised her Pippi Longstocking manuscript and entered it for the contest, along with a new effort, *All About the Bullerby Children*, in which she lovingly recreated her childhood in Vimmerby. *Pippi Longstocking* won first prize. *All About the Bullerby Children* failed to take an award but was bought for publication.

The first Pippi Longstocking book was well received by both critics and public and soon sold out. However, a year later, the follow-up, *Pippi Goes Aboard*, caused a furor, with Lindgren accused of undermining the authority of parents and teachers.

Professor John Landquist, writing in the evening newspaper *Aftonbladet* accused Lindgren of "crazed fantasy" and said Pippi's adventures were "something disagreeable that scratches at the soul."

Today there is a different perspective. Viví Edström, professor of literature at the University of Stockholm, has described Pippi as "a child's projection of everything that is desirable" and claims her as a major influence on Swedish literature.

"In the still prim and moralizing children's literature of the 1940s, Astrid Lindgren's breakthrough meant that children had a literature on their own terms," says Edström.

The third and last Pippi Longstocking book, *Pippi in the South Seas*, was published in 1948. In this, Pippi sails away to a Pacific island for a reunion with her father, returning to Sweden for Christmas, which she spends alone. It could be an allegory on the fate of nonconformists in Sweden, a country where the good of the collective has always been prized above that of the individual.

Physically, the model for Pippi was a red-haired, freckle-faced friend of daughter Karin, Sonja Melin, who today sells vegetables in Hötorgshallen, one of Stockholm's few surviving indoor markets. "I meet her now and again when I go out shopping," says Lindgren. "She was just so lively as a child. As soon as I saw her, I thought, 'That's my Pippi!'"

Lindgren has created many other well-loved and sometimes controversial characters in the 30 books she has written since.

Mio My Son, written in 1954 (perhaps significantly, two years after the death of husband Sture) is one of Lindgren's most ambitious books: a highly advanced fairy story that explores difficult themes such as fear and death.

In 1985 a journalist asked Lindgren on Swedish Radio: "Isn't *Mio My Son* actually a pretty nasty book?"

She replied, "Of course; that's why children love it."

While she has never attempted a "serious" adult novel ("I never really wanted to. I'm not sure I'd be any good at it."), she has not fought shy of exploring themes considered improper for children. In 1973 controversy raged once more over *The Brothers Lionheart*, in which a dying child dreams of meeting, in another world, the brother he idealizes who has died heroically in a fire. The two boys ride off to fight the forces of evil.

Shortly after this, in 1976, Lindgren, a lifelong voter for the Social Democrats, caused a still greater fuss when she became embroiled in a row with Sweden's Socialist government.

It all started with a demand from the tax authorities, which, she calculated, would, along with her social-insurance contributions, exceed her actual income. She wrote a fairy story for *Expressen*, the Stockholm newspaper. Its main character, Pomperipossa, has always loved her country and respected its rulers. Now she turns against them: "'O you, the pure and fiery social democracy of my youth, what have they done to you?' thought Pomperipossa, 'How long shall your name be abused to protect a dictatorial, bureaucratic, unjust, authoritarian society?'"

The barb went home, and in the Swedish parliament (*Riksdag*) the then finance minister, Gunnar Sträng (his surname translates into English as "Strict") reprimanded Lindgren. "The article is a combination of inspired fantasy and total ignorance of tax policy," he said. "Astrid Lindgren should stick to what she knows, namely making up stories."

Lindgren hit back: "He may not be good at arithmetic, but he's certainly good at telling fairy-tales. I think we should trade jobs, he and I."

In that year's general election the Social Democrats lost power, after more than 40 years in office. An analysis of the result by the influential Sifo public-opinion research institute named the controversy over Lindgren's story as a major contributory factor.

Ronia, the Robber's Daughter, published in 1981, returned to a "straight" fairy-tale format, the story of a boy and girl from two different, warring bands of robbers, who run away together. This was turned into an award-winning Swedish film by comedian/director Tage Danielsson. Eleven of her books have been filmed, and Lindgren herself still takes an active interest in each project.

She has been positively deluged with prizes, including in 1989 the Albert Schweitzer Award, for her work on behalf of animal rights. At a time in life when most people would be content to wind down, she joined forces with veterinary surgeon Kristina Forslund in a campaign to persuade Sweden to introduce more stringent rules on animal husbandry.

A string of articles and open letters soon brought the government to its knees. Prime Minister Carlsson announced new legislation that he dubbed "Lex Astrid" and called on Lindgren personally to tell her about it.

Despite the fact that the laws are considered the most advanced in the world, Lindgren is not satisfied. She describes them as "toothless." "They are full of loopholes," she says. "Now we have to fight to get them tightened up."

Although hampered by failing eyesight, she began the 1990s with a new children's play written for Stockholm's Royal Dramatic Theater, plans to film *The Brothers Lionheart*, and thoughts of writing a new book.

"It depends whether I feel inspired. I write quite quickly, in shorthand at first, then I type it. I do a chapter, then rewrite until it flows properly. After that I continue with the next one. A word processor? I couldn't use one of those; I'm not a bit technically minded, I'm afraid.

"I really don't know what I would have been if I had not become an author." She smiles, perhaps thinking of her battles with authority, the Pippi Longstocking side of her personality coming to the fore. "Maybe I could have been a lawyer. I might have been rather good at that."

3   Stockholm

Set at the point where the waters of Mälaren (Lake Mälar) rush into the Baltic, Stockholm is one of Europe's most beautiful capitals. Nearly 1.6 million people now live in the greater Stockholm area, yet it remains a quiet, almost pastoral city.

Built on 14 small islands among open bays and narrow channels, Stockholm is a handsome, civilized city, filled with parks, squares, and airy boulevards, yet it is also a bustling, modern metropolis. Glass-and-steel skyscrapers abound, but you are never more than five minutes' walk from twisting medieval streets and waterside walks.

The first written mention of Stockholm dates from 1252, when a powerful regent named Birger Jarl built a fortified castle and city here. King Gustav Vasa took it over in 1523, and King Gustavus Adolphus made it the heart of an empire a century later.

During the Thirty Years' War (1618–48), Sweden gained importance as a Baltic trading state, and Stockholm grew commensurately. But by the beginning of the 18th century, Swedish influence had begun to wane, and Stockholm's development had slowed. It did not revive until the Industrial Revolution, when the hub of the city moved north from the Old Town area.

Nowadays most Stockholmers live in high-rise suburbs dotted in the pine forests and by lakesides around the capital, linked to it by a highly efficient infrastructure of roads, railways, and one of the safest subway systems in the world. Air pollution is minimal and the city streets are relatively clean and safe.

Essential Information

Important Addresses and Numbers

Tourist Information
The main tourist office, **Stockholm Information Service,** in the center of the city at **Sverigehuset** (Sweden House; Kungsträdgården, Box 7542, S–103 93 Stockholm, tel. 08/789–2000) is open every day. Here you will find information on current events, sightseeing, one-day tours, maps, and books. Bookings can be made for tours.

The free publication *Stockholm This Week* is available at most hotels and tourist centers. The Saturday edition of the daily newspapers *Dagens Nyheter* and *Svenska Dagbladet* carry current listings of events, films, restaurants, and museums (in Swedish, of course).

Embassies
U.S. Embassy: Strandvägen 101, tel. 08/783–5300. **Canadian Embassy:** Tegelbacken 4, tel. 08/237920. **U.K. Embassy,** Skärpögatan 6–8, tel. 08/6670140.

Emergencies
Dial 90000 for emergencies. This covers police, fire, ambulance, and medical help, and sea and air rescue services.

Doctors
There is a 24-hour national health service emergency number (tel. 08/449200) and private care via City Hälsocentral (tel. 08/206990).

Dentists
There is an emergency clinic at St. Erik's Hospital, open 8 AM–7 PM, with provision for acute cases until 9 PM (tel. 08/6541117). The emergency number is 08/6540590.

English-Language Bookstores
Nearly all bookshops stock English-language books. The best selections are at **Hedengren's** (Sturegallerian shopping com-

plex, tel. 08/611–5132) and **Akademibokhandeln** (Mäster Samuelsgatan 32, near city center, tel. 08/237990). For English-language newspapers and magazines, try the **Press Center** (Gallerian, Hamngatan, tel. 08/723–0191) or one of the newsstands at Central Station.

Late-Night **C. W. Scheele** (Klarabergsgatan 64, tel. 08/218934 or 08/218280)
Pharmacies is open all night.

Travel Agencies **American Express** is at Birger Jarlsgatan 1 (tel. 08/235330). **SJ,** the state railway company, has its main ticket office at Central Station (Vasagatan 1, tel. 020/757575). For air travel, contact **SAS** (Klarabergsviadukten 72, accessible from Central Station, tel. 020/910150). For other travel agencies, see the yellow pages under *Resor-Resebyråer*.

Arriving and Departing by Plane

Airport Stockholm's **Arlanda** Airport was opened in 1960 at first solely for international flights, but it now also contains the domestic terminal. Arlanda is 41 kilometers (26 miles) from the center of Stockholm and is linked to it by freeway.

Between the Buses leave both the international and domestic terminals ev-
Airport and ery 10 to 15 minutes from 7:10 AM to 10:30 PM and run to the city
City Center terminal at Klarabergsviadukten next to the central railway sta-
By Bus tion. The trip costs SKr50. For more information, call 08/6001000.

By Taxi If you look for a taxi with a large SKr250 sign on the back or side window, or ask for *fast pris* (fixed price), the fare will be SKr250. SAS operates a shared limousine to any point in central Stockholm. This will cost between SKr185 and SKr280, depending upon distance. If two or more people travel to the same address together in a limousine, only one pays the full rate; the others pay half price. For more information and bookings, call 08/797–3700.

Arriving and Departing by Car, Train, and Bus

By Car You will approach the city by either the E3 highway from the west or the E4 from the north or south. The roads are clearly marked and well sanded and plowed during winter.

By Train All trains arrive at Stockholm's Central Station (Vasagatan, tel. 08/762–2000) in downtown Stockholm. From here regular commuter trains serve the suburbs, and an underground walkway leads to the central subway station.

By Bus Buses arrive at various points, all close to the central railway station. There are numerous companies, but the principal one, with services to most parts of the country, is run by **Eurolines,** also known as Continentbus (tel. 08/234810).

Getting Around

The most effective way to get around the city is to purchase a *Stockholmskort* (Key to Stockholm) card. Besides giving unlimited transportation on city subway, bus, and rail services, it offers free admission to 50 museums and several sightseeing trips. The card costs SKr150 for 24 hours, SKr300 for two days, and SKr450 for three days. It is available from the tourist center at Sweden House in Kungsträdgården and from the Hotellcentralen accommodations bureau at Central Station.

Otherwise, tickets may be bought on buses or at the subway barrier. The minimum fare is SKr12. It is cheaper to buy a discount coupon from one of the many Pressbyrån newsstands. The standard discount coupon valid for both subway and buses costs SKr80 and is good for a fixed number of trips (approximately 10) within the greater Stockholm area during an unlimited period of time. If you plan to travel within the greater Stockholm area extensively during a 24-hour period, you can purchase an SKr60 ticket; an SKr150 ticket will allow for 72 hours of travel. People under 18 or over 65 pay a reduced fare. The 24-hour card entitles the holder to admission to Skansen, Gröna Lund, and Kaknäs Tower.

Maps and timetables for all city transportation networks are available from the SL information desks at Sergels Torg. Information is also available by phone (tel. 08/6001000).

By Car Rental cars are readily available in Sweden and relatively inexpensive. Because of the availability and efficiency of public transport, there is little point in using a car within the city limits. However, if you are traveling elsewhere in Sweden, roads are uncongested and well marked, but gasoline is expensive (SKr7 per liter at press time). All major car-rental firms are represented, including **Avis** (Ringvägen 90, tel. 08/6449980) and **Hertz** (Vasagatan 26, tel. 08/240720.)

By Bus and Subway Stockholm has excellent bus and subway service. The subway stations are marked by a blue-on-white T (short for *Tunnelbanan*, or subway). The subway covers more than 60 route miles, and trains run frequently between 5 AM and 2 AM. There are also several night buses.

By Taxi Stockholm's taxi service is efficient but overpriced. To order a cab from one of the three taxi companies, telephone **Taxi Stockholm** (tel. 08/150000), **Taxi 1** (tel. 08/6700000), or **Taxikurir** (tel. 08/300000). **Taxi Stockholm** has an immediate charge of SKr23 whether you hail a cab or order one by telephone. A trip of 10 kilometers (6 miles) costs SKr80 between 6 AM and 7 PM, SKr90 at night, and SKr100 on weekends. If you call a cab, ask the dispatcher to quote you a fast pris, which is usually lower than the meter fare.

Opening and Closing Times

Banks **Banks** are open weekdays 9:30 AM to 3 PM, but some stay open until 5:30 on most days. The bank at Arlanda Airport is open every day with extended hours, and the Forex currency-exchange offices also have extended hours.

Museums The opening times for **museums** vary widely, but most are open from 10 AM to 4 PM weekdays and over the weekend but closed on Monday. Consult the guide in *På Stan*, the entertainment supplement published in *Dagens Nyheter's* Saturday edition.

Stores **Shops** are generally open weekdays from 9 AM, 9:30 AM, or 10 AM until 6 PM and Saturday from 9 AM to 1 or 4 PM. Most of the large department stores stay open later in the evenings and some open on Sunday. Several supermarkets open on Sunday, and there is a reasonable number of late-night food shops.

Guided Tours

Orientation A bus tour in English and Swedish covering all the main points of interest leaves each day at 11 AM from the Tourist Center at Sverigehuset and costs SKr135. Other more comprehensive tours, taking in museums, the Old Town, and City Hall, cost SKr200. Tickets are available at the Tourist Center (Kungsträdgården).

City Sightseeing (tel. 08/117023) runs several tours, including the "Domestic Stockholm" tour of the Cathedral and City Hall and the "Royal Stockholm" tour, which features visits to the Royal Palace and the Treasury.

Stockholm Sightseeing (tel. 08/240470) also runs combined boat and bus tours from outside the Grand Hotel and City Hall.

Boat Tours Strömma Bolaget and Stockholm Sightseeing (Skeppsbron 22, tel. 08/233375) runs a variety of boat and bus sightseeing tours of Stockholm. Boats leave from the quays outside the Royal Dramatic Theater, the Grand Hotel, and City Hall.

Personal Guides Individual city guides may be hired from Stockholm Information Service's Guide Centralen (c/o Hotell centralen, Centralstationen, Nedrebotten, S–111 20 Stockholm, tel. 08/240880), but be sure to book well in advance. Costs average SKr975 for a three-hour tour.

Walking Tours A walking tour of the Old Town leaves every evening at 6:30 from June to mid-September, from the Obelisk, Slottsbacken (Palace Hill).

Exploring Stockholm

Highlights for First-Time Visitors

Djurgården (*see* Tour 4)
Drottningholm Palace (*see* Tour 3)
Gamla Stan (Stockholm's Old Town) (*see* Tour 2)
Kungliga Slottet (Royal Palace) (*see* Tour 2)
Stadshuset (City Hall) (*see* Tour 3)
Skansen (*see* Tour 4)
Vasa Museum (*see* Tour 4)

The center of Stockholm is Sergels Torg, a modern, sunken square. Past the Parliament building on Helgeands Holmen (Holy Ghost Island) and over the tumbling Strömmen (the Current), where Lake Mälar empties into the Baltic, lies the superbly well preserved medieval Gamla Stan (Old Town). Behind the island of Skeppsholmen another stretch of water laps Strandvägen, the waterfront for Östermalm, the upscale residential area. At the end of Strandvägen, a bridge takes you over to Djurgården. Directly south of Gamla Stan is Södermalm (known as Söder), the south island.

Numbers in the margin correspond to points of interest on the Stockholm map.

Tour 1: Modern Stockholm

The heart of the city, Sergels Torg, named for Johan Tobias Sergel (1740–1814), one of Sweden's greatest sculptors, is

dominated by modern, functional buildings that include
❶ **Kulturhuset** (the House of Culture), a library, theater, and exhibition center, with an excellent restaurant. Make a slight detour to visit the Åhléns department store, then walk north, along the pedestrian street Sergelgatan in the shadow of five identical concrete-and-glass skyscrapers to **Hötorget** (the Hay
❷ Market), where you'll find **Konserthuset** (the Concert House), a colorful outdoor fruit and vegetable market, and the PUB department store. You might also like to visit **Hötorgshallen,** an underground, old-fashioned food hall, with relatively inexpensive restaurants.

Head east over Sveavägen, where you can make a brief detour to see the spot where Olof Palme was assassinated in 1986 and to visit his grave in Adolf Fredrik's Churchyard nearby.

Next, walk down **Kungsgatan,** Stockholm's main shopping street, to Stureplan. In **Stureplan** you'll find Sturegallerian, a fine modern shopping precinct. South along **Birger Jarlsgatan,** a street named for the nobleman generally credited with founding Stockholm around 1252, there are still more interesting shops and restaurants. When you reach Nybroplan, take a look
❸ at **Kungliga Dramatiska Teatern** (the Royal Dramatic Theater), an imposing building with a gilded roof that faces out over the Baltic harbor. Here occasional productions by Ingmar Bergman, the country's leading director, provoke the imagination.

❹ Heading west up Hamngatan, drop in at **Hallwylska Museet** (the Hallwyl Museum), a private turn-of-the-century palace, with imposing wood-panel rooms, housing a collection of furniture, paintings, and musical instruments in a bewildering mélange of styles assembled by the Countess von Hallwyl, who left it to the state on her death. *Hamngatan 4, tel. 08/666–4499. Admission: SKr40. English guided tour June–July, Sun. and Mon. 1 PM; Sept.–May, Sun. 1 PM.*

Not far along Hamngatan stands **Kungsträdgården,** a park since 1562 but previously the royal kitchen garden. There are usually public concerts and events here in the summer.

❺ On the park you will find **Sverigehuset** (Sweden House), with its excellent tourist center, and on the opposite side of the street the NK department store.

If you have time, head down Kungsträdgårdsgatan to Blasieholmshamnen quay, passing the **Grand Hotel** (where Nobel laureates are accommodated each year) and visit the
❻ **National Museum,** with its fine collection of old masters, including some of Rembrandt's major works. *Södra Blasieholmshamnen, tel. 08/666–4250. Admission: SKr40, free Fri. Open Wed., Fri., Sat., Sun. 11–5; Tues., Thurs. 11–9.*

Cross the footbridge to the idyllic island **Skeppsholmen,** where
❼ you'll find two museums. **Östasiatiska Museet** (the Museum of Far Eastern Antiquities), has an arresting collection of Chinese and Japanese Buddhist sculptures and artifacts. *Skeppsholmen, tel. 08/6664391. Admission: SKr30. Open Tues. 11–9, Wed.–Sun. 11–5.*

❽ A little farther along, **Moderna Museet** (the Modern Museum) features a good selection of contemporary art, including works by Picasso, Dali, and Modigliani. The museum has a fine, health-food-oriented canteen and a workshop for children.

Skeppsholmen, tel. 08/666-4250. Admission: SKr40, free Thurs. Open Tues.-Thurs. 11-8; Fri.-Sun. 11-5.

❾ The adjoining island, **Kastellholmen,** is a pleasant place for a stroll, especially on a summer evening, with fine views of Gamla Stan's seafront, across the Baltic harbor.

Tour 2: Gamla Stan (The Old Town)

Gamla Stan sits on a cluster of small islands between two of Stockholm's main islands and is the site of the medieval city. The narrow twisting cobbled streets are lined with superbly preserved old buildings.

❿ Start at the refurbished stone **Riksdagshuset** (Parliament Building) on **Helgeandsholmen** (Holy Ghost Island). It dates from the end of the 19th century. *Admission free. English guided tours Jan.-June, weekends 1:30; June-Aug., weekdays 12:30, 3.*

⓫ Cross the bridge to **Kungliga Slottet** (the Royal Palace), a magnificent granite edifice designed by Nicodemus Tessin and completed in 1760. There is a fine view here of the Baltic harbor, with the *af Chapman* sailing-ship youth hostel and the Grand Hotel and National Museum in the background. The **State Apartments** feature fine furnishings and Gobelins tapestries. **Livrustkammaren** (the Royal Armory) boasts an outstanding collection of weaponry and royal regalia, while **Skattkammaren** (the Treasury) houses the crown jewels, which are no longer used, even on ceremonial occasions, in this self-consciously egalitarian country. *Admission: State Apartments SKr25; treasury and royal armory SKr40; treasury and armory open Mon.-Sat. 11-3, Sun. noon-4. State apartments open Tues.-Sat. 10-3, Sun. noon-3.*

It is only a short walk from the palace to Stockholm's 15th-century Gothic cathedral, **Storkyrkan** (the Great Church), where Swedish kings were crowned until 1907. It contains a dramatic wooden statue of St. George slaying the dragon, carved by Bernt Notke of Lübeck in 1489, and the *Parhelion,* a painting of Stockholm dating from 1520, the oldest in existence.

Walk a few yards on Källargränd to the front of Storkyrkan or on Trångsund to the rear until you reach **Stortorget** (the Great Square), which is small but marvelously atmospheric, fronted by magnificent old merchants' houses. Here in 1520 the Danish King Christian II ordered a massacre of Swedish noblemen, paving the way for a national revolt against foreign rule and the founding of Sweden as a sovereign state under King Gustav Vasa, who ruled from 1523 to 1560.

⓭ In **Stockholms Fondbörs** (the Stock Exchange), which also fronts onto the square, the Swedish Academy meets each year to decide the winner of the Nobel Prize for literature. The Stock Exchange itself is computerized and rather quiet. There are no tours in English, but there is a film about the Stock Exchange in Swedish. *Stockholms Fondbörs, Källargränd 2, Stockholm, tel. 08/613-8892.*

⓮ Passing among ancient buildings, you walk down Svartmangatan to **Tyska Kyrkan** (the German Church), with its magnificent oxidized copper spire and airy interior. Then go down

Hennes and Mauritz Apotek

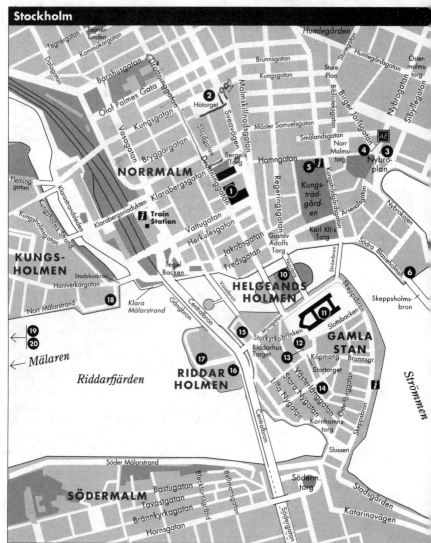

Stockholm

Galerian

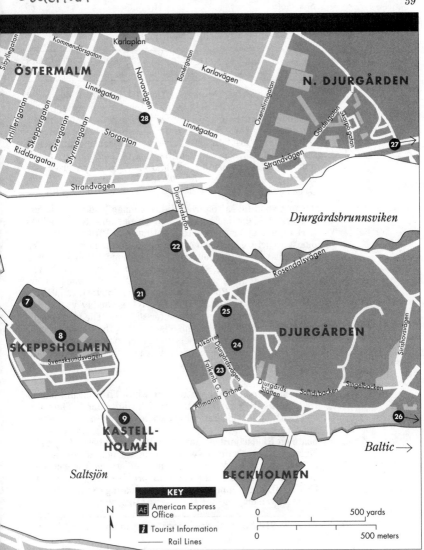

Tyska Brinken to Västerlånggatan, where you can walk north, checking out pricey fashion boutiques.

Time Out On Västerlånggatan you can stop for a coffee and a pastry in **Grå Munken** (the Gray Monk) coffee house.

⓯ Cut down Storkyrkobrinken to the 17th-century **Riddarhuset** (the House of Nobles), built in the Dutch Baroque style. Before the abolition of the aristocracy early in the 20th century, it was the gathering place for the First Estate of the realm. Hanging from its walls are 2,325 escutcheons, representing all the former noble families of Sweden. Because of the building's excellent acoustic properties, Riddarhuset is often used for concerts. *Riddarhuset, tel. 08/100857. Admission: SKr20. Open weekdays 11:30–12:30.*

⓰ A short walk takes you over Riddarholmen bridge to **Riddarholmen** (the Island of Knights), on which stands **Riddarholmskyrkan,** a Greyfriar monastery dating from 1270. The second-oldest structure in Stockholm, it has been the burial place for 17 Swedish kings over four centuries. The most famous figures buried here are King Gustavus Adolphus, hero of the Thirty Years' War, and the warrior king Karl XII, renowned for his daring invasion of Russia, who finally fell in Norway in 1718. The latest king to be put to rest here was Gustav V, in 1950. Normally the church is not used for services. The various rulers' sarcophagi, usually embellished with their monograms, are visible in the small chapels given over to the various dynasties. The redbrick structure is distinguished by its delicate iron fretwork spire. *Admission: SKr10. Open May–Aug. 10–3, Sun. 1–3.*

⓱ Riddarholmen is also the site of the white 17th-century palace that houses the **Svea Hovrätt** (Swedish High Court). The quiet and restful quayside here is an excellent place to end an afternoon's sightseeing, sitting by the water's edge, watching the boats on **Riddarfjärden** (Bay of Knights) and beyond it, Lake Mälar. It affords a fine view of the lake, the magnificent arches of **Västerbron** (the West Bridge) in the distance, the southern heights, and above all the imposing profile of Stadshuset (the City Hall), which appears almost to be floating on the water. At the quay you may see one of the Göta Canal ships.

Tour 3: Stadshuset and Drottningholm

Stockholm's City Hall and Drottningholm Palace, outstanding embodiments of Swedish architecture and sensibilities from different centuries, share access from Mälaren.

⓲ Start at the redbrick **Stadshuset,** a powerful symbol of Stockholm, among the most impressive pieces of modern architecture in Europe. Completed in 1923, it was created by Rangnar Östberg, one of the founders of the National Romantic movement. It is both functional (headquarters for the city council) and ornate (its immense Blue Hall is the venue for the Nobel Prize dinner each December, Stockholm's principal social event). A trip to the top of the 348-foot tower, most of which can be achieved by elevator, is rewarded by a breathtaking panorama of the city and Riddarfjärden. *Hantverkargatan 1, tel. 08/ 785–9074. Admission to tower: SKr10. Tour of Stadshuset and* *tower: SKr25; tours at 10 and noon Sat. Tower open May–Sept., daily 10–4:30.*

Time Out After climbing the tower, relax on Stadshuset's fine grass terraces, which lead down to the bay, or perhaps have lunch in **Stadshuskällaren** (the City Hall Cellar, tel. 08/650–5454), whose kitchen prepares the annual Nobel banquet.

Walk the short distance over Stadshusbron (City Hall Bridge) to the quayside at **Klara Mälarstrand,** from which boats leave ⑲ regularly for **Drottningholms Slott** (Queen's Island Castle), a miniature Versailles dating from the 17th century on an island in Mälaren some 45 minutes from the city center. The royal family once used it as their summer residence, but, tiring of the immensity of the Royal Palace, they moved permanently to one wing of Drottningholm in the 1970s. Drottningholm is one of the most delightful of European palaces, embracing all that was best in the art of living practiced by mid-18th-century royalty. The interiors are from the 17th, 18th, and 19th centuries, and most are open to the public. *Drottningholms Slott, tel. 08/ 759–0310. Admission: SKr30. Open May–Aug., daily 11–4:30; Sept., weekdays 1–3:30.*

The lakeside gardens of Drottningholm are its most beautiful ⑳ asset, containing **Drottningholms Slottsteater** (the Court Theater), the only complete theater to survive from the 18th century anywhere in the world. It was built by Queen Lovisa Ulrika in 1766 as a wedding present for her son Gustav III. It fell into disuse after his assassination at a masked ball in 1792, but in 1922 it was rediscovered. There is now a small theater museum here as well. To obtain tickets for a performance, you must book well in advance. A word of caution: the seats are extremely hard—take a cushion. *Castle tel. 08/759–0310. Admission: SKr30. Open May–Aug., weekdays 11:30–4:30, Sun. 11:30–4:30; Sept. 12:30–3:30.*

Tour 4: Djurgården and Skansen

Djurgården is Stockholm's pleasure island. On it you will find the outdoor museum Skansen, the Gröna Lund amusement park, and the *Vasa*, a 17th-century warship raised from the bottom of the harbor in 1961, as well as other delights.

You can reach **Djurgården** by sea aboard the small ferries that leave from **Slussen** at the southern end of Gamla Stan or from **Nybrokajen** (the New Bridge Quay) in front of the **Kungliga Dramatiska Teater.** Alternatively, starting at the theater, stroll down the **Strandvägen** quayside, taking in the magnificent old sailing ships permanently anchored here and the fine views over the harbor, and then cross **Djurgårdsbron** (the Djurgården Bridge) to the island. Your first port of call should ㉑ be the **Vasa Museet,** where you can see the *Vasa*, a warship that sank on its maiden voyage in 1628, was forgotten for three centuries, then located in 1956, and raised from the seabed in 1961. Its hull was found to be largely intact, because the Baltic's brackish waters do not support worms that otherwise eat ship's timbers. Now largely restored to her former, if brief, glory, the man-of-war resides in a handsome new museum. *Galärvarvet, Djurgården, tel. 08/666–4800. Guided tours in English every hour. Admission: SKr40 adults, SKr10 children. Open daily 10–5 (Wed. 10–8).*

㉒ Close by is the **Nordiska Museet** (the Nordic Museum), housed in a splendid late-Victorian structure, worth a quick visit for an insight into Swedish folklore. Its collection includes peasant costumes from every region of the country and exhibits on the Sami (pronounced **sah**-mee; Lapps), formerly seminomadic reindeer herders who inhabit the far north. *Djurgårdsvägen 6–16, tel. 08/666-4600. Admission SKr50. Open Tues., Wed., Fri. 10–4, Thurs. 10–8, weekends 11–4.*

㉓ Just down the road is **Gröna Lund,** an amusement park that features a range of carnival rides, though on a smaller scale than both Copenhagen's Tivoli and Göteborg's Liseberg. *Djurgårdsvägen, tel. 08/665-7000. Admission: SKr35 adults, children 12 years and under free. Open mid-Apr.–late Aug.*

㉔ Cross Djurgårdsvägen to **Skansen,** a must for any visitor to Stockholm. The world's first open-air museum, it was founded by philologist and ethnographer Artur Hazelius (who is also buried here) in 1891 to preserve traditional Swedish architecture, including farmhouses, windmills, barns, a working glassblower's hut, and churches, brought from all parts of the country. Not only is Skansen a delightful trip out of time in the center of a modern city, it also provides an easily assimilated insight into the life and culture of Sweden's various regions. In addition, the park contains a zoo, a circus, an aquarium, a theater, and cafés. *Djurgårdsslätten 49–51, tel. 08/663-0500. Admission: SKr20 adults (except weekends, SKr30), children under 14 free. Open Sept.–Apr. daily 9–5; May–Aug., daily 9–10.*

Time Out   For a snack with a view, try the **Solliden Restaurant** at Skansen. The museum also offers a selection of open-air snack bars and cafés; Gröna Lund has four different restaurants.

㉕ The charmingly archaic **Biologiska Museet** (Biological Museum), in the shadow of Skansen, has a collection of stuffed animals in various simulated environments. *Hazeliusporten, tel. 08/661-1383. Admission: SKr6. Open daily 10–3.*

㉖ Djurgården's treasure is **Waldemarsudde,** the beautiful turn-of-the-century home of Sweden's Prince Eugen, an accomplished painter, who died in 1947. His mansion, bequeathed to the Swedish people, maintains an important collection of Nordic paintings from 1880 to 1940 in addition to the prince's own works. Its grounds are a delight. *Prins Eugens väg 6, tel. 08/662-1833. Admission: SKr30. Open Tues.–Sun. 11–5; Tues. and Thurs. 7–9.*

㉗ Finally, eastward on Norra Djurgården is **Kaknästornet,** the radio and television tower, completed in 1967 and, at 511 feet, the highest building in Scandinavia. Here you can eat a meal in a restaurant 426 feet above the ground and enjoy panoramic views of the city and the archipelago. *Mörkakroken, off Kaknäsvägen, tel. 08/667-8517. Admission: SKr20. Open Apr. 15–Sept. 15, daily 9 AM–10:30 PM.*

Cross the Djurgården bridge and proceed up Narvavägen to **㉘** **Historiska Museet** (the Museum of National Antiquities), which houses important collections of Viking gold and silver treasures. **Myntkabinettet** (the Royal Cabinet of Coin), in the same building, boasts the world's largest coin. *Narvavägen 13–17,* *tel. 08/783–9400. Admission to both: SKr50. Open Tues., Wed., and Fri. noon–5; Thurs. noon–8; weekends 10–5.*

Short Excursions from Stockholm

Numbers in the margin correspond to points of interest on the Excursions from Stockholm map.

Skärgården Skärgården (the archipelago) is Stockholm's greatest natural asset: more than 25,000 islands and skerries, many uninhabited, spread across an almost tideless sea of clean, clear water. To sail lazily among these islands aboard an old steamboat on a summer's night is a timeless delight.

Regular ferry services depart from the quayside in front of the Grand Hotel. Cruises on a variety of boats leave from the harbor in front of the Royal Palace or from Nybrokajen, across the road from the Royal Dramatic Theater.

For the tourist with limited time, one of the simplest ways to get a taste of the archipelago's delights is to take a one-hour ❶ ferry trip to **Vaxholm,** an extremely pleasant, though sometimes crowded, mainland seaside town of small, red-painted wooden houses. It is the site of a fortress guarding the approaches to Stockholm. The fortress, **Vaxholms Kastell,** houses a small museum, **Vaxholms Kastell Museum,** showing the defense of Stockholm over the centuries. *Tel. 08/541–30107. Admission: SKr20 or SKr45 including boat fare. Open May 15–Aug. 31, daily noon–3:45; July 3–14, daily 11–6 (when a pontoon bridge temporarily links the island with the mainland). Group admission also at other times by arrangement.*

A more authentic way of getting to know the archipelago is to seek out the *Blidösund.* A coal-fired steamboat built in 1911 that was in regular service for 50 years, it is now run by a small group of enthusiasts, who take parties of around 250 merrymakers on evening cruises. The *Blidösund* leaves from a berth close to the Royal Palace in Stockholm. *SS Blidösund, Skeppsbron 10, tel. 08/117113 or 08/202186. Fare: SKr100. Season: May–Sept.; departs Mon.–Thurs. at 7:30, returns at 11:15.*

The finest of the other steamboats is *Björkfjärden,* which leaves from Nybrokajen, close to the Strand Hotel. *Björkfjärden, Ångfartyget, St. Nygatan 45, tel. 08/233375. Fare: SKr100. Season: June–Aug.*

Mälaren Boats plying the lake leave from a quay close to City Hall. There are regular services and excursions to various points, but the most delightful way to experience the true vastness of ❷ Sweden's third-largest lake is the trip to **Mariefred** aboard the coal-fired steamer of the same name, built in 1903 and still going strong. *Round-trip fare, SKr150; one-way, SKr100. Limited service from May, regular sailings from June. For boat schedules, contact Mariefred Tourist Office, tel. 0159/29790.*

The principal attraction in Mariefred, an idyllic little town of mostly timbered houses, is the 16th-century **Gripsholm Slott** (castle), which contains fine Renaissance chambers, a superbly atmospheric theater dating from the late 1700s, and Sweden's royal portrait collection. *S–64700, tel. 0159/10194. Admission: SKr30. Open May, June, Aug., daily 10–4; July, daily 10–5;*

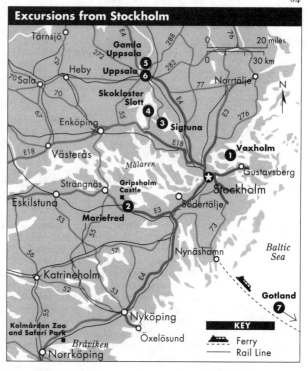

Excursions from Stockholm

Apr. Tues.–Sun. 10–3; Sept., Tues.–Sun. 10–4; Jan.–Mar. and Oct.–Dec., weekends 12–5.

You can also travel by narrow-gauge steam railway from Mariefred to a junction on the main line to Stockholm, returning to the capital by ordinary train.

Sigtuna
3
This extremely picturesque and restful little town of 5,000 is idyllically located some 30 kilometers (20 miles) from Stockholm on a northern arm of Lake Mälar. **Sigtuna** was the principal trading post of the Svea, the tribe that settled Sweden after the last Ice Age. After it was sacked by Estonian pirates, its merchants founded Stockholm sometime in the 13th century. Little remains of Sigtuna's former glory, beyond parts of the principal church. The town hall dates from the 18th century, the main part of town from the early 1800s, and there are two houses said to date from the 15th century. Sigtuna can be reached by taking a commuter train from Stockholm's Central Station to Märsta, where you change to Bus 570 or 575. From June to August it can also be reached by boat from the quay near City Hall. The fare is approximately SKr60.

Skokloster Slott
4
About 20 kilometers (12 miles) to the northeast of Sigtuna off the E18 highway lies **Skokloster Slott**, a Baroque castle that was the home of a celebrated Swedish soldier, Field Marshal Carl Gustav Wrangel. It is exquisitely furnished with the spoils of his successful campaigns in Europe in the 17th century. *S–14800 Bålsta, tel. 018/386077. Admission: SKr40. Open May–Aug. 31, daily 11–4. Special tours for groups can be arranged in September.*

What to See and Do with Children

In addition to **Skansen** and the **Gröna Lund** amusement park, (*see* Tour 4, *above*) the **Stockholms Leksaksmuseet** (Toy Museum) features a collection of toys and dolls from all over the world and has a playroom for children. *Mariatorget 1, Södermalm, tel. 08/6416100. Admission: SKr25 adults, SKr10 children. Open Tues.–Fri. 10–4, Sat.–Sun. 12–4.*

See also the Saturday *Dagens Nyheter* newspaper for details of children's events at other museums.

Off the Beaten Track

Hidden away over a grocery store, **Strindbergsmuseet Blå Tornet** (Strindberg Museum, Blue Tower) is dedicated to Sweden's most important author and dramatist (1849–1912). This was actually August Strindberg's home from 1908 until his death, and the interior has been lovingly reconstructed with authentic furnishings and other objects (including his pen). It also has a library, a press, and picture archives and arranges literary, musical, and theatrical events. *Drottninggatan 85, tel. 08/113789. Admission: SKr20. Open Tues. 10–4 and 6–8; Thurs.–Sat. 10–4; Sun. 12–4.*

Millesgården is another home that has become a museum dedicated to its former owner, in this case American-Swedish sculptor Carl Milles (1875–1955). His works and his collection of the works of other artists are displayed in the house, and his sculptures top columns on terraces in a magical garden high above the harbor and the city. *Carl Milles väg 2, Lidingö, tel. 08/731–5060. Admission: SKr30. Open: May–Sept., daily 10–5; June–Aug., Wed. 10–9; Oct.–Apr., Tues.–Sun. 11–4.*

Shopping

Shopping Districts The three main department stores are situated in the central city area, as are the **Gallerian** and **Sturegallerian** shopping malls. However, there are interesting boutiques and galleries in **Västerlånggatan,** the main street of the Old Town, and some excellent handicrafts and art shops line the raised sidewalk at the start of **Hornsgatan** in Söder.

Department Stores Sweden's leading department store, **NK** (the initials, pronounced ***enn-koh***, stand for *Nordiska Kompaniet*), is located in Hamngatan, just across the street from Kungsträdgården (tel. 08/762–8000). The **Åhléns** department store (tel. 08/246000) is only a short distance up Hamngatan at Klarabergsgatan. **PUB** (the initials of founder Paul U. Bergström) is at Hötorget (tel. 08/791–6000). Greta Garbo worked here before she went into films.

Street Markets There is a **flower and fruit market** every day at **Hötorget** and a **fleamarket** at the suburb of **Skärholmen.** The best streets for **bric-a-brac** and **antiques** are **Odengatan** and **Roslagsgatan** (Odenplan subway station).

Specialty Stores The principal local auction houses are **Lilla Bukowski**
Antiques (Strandvägen 7, tel. 08/6140800), **Beijers Auktioner** (Birger Jarlsgatan 6, tel. 08/6117870), and **Stockholms Auktionsverk** (Jakobsgatan 10, tel. 08/142440).

Books Both **Hedengrens** (Sturegallerian, tel. 08/611–5132) and **Akademibokhandeln** (Mäster Samuelsgatan 32, tel. 08/214890) have excellent selections of English-language and Swedish books. **Hemlins** (Västerlånggatan 6, in the Old Town, tel. 08/106180) carries foreign titles and antique books.

Crystal Swedish crystal is available at a number of stores, among them **Nordiska Kristall** (Kungsgatan 9, tel. 08/104372), **Svenskt Glas,** (Birger Jarlsgatan 8, tel. 08/6797909), **New Scandinavian Design** (Tegelbacken 4, tel. 08/219211), and **NK** (*see* Department Stores, *above*). All feature everything from small bowls to major art works at prices that range from SKr144 to SKr88,000.

Handicrafts Swedish handicrafts from all over the country are available at **Svensk Hemslöjd** (Sveavägen 44, tel. 08/232115). **Stockholms Läns Hemslöjdsförening** (Drottninggatan 14, tel. 08/761–1717) also has an excellent selection. Prices are high, but so is the quality.

Men's Clothing For suits and evening suits for both sale and rental, **Hans Allde** (Birger Jarlsgatan 58, tel. 08/200835) provides good, old-fashioned service. For shirts, there is **La Chemise** (Smålandsgatan 11, tel. 08/6111494).

Women's Clothing There are many boutiques in **Biblioteksgatan** and **Västerlånggatan** in Gamla Stan, in addition to stores such as **Twilfit** (Nybrogatan 11, tel. 08/662–3817; Gallerian, tel. 08/216221; and Gamla Brogatan 36–38, tel. 08/201954). **Hennes & Mauritz** (Hamngatan 14 and 22; Drottninggatan 53 and 56; Hötorget 1–3; Sergelgatan 1, 11, 22; and Sergels Torg 12; all tel. 08/796–5500) is one of the few Swedish-owned clothing stores to have achieved international success.

Sports and Fitness

Participant Sports

Bicycling Stockholm is well supplied with bicycle routes and, except during peak traveling times, bikes may be taken aboard commuter trains for excursions to the suburbs. **Cyckelfrämjandet** (tel. 08/321680), a local bicyclists' association, publishes an English-language guide to cycling trips. Bicycles may be rented from **Cykel & Mopeduthyrning** (Strandvägen at Kajplats 24, tel. 660–7959) or from **Skepp & Hoj** (Gälarvärvsvägen 10, tel. 08/660–5757). Rental costs average around SKr80 per day.

Golf There are numerous golf courses around Stockholm, among them **Lidingö Golf Club** (Sticklinge on Lidingö, tel. 08/765–7911) and **Nacka Golfbana** (Nacka, tel. 08/773–0431).

Health and Fitness Centers Keeping fit is an obsession with Swedes. **Friskis & Svettis** (Eriksgatan 63, 100 28 Stockholm, tel. 08/6520470) is a legendary local gym specializing in aerobics. Farther along the same road is the **Atalanta Girls Gym** (Eriksgatan 34, tel. 08/6506625). For relatively inexpensive massage, try **Axelsons Friskvård** (Gästrikegatan 12, tel. 08/338988). Otherwise, consult the yellow pages under "Frisk-, hälsovård."

Jogging Numerous parks and footpaths dot the central city area, among them **Haga Park,** which also has canoe rentals, **Djurgården,** and **Liljans Skogen.** An interesting track runs alongside the

Karlbergssjö; it can be reached from an alleyway and steps at the side of Eriksbron (the Eric Bridge).

Swimming In the center of town, **Centralbadet** (Drottninggatan 88, tel. 08/ 242402), newly renovated, boasts an extra-large pool and numerous other facilities. **Sturebadet** (Sturegalleriet, tel. 08/ 6796700) also has excellent facilities.

Tennis There are many fine tennis courts in and around Stockholm. **Kungliga Tennishallen** (the Royal Tennis Hall, Lidingövägen 75, tel. 08/667–0350) is where former champion Björn Borg plays. Another good venue is **Tennisstadion** (Fiskartorpsvägen 20, tel. 08/215454).

Spectator Sports

There are two main sports stadiums in Stockholm, featuring soccer in summer and ice hockey in winter. The **Globe** (Box 10055, S–12127, tel. 08/725–1000), at 281 feet claimed to be the world's tallest spherical building, has its own subway station just across the water from Söder. The Stockholm Open Tennis Tournament is held here each November. To the north there is **Råsundastadion** (Solnavägen 51, Solna, tel. 08/735–0900).

Beaches

The best bathing places in central Stockholm are on the island of **Långholmen** and at **Rålambshov** at the end of Norr Mälarstrand. Both are grassy or rocky lakeside hideaways. Topless sunbathing is virtually de rigueur.

Dining

Recently restaurant prices have declined and a greater selection of less expensive restaurants has appeared on the scene. Even the higher-priced restaurants in Stockholm have kept their prices down. One factor has been the decrease in the value-added tax on restaurant food from 25% to 21%. Among Swedish dishes, the best bets are fish, particularly salmon, and the smörgåsbord buffet, which is usually a good value. Many restaurants close for either July or August, and most close at Christmas and New Year. It is advisable to telephone first to check that the restaurant is open. Unless otherwise stated, casual dress is acceptable. (For rates, *see* Staying in Sweden in Chapter 1.)

Highly recommended restaurants are indicated by a star ★.

Very Expensive

Grands Franska Matsalen. This classic French restaurant in the Grand Hotel has an inspiring view of the Old Town and the Royal Palace across the inner harbor waters. The food is equally inspiring, and the presence of Sweden's Chef of the Year for 1989, Roland Persson, has only improved matters. The duckling in coriander with honey-and-cinnamon sauce, and the medallions of deer with shiitake mushrooms in wild-berry cream sauce are highly recommended. The thick carpets and elegant decor should be matched by your thick wallet. *Grand Hotel, Blasieholmshamnen 8, tel. 08/221020. Reservations required. Jacket and tie required. AE, DC, MC, V.*

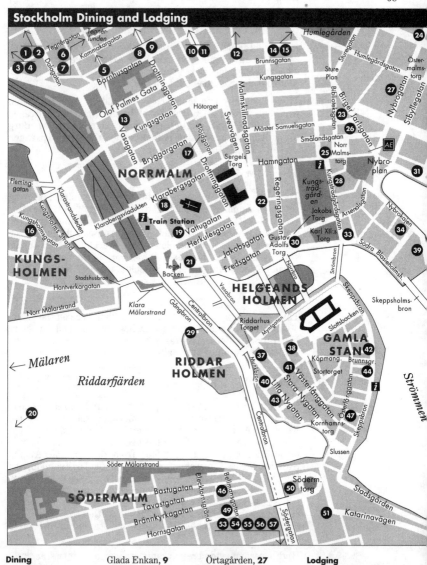

Stockholm Dining and Lodging

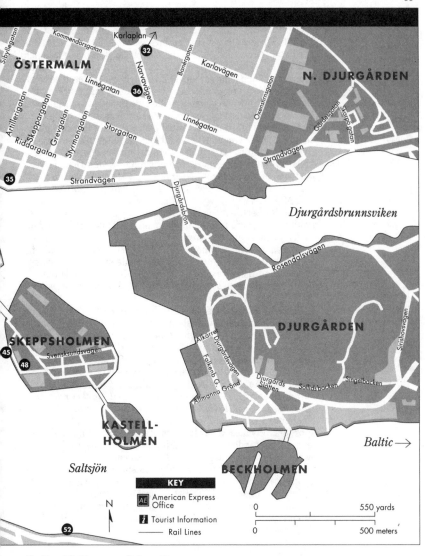

Continental, **18**

Diplomat, **31**

Grand, **33**

Gustav af Klint, **52**

Hotel City, **17**

Hotel Gamla Stan, **43**

Lady Hamilton, **38**

Långholmen, **20**

Lord Nelson, **41**

Mälardrottningen, **29**

Mornington, **24**

Reisen, **42**

Royal Viking, **21**

Scandic Crown, **50**

Sergel Plaza, **22**

Skeppsholmen, **48**

Stockholm, **25**

Strand, **34**

Tegnérlunden, **6**

Victory, **40**

Operakällaren. Stockholm's best-known restaurant has a magnificent location in the Opera House at the end of Kungsträdgården. Operakällaren started business in 1787, so the tone is predictably snobbish but not intrusively so. The decor is lavish Old World style, with deep Oriental carpeting, shiny polished brass, and handsome carved-wood chairs and tables. The crystal chandeliers are said to be Sweden's most magnificent, and the high windows on the south side give fine views of the Royal Palace. Top selections on the grand smörgåsbord table with pickled herring, rollmops (rolled herring), reindeer and elk in season, and ice cream with cloudberry (a yellow blackberry native to Scandinavia) sauce. Resting on its laurels, Operakällaren tends to be more a Swedish institution than a great gastronomic experience. *Operahuset, Jakobs Torg 2, tel. 08/ 111125. Reservations required. Jacket and tie required. AE, DC, MC, V.*

★ **Paul & Norbert.** Among the best culinary spots in Stockholm, Paul and Norbert is a quaint, romantic restaurant located on the city's most elegant avenue and overlooking one of its most picturesque bays. It is noted for its French-style preparations of indigenous wild game such as reindeer, elk, partridge, grouse, and fish of various kinds. The decor is rustic but refined. *Strandvägen 9, tel. 08/6638183. Reservations required. AE, DC, MC, V. Closed weekends.*

Ulriksdalsvärdshus. This beautifully situated country inn, built in 1868, offers both Swedish and international cuisine, but is particularly noted for its lunchtime smörgåsbord. It provides a specifically Swedish experience in the park of an 18th-century palace, overlooking orchards and a peaceful lake. The interior is traditional, and guests even stand and sing the Swedish national anthem as the flag is lowered. *Ulriksdals Slottspark, Solna, tel. 08/850815. Reservations advised. Jacket required. AE, DC, MC, V. Closed Christmas. No dinner Sun.*

★ **Wedholms Fisk.** Noted for its fresh seafood dishes, Wedholms appropriately faces a bay in the center of Stockholm. High ceilings, large windows, and tasteful modern paintings from the owner's personal collection create a spacious, sophisticated atmosphere. The traditional Swedish cuisine is simple, straightforward, generous, and delicious, and consists almost exclusively of seafood. Try the poached sole in lobster-and-champagne sauce or the Pilgrim mussels Provençal. *Nybrokajen 17, tel. 08/6117874. Reservations advised. AE, DC, MC, V. Closed Sun.*

Expensive

Aurora. Extremely elegant, if a little staid, this Old Town cellar restaurant is set in a beautiful 300-year-old house. A largely foreign clientele enjoys top-quality Swedish and international cuisine served in intimate small rooms. The adjacent Old City Club, under the same management, is open for moderate-price lunch Monday through Friday. *Munkbron 11, tel. 08/219359. Reservations required. Jacket and tie required. AE, DC, MC, V. Closed Sun.*

Blå Gåsen. This is a classic Östermalm restaurant: very classy, cozy, and costly. The Swedish/French food is excellent, the service usually impeccable. *Karlavägen 28, tel. 08/6110269. Reservations advised. Jacket and tie required. AE, DC, MC, V.*

★ **Clas på Hörnet.** In the small, intimate ground floor of a restored inn built in 1739, this restaurant is only a little off the beaten track but well worth seeking out for its extremely pleasant, relaxed, and old-fashioned atmosphere. It offers a choice of Swedish or international cuisine, including outstanding *stromming* (Baltic herring). *Surbrunnsgatan 20, tel. 08/165136. Reservations required. Jacket and tie required. AE, DC, MC, V. Closed Christmas.*

Den Gyldene Freden. Sweden's most famous old tavern, "Freden" has recently been restored after being closed for many years. The building dates from 1721 and the restaurant from the following year. The haunt of bards and barristers, artists and ad people, Freden could probably serve sawdust and still be popular, but the staff is worthy of the restaurant's hallowed reputation. The cuisine has a Swedish orientation, but Continental influences are spicing up the menu. Season permitting, try oven-baked fillets of turbot, served with chanterelles and cèpes. The gray hen fried with spruce twigs and dried fruit is another good selection. The menu changes regularly and the friendly staff will gladly make recommendations. *Österlånggatan 51, tel. 08/109046. Reservations advised. AE, DC, MC, V. Closed Sun. No lunch.*

Edsbacka Krog. In 1626, Edsbacka became Stockholm's first licensed inn. This out-of-town Continental/Swedish restaurant boasts reliably superb culinary standards. With its exposed, rough-hewn beams, plaster walls, and open fireplaces, it has the feel of a country inn for the gentry. The owner, Christer Lindström, is an award-winning chef; his tarragon chicken with winter vegetables is worth the occasional long wait. *Sollentunavägen 220, Sollentuna, tel. 08/963300. Reservations advised. AE, DC, MC, V. Closed Sun. No lunch Sat.*

Greitz. Home-style Swedish cuisine is served in this classy and comfortable restaurant. Try the *Sotare* (grilled Baltic herring with parsley and butter). Also good is the *burbot* (local whitefish) stewed in wine with burbot roe and croutons. The decor is revamped cafe style, with the once-stained wood paneling around the room now painted a trendy burgundy red. *50 Vasagatan, tel. 08/234820. Reservations advised. Jacket and tie advised. AE, DC, MC, V. Closed Sun.*

Invito. This elegant and airy Italian restaurant in Östermalm has a pleasant dining room on the ground floor and atmospheric cellar rooms below. *Engelbrektsgatan 37, tel. 08/203934. Reservations required. Jacket and tie required. AE, DC, MC, V.*

Källaren Diana. Something of an institution, this is a great restaurant for authentic Swedish cuisine at the highest level. Located in an atmospheric Gamla Stan cellar, it is noted for such Swedish specialties as cuts of elk and reindeer meat and cloudberry desserts. Nowadays in summer customers may be predominantly foreign or businesspeople from the provinces. *Brunnsgränd 2, tel. 08/107310. Reservations advised. Jacket required. AE, DC, MC, V.*

KB. The most urbane of Stockholm's quality restaurants serves Swedish country fare, painstakingly prepared. The middle-aged waitresses are familiar in the best sense, and the patrons are among the city's most relaxed. There are soft, fitted benches around the smallish dining room, and another, more casual dining room in the bar next door, where you might try the excellent *mejramkorv* (marjoram sausage). Chef Örjan Klein pushes low-cal, low-fat dishes in the best modern tradition (i.e., with visible homage to France). Try the pot-au-feu with chicken and almond potatoes, or the Swedish freshwater crayfish in season. *Smålandsgatan 7, tel. 08/6796032. Reservations advised. AE, DC, MC, V. Closed Sun. No lunch Sat.*

Stallmästaregården. A historic old inn with an attractive courtyard and garden, Stallmästaregården is located in the Haga Park, half an hour from the city center. The fine summer meals are served in the courtyard overlooking the waters of Brunnsviken. *Norrtull, near Haga, tel. 08/6101300. Reservations advised. AE, DC, MC, V.*

Moderate

★ **Bakfickan.** The name means "hip pocket" and is appropriate because this restaurant is tucked round the back of the Opera House complex. It's a budget-price alternative to the nearby Operakällaren and is particularly popular at lunchtime, offering Swedish home cooking and a range of daily dishes. Counter and table service are available. *Operahuset, Jakobs Torg 2, tel. 08/242700. No reservations. AE, DC, MC, V. Closed Sun.*

Butler's. The menu is short but dependable, specializing in eclectic lamb dishes from southern Europe. Try the saddle of lamb with mixed vegetables Provençal, or the steak tournedos in creamy mustard sauce with garlic and mushrooms. The checkered tablecloths and the French bistro chairs give Butler's an indefinable Continental atmosphere. Butler's is noisy but very trendy for lunch. *Rörstrandsgatan 11, tel. 08/321823. Reservations advised. AE, DC, MC, V. No lunch on weekends.*

De Fyras Krog. The Inn of the Four Estates in Södermalm boasts a good traditional Swedish menu and an intimate, cozy atmosphere. *Tavastgatan 22, tel. 08/6586405. Reservations advised. AE, DC, MC, V.*

Hannas Krog. What started out as an interesting neighborhood spot has become one of Söder's trendiest restaurants. Ranging from Caribbean shrimp specialties to Provençal lamb dishes, the food is good, if a bit pricey. Service is consistent with the restaurant's crowded and relaxed atmosphere. *Skånegatan 80, tel. 08/6438225. Reservations required. AE, DC, MC, V.*

★ **Nils Emil.** This bustling restaurant in Södermalm is known for delicious Swedish cuisine and generous helpings at reasonable prices. It attracts members of the royal family on a regular basis. The paintings of personable owner/chef Nils Emil's island birthplace in the Stockholm Archipelago are by a well-known Swedish artist. *Folkungagatan 122, tel. 08/407209. Reservations required. Jacket and tie advised. AE, DC, MC, V.*

Prinsen. Established in 1897, this lively restaurant has remained an unpretentious, unchanging presence in a fashionable area given to overtrendiness—one reason for Prinsen's popularity with the city's writers, musicians, and artists. The food is primarily robust, if plain, Swedish and French fare, served by attentive waiters negotiating narrow aisles and crowded booths. *Mäster Samuelsgatan 4, tel. 08/6111331. Reservations advised. AE, DC, MC, V.*

Rolfs Kök. Small and modern, this restaurant combines an informal atmosphere with excellent Swedish/French cuisine at reasonable prices. The lamb is usually a good bet. *Tegnérgatan 41, tel. 08/101696. No reservations. AE, DC, MC, V.*

Söders Hjärta. Conveniently located on Söder just across from a floodlit church, this bistro is not far from the Slussen subway station. The cuisine is Stockholm standard, but the adjacent large bar is cheerful and friendly. *Bellmansgatan 22, tel. 08/ 6401462. Reservations required. AE, DC, MC, V.*

Tranan. A young, Yuppie crowd uses Tranan for its bar, which often features live music, and for its unpretentious restaurant. The stark walls and checkered floor are from Tranan's days as a workingman's beer parlor. Chef Rolf Durr improvises the menu almost daily. Traditional Swedish dishes such as boiled pork sausage and mashed turnip with lashings of sweet mustard are more delicious than they sound. *Karlbergsvägen 14, tel. 08/300765. Reservations advised. AE, DC, MC, V.*

★ **Wasahof.** Popular with newspaper reporters, copywriters, and advertising types, Wasahof is noted for its friendly, bistrolike atmosphere. Often packed and smoky on weekday nights, it offers a tasty menu once you squeeze past the crowded bar. *Dalagatan 46, tel. 08/323440. Reservations advised. AE, DC, MC, V.*

Inexpensive

Cassi. This centrally located restaurant specializes in French cuisine at reasonable prices. *Narvavägen 30, tel. 08/661–7461. Reservations advised. MC. Closed Sat.*

Glada Enkan. This so-called artists' restaurant, housed in a former widow's home in Vasastan, serves excellent food and wine at (for Sweden) reasonable prices. It's a short walk from the Odenplan subway station. *Norrtullsgatan 45, tel. 08/ 339575. No reservations. AE, V.*

Open Gate. Located near the Slussen locks, on the south side of Stockholm Harbor, this is a popular, trendy Art Deco Italian-style trattoria that attracts a youngish crowd. Pasta dishes are the house specialty. *Högbergsgatan 40, tel. 08/6439776. No reservations. AE, DC, MC, V.*

★ **Örtagården.** This is a truly delightful vegetarian, no-smoking restaurant above the Östermalmstorg food market. The excellent-value buffet includes soups, salads, and hot dishes and is served in a turn-of-the-century atmosphere. *Nybrogatan 31, tel. 08/662–1728. No reservations. DC, MC, V.*

Lodging

In spite of the prohibitively expensive reputation of Stockholm's hotels, great deals can be found during the summer, when prices are substantially lower and numerous discounts are available. Some 60 hotels offer the **"Stockholm Package,"** providing accommodations for one night, breakfast, and a card giving free admission to museums and travel on public transport. Costs run from SKr305 to SKr655. Details are available from travel agents, tourist bureaus, or **Stockholm Information Service** (Box 7542, S–103 93 Stockholm, tel. 08/789–2000), or from Hotel Centralen (Centralstationen, S–111 20 Stockholm, tel. 08/240880). All rooms in the hotels reviewed are equipped with shower or bath unless otherwise noted. (For rates, *see* Staying in Sweden in Chapter 1.)

Highly recommended hotels are indicated by a star ★.

Very Expensive

Amaranten. A little out of the way, on the island of Kungsholmen, this large, modern Reso hotel is, however, just a few minutes' walk from Stockholm's central train station. Built in 1969, it was refurbished in 1988. A roof garden is featured atop the "executive tower," which contains 52 rooms. The brasserie-style restaurant offers cuisine with a French touch. *Kungsholmsgatan 31, Box 8054, 104 20, tel. 80/654–1060, fax 08/652–6248. 410 rooms. Facilities: restaurants, piano bar, pool, sauna, solarium. AE, DC, MC, V.*

Berns. In a successful attempt to distinguish itself from the rest of the crowd, the 130-year-old Berns opted for a Spartan look in its 1989 renovation. Indirect lighting, modern Italian furniture, and expensive marble, granite, and wood inlays now dominate the decor of the public areas and guest rooms. It was one of August Strindberg's haunts; guests can breakfast in the Red Room, immortalized by his novel of the same name. *Näckströmsgatan 8, S–111 47, tel. 08/614–0700 or 800/448–8355, fax 08/611–5175. 59 rooms, 3 suites. Facilities: restaurant, bar. AE, DC, MC, V.*

Continental. Located in the city center across from the train station, the Continental is a reliable hotel that is especially popular with American guests. First opened in 1966, it was renovated in 1992. It offers four restaurants in different price brackets, all of which have also been renovated. *Klara Vattugränd 4, S–101 21, tel. 08/244020, fax 08/113695. 250 rooms with bath. Facilities: 4 restaurants. AE, DC, MC, V.*

Diplomat. Located within easy walking distance of Djurgården, this elegant hotel is less flashy than most in its price range. Rooms facing the water have magnificent views over Stockholm Harbor. Originally a turn-of-the-century house, it was converted to its present use in 1966. The sometimes slow and indifferent service is partially compensated for by its calm and dignified atmosphere. *Strandvägen 7C, S–104 40, tel. 08/663–5800, fax 08/783–6634. 133 rooms. Facilities: restaurant, bar, sauna, office, conference room. AE, DC, MC, V. Closed Christmas and New Year's Day.*

Grand. The city's showpiece hotel is an 1874 landmark on the quayside at Blasieholmen, just across the harbor from the Royal Palace. Visiting political dignitaries and Nobel Prize winners are accommodated here. The gracious Old World atmosphere extends to the comfortable and well-furnished rooms. One of the hotel's best features is a glassed-in veranda overlooking the harbor, where an excellent smörgåsbord buffet is served. *Södra Blasieholmshamnen 8, Box 164 24, S–103 27, tel. 08/221020, fax 08/218–6880. 299 rooms, 20 suites. Facilities: restaurant, piano bar, shop, conference and banquet rooms. AE, DC, MC, V.*

★ **Lady Hamilton.** This small but charming hotel is in a house dating from 1470 near the Royal Palace in the Old Town. Converted to its present use in 1980, it boasts an extensive collection of antiques, including one of George Romney's portraits of Lady Hamilton, the English beauty who was the mistress of Lord Nelson at the beginning of the 19th century. *Storkyrkobrinken 5, S–111 28, tel. 08/234680, fax 08/111148. 34 rooms. Facilities: cafeteria, sauna, minipool. AE, DC, MC, V. Closed Christmas.*

Reisen. This Reso hotel, dating from 1819, successfully manages to combine elegance with modernity. It has a magnificent central location on the Old Town waterfront. The rooms have all been modernized and are well furnished, while the swimming pool is built under medieval arches. The Quarter Deck restaurant serves high-quality Swedish-French food, and the piano bar attracts a lively crowd at night. *Skeppsbron 12–14, S–111 30, tel. 08/223260, fax 08/201559. 114 rooms. Facilities: 2 restaurants, 2 bars, indoor pool, sauna, conference rooms. AE, DC, MC, V. Closed Christmas and New Year's Day.*

Royal Viking. Only yards from Central Station and from the airport bus terminal, the SAS-owned Royal Viking was built in 1984. The large atrium lobby is spacious, and the split-level lounge is elegant. Last renovated in early 1990, the guest rooms lack nothing except space; they have attractive natural textiles and artwork, sturdy writing desks, minibars, separate seating areas, and plush robes in the large bathrooms. Triple-glazed windows and plenty of insulation keep traffic noise to a minimum, but check whether the current bar pianist is the exuberant type before taking a room on the atrium. The staff is young and inexperienced, and service is at best formal. *Vasagatan 1, S–101 24, tel. 08/141000 or 800/448–8355, fax 08/108180. 319 rooms. Facilities: 3 restaurants, 2 bars, nightclub, indoor pool, sauna, solarium, massage, conference rooms, SAS ticket counter and check-in, rooms for disabled guests. AE, MC, V.*

Sergel Plaza. This stainless-steel-paneled high-rise became a (Reso) hotel in 1984. The lobby is welcoming, with cane chairs in a pleasantly skylighted seating area. Well-lighted rooms are practical but lack the luxury feel the price tag might lead you to expect; the decor is almost disappointing, with run-of-the-mill furnishings and too many grays. The location is central, right on the main pedestrian mall, but most windows view only office buildings. The best rooms are high up, with a view of the inner-city rooftops and beyond. *Brunkebergstorg 9, S–164 11, tel. 08/226600 or 800/843–6664, fax 08/215070. 406 rooms. Facilities: restaurant, 2 bars, rooms for nonsmokers and the disabled, conference rooms. AE, DC, MC, V.*

Strand. This Old World yellow-brick hotel, built in 1912 for the Stockholm Olympics, was completely and tastefully modernized after its purchase by SAS in 1986. The waterside location is right across from the Royal Dramatic Theater. No two of its rooms are the same; many are furnished with antiques and have rustic touches such as flower painting on woodwork and furniture. *Nybrokajen 9, Box 163 96, S–103 27, tel. 08/678–7800, fax 08/611–2436. 138 rooms. Facilities: restaurant, sauna, kiosk, conference rooms. AE, DC, MC, V.*

Victory. Slightly larger than its brother and sister hotels, the Lord Nelson and Lady Hamilton, this is an extremely atmospheric lodging place in a building that dates from 1640 in the Old Town. It also houses a noted restaurant, Lejontornet, which boasts an extensive wine cellar. *Lilla Nygatan 5, S–111 28, tel. 08/143090, fax 08/202177. 48 rooms. AE, DC, MC, V.*

Expensive

★ **Anno 1647.** The name is the date the building was erected. A small, pleasant, friendly hotel on Söder, the south island, it is three stops on the subway from the city center. *Mariagränd 3, S–116 21, tel. 08/6440480, fax 08/6433700. 42 rooms, 30 with baths. Facilities: restaurant serving light foods only. AE, DC, MC, V.*

Birger Jarl. This is one for nondrinkers: a hotel with no liquor license that is connected to a neighboring church, with weekly services in English. The modern, characteristically Scandinavian hotel opened in 1974. It is a quiet, unpretentious place, only a short walk from Stureplan. *Tulegatan 8, S–104 32, tel. 08/151020, fax 08/317366. 248 rooms. Facilities: cafeteria, fitness center, sauna. AE, DC, MC, V.*

Clas på Hörnet. This may be the most exclusive—and smallest—hotel in town: 10 rooms (eight doubles) in an 18th-century inn converted into a small hotel in 1982. The rooms, comfortably furnished with antiques of the period, go quickly. The restaurant (*see* Dining, *above*) is worth a visit in its own right; a bar opened in 1991 in the adjacent glassed-in pavilion. *Surbrunnsgatan 20, S–113 48, tel. 08/165130, fax 08/612–5315. Facilities: restaurant, bar. AE, DC, MC, V.*

Lord Nelson. A small hotel with nautical atmosphere right in the middle of the Old Town, this is in the same hotel family as the Lady Hamilton and the Victory. Space is at a premium, and the rooms are little more than cabins, though service is excellent. Noise from merrymakers in the pedestrian street outside can be a problem during the summer. *Västerlånggatan 22, S–111 29, tel. 08/232390, fax 08/101089. 31 rooms. Facilities: sauna, conference room. AE, DC, MC, V.*

Mälardrottningen. One of the more unusual places to stay in Stockholm, *Mälardrottningen* (Queen of Lake Mälar), a Sweden Hotels property, was once Barbara Hutton's yacht. Since 1982, it has been a quaint and pleasant hotel, with a crew as service-conscious as any in Stockholm. Tied up on the freshwater side of Gamla Stan, it is minutes from everything. The small suites are suitably decorated in a navy-blue and maroon nautical theme. Some of the below-deck cabins are a bit stuffy. Its chief assets are novelty and absence of traffic noise. *Riddarholmen 4, S–111 28, tel. 08/243600 or 800/448–8355, fax 08/243676. 59 rooms. Facilities: restaurant, grill, bar, conference rooms. AE, DC, MC, V.*

Mornington. A quiet, modern (Best Western) hotel that prides itself on a friendly atmosphere, the Mornington is within easy walking distance of Stureplan and downtown shopping areas and particularly handy to Östermalmstorg, with its food hall. *Nybrogatan 53, S–102 44, tel. 08/663–1240, fax 08/662–2179. 141 rooms. Facilities: restaurant, bar, rooms for the disabled and nonsmokers, 4 conference rooms, sauna, steam baths. AE, DC, MC, V.*

Scandic Crown. Working with what appears to be a dubious location (perched on a tunnel above a six-lane highway), the Scandic Crown has pulled a rabbit out of a hat. The hotel was built in 1988 on special cushions; you know the highway is there, but it intrudes only minimally, mainly in view. The intriguing labyrinth of levels, separate buildings, and corridors is filled with such details as a rounded stairway lighted from between the steps. The guest rooms are exquisitely designed and decorated in modern style, with plenty of stainless steel and polished wood inlay to accent the maroon color scheme. The hotel is easily accessible from downtown. *Guldgränd 8, S–104 65, tel. 08/702–2500, fax 08/6428358. 264 rooms. Facilities: 2 restaurants, bar, shops. AE, DC, MC, V.*

Moderate

Alfa. About 20 minutes from the city center, Alfa is a medium-size, medium-class hotel. Opened in 1972, it has recently been refurbished. *Marknadsvägen 6, S–121 09, tel. 08/810600. 104 rooms with bath. Facilities: restaurant. AE, DC, MC, V.*

Bema. This small hotel has a reasonably central location, on the

519 M.P.H.

190 M.P.H.

75 M.P.H.

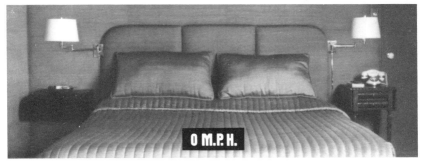

0 M.P.H.

WE LET YOU SEE EUROPE AT YOUR OWN PACE.

Regardless of your personal speed limits, Rail Europe offers everything to get you over, around and through anywhere you want in Europe. For more information, call your travel agent or 1-800-4-EURAIL.

OFFICIAL DISTRIBUTOR
Rail Europe
OF THE EURAIL PASS

We can wire money to every major city in Europe almost as fast as you can say, "Zut alors! J'ai perdu mes valises".

How fast? We can send money in 10 minutes or less, to 13,500 locations in over 68 countries worldwide. That's faster than any other international money transfer service. And when you're *sans* luggage, every minute counts.

MoneyGram from American Express® is available throughout Europe. For more information please contact your local American Express Travel Service Office or call: 44-71-839-7541 in England; 33-1-47777000 in France; or 49-69-21050 in Germany. In the U.S. call 1-800-MONEYGRAM.

MoneyGram

INTERNATIONAL MONEY TRANSFERS.

Ten-minute delivery subject to local agent hours of operation. Local send/receive facilities may also vary. ©1993 First Data Corporation.

ground floor of an apartment block near Tegnérlunden. *Upplandsgatan 13, S–111 23, tel. 08/2332675, fax 08/205338. 12 rooms with showers. Facilities: breakfast. AE, DC, MC, V.*

Hotel City. A large, modern-style hotel built in the 1940s but modernized in 1982–83, the City is located near the city center and Hötorget market. Breakfast is served in the atrium Winter Garden. *Slöjdgatan 7, S–111 81, tel. 08/222240, fax 08/208224. 300 rooms with bath. Facilities: restaurant, café, sauna, rooms for the disabled. AE, DC, MC, V.*

Hotel Gamla Stan. A quiet, cozy hotel in the area of town for which it was named, the Gamla Stan has recently been renovated and each of its 51 rooms is uniquely decorated. *Lilla Nygatan 25, tel. 08/24450, fax 08/216483. Facilities: breakfast included. AE, DC, MC.*

Stockholm. Occupying the upper floors of a downtown office building, this Sweden Hotels property has mainly modern decor offset by traditional Swedish furnishings that help create its friendly atmosphere. *Norrmalmstorg 1, S–111 46, tel. 08/6781320, fax 08/611–2103. 92 rooms. Facilities: breakfast. AE, DC, MC, V.*

Tegnérlunden. An extremely good bet for the budget tourist, this moderate-size hotel (owned by Sweden Hotels) is situated only a short walk from the city center opposite a small park, close to the Strindberg Museum. *Tegnérlunden 8, S–113 59, tel. 08/349780, fax 08/327818. 104 rooms. Facilities: rooms for nonsmokers. AE, DC, MC, V.*

Inexpensive

Alexandra. Although it is in the Södermalm area, to the south of the Old Town, the Alexandra is only five minutes by subway from the city center. It is a small, modern hotel, opened in the early 1970s and renovated in 1988. Only breakfast is served. *Magnus Ladulåsgatan 42, S–118 27, tel. 08/840320. 79 rooms with bath. Facilities: sauna, solarium. AE, DC, MC, V. Closed Christmas and New Year's Day.*

Gustav af Klint. A "hotel ship" moored at Stadsgården quay, near Slussen subway station, the *Gustav af Klint* is divided into two sections—a hotel and a hostel. It was refurbished in 1989. There is a cafeteria and a restaurant, and you can dine on deck in summer. *Stadsgårdskajen 153, S–116 30, tel. 08/404077. 28 cabins, none with bath. AE, DC, MC, V. Closed Christmas and New Year's Day.*

Youth Hostels Don't be put off by the "youth" bit: There's actually no age limit. The standards of cleanliness, comfort, and facilities offered are usually extremely high.

af Chapman. This is a sailing ship built in 1888 that is permanently moored in Stockholm Harbor, just across from the Royal Palace. It is a landmark in its own right. *Västra Brobänken, Skeppsholmen S–111 49, tel. 08/6795015. 136 beds, 2- to 6-bed cabins. Facilities: breakfast.*

Bosön. Out of the way on the island of Lidingö, this hostel is pleasantly situated close to the water. *Bosön, S–181 47 Lidingö, tel. 08/767–9300. 26 beds; 2- to 3-bed rooms. Facilities: breakfast, cafeteria, washing machine, sauna, canoes for rent. V.*

Långholmen. This former prison, built in 1724, was converted into a combined hotel and hostel in 1989. It is located on the island of Långholmen, which has popular bathing beaches. The hotel serves Swedish home cooking. *Långholmen, Box 9116, S–102 72,tel. 08/668–0510. Summer weekends: 254 beds (hotel: 101 2- to 4-bed rooms, all but 10 with showers and WC). Sept.–May, weekdays: 26 beds with shared bath. 32 beds adapted for the disabled. Facilities: cafeteria, restaurant, laundry room, sauna, beach. AE, DC, MC, V.*

Skeppsholmen. A former craftsman's workshop in a pleasant and quiet part of the island, it was converted into a hostel for the overflow from the *af Chapman*, which is an anchor's throw away. *Skeppsholmen, S–111 49, tel. 08/6795017. 152 beds, 2- to 4-bed rooms. Facilities: special rooms for disabled guests, breakfast. No credit cards.*

Camping There are camping sites at Enskede (tel. 08/773–0100), Haninge (tel. 08/745–8259), Slagsta (tel. 0753/77788), Bredäng (tel. 08/977071), and Sollentuna (tel. 08/353475). Camping in the Stockholm area costs SKr50–SKr100 per night.

The Arts and Nightlife

The Arts

Dance There are demonstrations of Swedish folk dancing in **Kungsträdgården** and at **Mosebacken** in Söder during the summer months. Consult the tourist office for details.

Film Foreign movies are not dubbed. The best-quality cinema in town is the **Grand** (Sveavägen, tel.08/112400). The cinema at **Filmhuset** (Borgvägen 1–5, tel. 08/665–1100), headquarters of the Swedish Film Institute, usually has a good program. A curiosity is **Folkets Bio** (The People's Cinema) (Vegagatan 17, tel. 08/736–0035), a leftover from more idealistic times, which shows films that don't get general release.

Music Free concerts are held in **Kungsträdgården** every summer. For details, contact the tourist office. International orchestras often visit **Konserthuset** (Hötorget 8, tel. 08/102110), the main concert hall.

Opera **Operan** (the Royal Opera House) (Jakobs Torg 2, tel. 08/248240), dating from 1898, continues a tradition going back to 1755, when Queen Lovisa Ulrika introduced opera to her subjects. Sweden has continued to produce such names as Jenny Lind, Jussi Björling, and Birgit Nilsson. **Folkoperan** (Hornsgatan 72, tel. 08/6585300), a lively, modern company with its headquarters in Söder, features "opera in the round." It rides roughshod over traditional methods of presentation and interpretation of the classics, generally to scintillating effect.

Theater **Kungliga Dramatiska Teatern** (or Dramaten: the Royal Dramatic Theater) (Nybroplan, tel. 08/667–0680) sometimes stages productions of international interest, even though they are in Swedish. These include works directed by Ingmar Bergman. The **Regina Theater** (Drottninggatan 71a, tel. 08/207000) stages English-language productions.

Nightlife

The hub of Stockholm's nightlife is Kungsträdgården, where several popular bars and discothèques line the western edge of the park. On weekends these spots are often packed with tourists and locals.

Bars If you prefer exploring areas not entirely swamped by crowds, you will find a bar-hopping visit to Södermalm rewarding. Start at **Mosebacke Etablissement** (Mosebacke torg 3, tel. 08/ 641–9020), a combined indoor theater and outdoor café with a spectacular view of the city. Wander along Götagatan with its lively bars and head for the **Pelikan Restaurant** (Blekingegatan 40, tel. 08/743–0695), a former beer hall and now an unpretentious but well-priced restaurant and bar. The trendy **Hannas Krog** (Skånegatan 80, tel. 08/767–5211) features a bar in the cellar with low lights, little furnishing, loud music, and people dressed in black.

Piano bars are also part of the Stockholm scene. Try the **Anglais Bar** at the Hotel Anglais (tel. 08/6141600) or the **Clipper Club** at the Hotel Reisen, Skeppsbron (tel. 08/223260).

Cabaret Stockholm's biggest nightclub, **Börsen** (Jakobsgatan 6, tel. 08/ 787–8500), offers high-quality international cabaret shows. Another popular spot is the **Cabaret Club**, Barnhusgatan 12 (tel. 08/110608; reservations advised). Drag shows are the main attraction at **Studion** (St. Eriksplan 4, tel. 08/344454).

Casinos These simply do not exist as such. Many hotels and bars have a roulette table and sometimes blackjack, operating according to Swedish rules aimed at restricting the amount you can lose.

Discos **Café Opera** (tel. 08/110026) enjoys a magnificent locale in the Opera Building at the end of Kungsträdgården. A popular meeting place for young and old alike, it features a restaurant, roulette tables, and the longest bar in town, with a disco that starts at midnight, closing at 3 AM. **Daily News** (tel. 08/215655), a glitzy disco located at the other end of Kungsträdgården near the Sweden House, has a restaurant and is open until 3 AM. **King Creole** (Kungsgatan 18, tel. 08/244700) offers big-band dance music alternating with rock. **Berns** (Berzeli Park, tel. 08/ 614–0550), an elegant restaurant and bar located in a renovated period building with a large balcony facing the Stockholm Royal Theater, turns into a lively discothèque at night. Other hot spots are **Sture Compagniet** (Sturegatan 4, tel. 08/ 6117800) and **Sloppy's** (Horngsgatan 136, tel. 08/845610).

Gay Bars **Pride** (Sveavägen 57, tel. 08/315533) has a restaurant, café, bookshop, and disco, run by homosexuals for homosexuals. It's all totally respectable by local standards and backed by grants from the authorities.

Jazz Clubs The best venue is **Fasching** (Kungsgatan 63, tel. 08/216267), close to the city center and featuring international and local bands. **Stampen** (Stora Nygatan 5, tel. 08/205793), an overpriced but atmospheric club in the Old Town, features traditional jazz nightly.

Rock Clubs The best local and international groups can be seen at **Berns** (Berzeli Park, tel. 08/6140720); **Galaxy** (on Strömsburg, an islet in the middle of Strömmen, tel. 08/215400); **Ritz** (Götgatan 51, on Söder, subway: Medborgarplatsen; tel. 08/6424737); **Lido** (on Söder, at Hornsgatan 92, subway: Zinkensdamm; tel. 08/ 6682333); and **Krogen Tre Backar** (off Sveavägen at Tegnérgatan 12–14, tel. 673–4400).

Excursions from Stockholm

Uppsala

Sweden's principal university town vies for that position with Lund in the south of the country. August Strindberg, the nation's leading dramatist, studied here—and by all accounts hated the place. Ingmar Bergman, his modern heir, was born here. It is a historic site where pagan (and extremely gory) Viking ceremonies persisted into the 11th century. Uppsala University, one of the oldest and most highly respected institutions in Europe, was established here in 1477 by Archbishop Jakob Ulfson. As late as the 16th century, nationwide *tings*, early parliaments, were convened here. Today it is a quiet home for around 170,000 people, built along the banks of Fyris River, a pleasant jumble of old buildings dominated by its cathedral, which dates from the early 13th century.

Tourist Information The main **tourist office** (tel. 018/117500 or 018/274800) is at Fyris Torg in the center of town. In summer a small tourist information office is also open at Uppsala Castle.

Getting There
By Car Uppsala is an easy drive 67 kilometers (41 miles) north from Stockholm along the E4 motorway.

By Train There is regular train service from Central Station. The journey takes 45 minutes.

By Bus Buses leave the city terminal at Klarabergsviadukten on Friday and Sunday. For information, call 08/237190. There is direct bus service to Uppsala from Arlanda Airport.

Guided Tours You can explore Uppsala easily by yourself, but guided tours in English for groups can be arranged through the tourist office.

Numbers in the margin correspond to points of interest on the Excursions from Stockholm map.

Exploring Uppsala
❺ Ideally you should start your visit with a trip to **Gamla Uppsala** (Old Uppsala), 5 kilometers (3 miles) north of the town. Here under three huge **mounds** lie the graves of the first Swedish kings, Aun, Egil, and Adils, of the 6th-century Ynglinga dynasty. Close by in pagan times was a sacred grove containing a legendary oak from whose branches animal and human sacrifices were hung. By the 10th century, Christianity had eliminated such practices. A small church, which was the seat of Sweden's first archbishop, was built on the site of a former pagan temple. Today the archbishopric is in Uppsala itself, and the church, **Gamla Uppsala Kyrka**, is largely for the benefit of tourists. A small open-air museum nearby, **Disagården,** features old farm buildings, most of them from the 19th century. *Admission free. Open May–Sept., daily 9–5.*

Time Out You can drink mead brewed from a 14th-century recipe at the nearby **Odinsborg Restaurant.**

❻ Back in **Uppsala,** your first visit should be to Uppsala **Domkyrka** (Cathedral), whose twin towers (362 feet high) dominate the city. They are the same height as the length of the nave. Work on the cathedral was begun in the early 13th century; it was consecrated in 1435 and restored between 1885 and 1893. The cathedral remains the seat of Sweden's archbishop. It is important in the nation's history as the site of the tomb of Gustav Vasa, the king who established Sweden's independence in the 16th century. It also houses a silver casket containing the bones of St. Erik, Sweden's patron saint.

Work on **Uppsala slott** (Uppsala Castle) was started in the 1540s by Gustav Vasa, who intended it to symbolize the dominance of the monarchy over the church. It was completed under Queen Christina nearly a century later. Students gather here every April 30 to celebrate the Feast of Valborg and optimistically greet the arrival of spring.

In the excavated castle ruins, **The Vasa Vignettes,** scenes from the 16th century, are portrayed with effigies, costumes, light, and sound effects. *Admission: SKr35 adults, SKr15 children under 15. Open daily, mid-Apr.–late Sept.*

One of Uppsala's most famous sons, Carl von Linné, also known as Linnaeus, was a professor of botany at the university during the 1740s and created the Latin nomenclature system for plants and animals. The **Linné Museum** in his old botanical garden, **Linnéträdgården,** which has been restored to its former glory, is dedicated to his life and works. The orangery houses a pleasant cafeteria and is used for concerts and cultural events. *Svartbäcksgatan 27, tel. 018/136540. Admission to garden SKr10. Open May–Aug., daily 9–9; Sept.–Apr., daily 9–7. Admission to museum: SKr10. Open May–Sept., Tues.–Sun. 1–4.*

Uppsala Universitetet (the Uppsala University), founded in 1477, features the **Carolina Rediviva** (the university library), which contains a copy of every book published in Sweden, in addition to a large collection of foreign literature. One of its most interesting exhibits is the *Codex Argentus*, a silver Bible written in the 6th century.

Completed in 1625, the **Gustavianum,** which served as the university's main building for two centuries, is easy to spot by its remarkable copper cupola, now green with age. The building houses the ancient anatomical theater where lectures on human anatomy and public dissections took place. The Victoria Museum of Egyptian Antiquities and the Museums for Classical and Nordic Archeology are also in the building. *Akademigatan 3, tel. 018/182500. Admission: SKr20. Open daily noon–3.*

Dining **Domtrappkällaren.** Located in a 14th-century cellar near the cathedral, Domtrappkällaren features excellent French and Swedish cuisine. *Sankt Eriksgränd 15, tel. 018/130955. Reservations required. Dress: casual but neat. AE, DC, MC, V.*

Gotland

Gotland is Sweden's main holiday island, a place of wide, sandy beaches and wild cliff formations called *raukar.* Inland, there is verdant sheep-farming country and glades in which 35 different varieties of wild orchids thrive, attracting botanists from all over the world. Lying in the Baltic just 85 kilometers (53 miles) from the mainland, the island is 125 kilometers (78 miles) in length and 52 kilometers (32 miles) across at its widest point.

Gotland was first inhabited around 5000 BC, and by the time of the Roman Iron Age had become a leading Baltic trading center. Germans arrived later and built most of its churches in the 13th century. They established close trading links with the Hanseatic League in Lübeck. The Danes followed, and it was not until 1645 that Gotland finally became part of Sweden.

Tourist Information The main tourist office is at Bermeisterska huset, Hamngatan 4, Visby (tel. 0498/210982).

Getting There
By Plane Fifteen flights a day arrive in Gotland's airport from Stockholm. For information, call SAS (tel. 08/151000).

By Boat Car ferries sail from Nynäshamn, a small port on the Baltic an hour by car or rail from Stockholm (commuter trains leave regularly from Stockholm's Central Station for Nynäshamn), at 12:40 PM and 11:30 PM during the summer and at 11:30 PM only during the winter. The voyage takes about five hours. Boats also leave from Oskarshamn, farther down the Swedish coast and closer to Gotland. *Kungsgatan 48, Gotland City, tel. 08/236170 or 08/233180; Nynäshamn, tel. 08/5206400.*

Guided Tours Guided tours of the island and Visby, the capital, are available in English by arrangement with the tourist office.

Exploring Gotland
❼ If you have a limited time schedule, you may be content to visit Gotland's capital, **Visby,** a delightful, hilly town of about 20,000 people, in which medieval houses, ruined fortifications, and churches blend with cobbled lanes of fairy-tale cottages, their facades covered with roses reputed to bloom even in November because the climate is so gentle.

In its heyday Visby was protected by a wall, of which 3 kilometers survive today, along with 44 towers and numerous gateways. It is considered the best-preserved medieval city wall in Europe after that of Carcassonne in southern France. The north gate provides the best vantage point for an overall view of the wall.

The cathedral, **St. Maria Kyrka,** is the only one of the town's 13 medieval churches that is still intact and in use.

Near the harbor is **Det Gamla Apoteket** (the Old Apothecary), a late-medieval four-story merchant's house, where a silversmith now works and demonstrates his trade to visitors. *Strandgatan 28, tel. 0498/212889. Admission free. Open daily 9–5.*

In the same street you'll find **Burmeisterska huset,** the home of the Burmeister, or principal German merchant, which today houses the tourist office. *Strandgatan 9, tel. 0498/210982. Admission: free. Open weekdays 8–8, weekends 10–7.*

Fornsalen (the Fornsal Museum) contains examples of medieval artwork, hordes of silver from Viking times, and impressive picture stones that predate the Viking rune stones. *Strandgatan 14, S–62102, tel. 0498/247010. Admission: SKr20 adults, children under 16 free. Open mid-May–Sept., daily 11–6; Sept–mid-May, Tues.–Sun. noon–4.*

Celebrated during early August, **Medieval Week** is a city-wide festival marking the invasion by the Danish King Valdemar of the prosperous island on July 22, 1361. Medieval jousting, a "medieval" open market on Strandgatan, and a variety of street theater performances recreate the period.

The rest of the island is best explored by bicycle. Bicycles, tents, and camping equipment can be rented from **Gotlands Cykeluthyrning** (Skeppsbron 8, tel. 0498/14133). Details of Gotlandsleden, a 200-kilometer (120-mile) route around the island, which avoids military installations (off-limits to foreigners), are available from the tourist office.

The stalactite caves at **Lummelunda,** about 13 kilometers (8 miles) from Visby, are unique in this part of the world and are worth visiting, as is the **Krusmyntagården** (herb garden), 8 kilometers (5 miles) north of Visby, close to the sea.

There are approximately 100 old churches on the island that are still in use today, dating from Gotland's great commercial era. Outstanding among them are **Barlingbro,** dating from the 13th century, with vault paintings, stained-glass windows, and a remarkable 12th-century font; the exquisite **Dalhem,** constructed about 1200; **Gothem,** built during the 13th century, with a notable series of paintings of that period; **Grötlingbo,** a 14th-century church with stone sculpture and stained glass (note the 12th-century reliefs on the facade); **Tingstäde,** a mix of six building periods from 1169 to 1300; **Roma Kloster Kyrka** (Roma Cloister Church), the massive ruins of a Cistercian monastery founded in 1164; and **Öja,** decorated with paintings and housing a famous holy rood from the late 13th century.

Curious rock formations dot the coasts, and two bird refuges, **Stora** and **Lilla Karlsö,** stand off the coast south of Visby. The bird population consists mainly of guillemots, which look like penguins. Visits to these refuges are permitted only in the company of a recognized guide. (Stora Karlsö, tel. 0498/40500; Lilla Karlsö, tel. 0498/41139).

Dining **Gutekällaren.** Despite the name, this is not a cellar restaurant.
Visby Located aboveground in a building that dates from the 12th century, it features local specialties, many involving lamb. *Stora Torget 3, tel. 0498/210043. Reservations required. AE, DC, MC, V. Expensive.*
Lindgården. This atmospheric restaurant specializes in both local dishes and French cuisine. *Strandgatan 26, tel. 0498/ 218700. Reservations required. AE, DC, MC, V. Expensive.*

4 Göteborg

If you arrive in Göteborg (Gothenburg) by car, don't drive straight through the city in your haste to reach your coastal vacation spot; it is well worth spending a day or two exploring this attractive port. A quayside jungle of cranes and warehouses attests to the city's industrial might, yet within 10 minutes' walk of the waterfront is an elegant, modern city of broad avenues, green parks, and gardens. It is an easy city to explore: Most of the major attractions are within walking distance of one another, and there is an excellent streetcar network. In summer you can take a sightseeing trip on an open-air streetcar.

Sprawling, mostly modern Göteborg, with a population of 500,000, is Sweden's second-largest city. Its heart is Avenyn (the Avenue; actually Kungsportsavenyn, but over the years shortened to simply Avenyn), a 60-foot-wide, tree-lined boulevard that bisects the center of the city in a south–north direction, linking its cultural heart, Götaplatsen, at the southern end, with the main commercial area, now dominated by the huge, modern Nordstan shopping center. Also toward the northern end of Avenyn is the pleasant park of Trädgårds-föreningen (the Horticultural Society—called Trägårn), the best-known of the city's 20 parks.

Beyond Nordstan is the harbor, 22 kilometers (14 miles) of quays with warehouses and sheds covering more than 1.5 million square feet and spread along both banks of the Göta Älv (river), making Göteborg Scandinavia's largest port. It is also the home of Scandinavia's largest corporation, the automobile manufacturer Volvo (which means "I roll" in Latin), as well as of the roller-bearing manufacturer SKF and the world-renowned Hasselblad camera company.

Historically, Göteborg owes its existence to the sea. Tenth-century Vikings sailed from its shores, and a settlement was founded here in the 11th century. Not until 1621, however, did King Gustav II Adolf grant Göteborg a charter in order to establish a free-trade port on the model of others already thriving on the Continent. The west-coast harbor would also allow Swedish shipping to avoid Danish tolls exacted for passing through Öresund, the stretch of water separating the two countries. Foreigners were recruited to make these visions real: The Dutch were its builders—hence the canals that thread the city—and many Scotsmen worked and settled here, though they have left little trace.

Today Göteborg resists its second-city status by being a leader in terms of attractions and civic structures: The Scandinavium was until recently Europe's largest indoor arena; the Ullevi Stadium stages some of the Nordic area's most important concerts and sporting events; Nordstan is one of Europe's largest indoor shopping malls; and Liseberg, Scandinavia's largest amusement park in area, attracts some 2.5 million visitors a year. Over the Göta River is Älvsborgsbron, at 3,000 feet the longest suspension bridge in Sweden, and under it is the Tingstads Tunnel, at 62 feet the world's widest cut through rock for motor vehicles.

Göteborg is a pleasantly relaxed place from which to explore the west coast of Sweden, where wide, unspoiled beaches and a majestic rocky coastline alternate with timbered fishing villages. From here, too, you can set out on the Göta Canal, Sweden's "blue ribbon," down which barges once sailed laden with exports and imports, but which today provides a picturesque water journey through the Swedish countryside.

Essential Information

Important Addresses and Numbers

Tourist Information
The main tourist office is Göteborg's Turistbyrå (Kungsportsplatsen 2, S–411 10 Göteborg, tel. 031/100740). There is also an office at the Nordstan shopping center (Nordstadstorget, 411 05 Göteborg).

Consulates
U.K. Consulate: Götgatan 15, tel. 031/151327.

Emergencies
Dial 90000 (*see* Stockholm, *above*).

Doctors
Dial 031/415500 for information on medical services. Emergencies are handled by the **Sahlgrenska Hospital** (tel. 031/601000), **Östrasjukhuset** (tel. 031/374000), and **Mölndalssjukhuset** (tel. 031/861000). There is a private medical service at **City Akuten** (Drottninggatan, tel. 031/101010).

Dentists
The national health service emergency number is 031/803140; the private dental service emergency number is 031/117017.

Pharmacy
Vasen (Götgatan 12, tel. 031/804410), in the Nordstan shopping mall, is open 24 hours.

English-Language Bookstores
Nearly all bookshops stock English-language books. The broadest selection is at **Esselte's Eckersteins** store (Södra Larmgatan 11, tel. 031/171100).

Travel Agencies
The SJ main ticket office is located at Östra Hamngatan 35 (tel. 031/176860). For other travel agencies see the yellow pages under *Resor-Resebyråer*.

Arriving and Departing by Plane

Airports and Airlines
The airport, **Landvetter,** is approximately 26 kilometers (16 miles) from the city center. Among the airlines operating from it are **SAS** (tel. 020/910150), **British Airways** (tel. 020/781144), **Air France** (tel. 031/801110), and **Lufthansa** (tel. 031/805640).

Between the Airport and City Center
By Bus
Landvetter is linked to Göteborg by freeway. Buses leave Landvetter every 15 minutes, traveling to Drottningtorget near the central railway station and stopping at the SAS Park Avenue Hotel. The price of the trip is SKr50. For more information, call 031/801235.

By Taxi
A taxi to the city center will cost between SKr250 and SKr300. For SAS limousine service, call 031/942424.

Arriving and Departing by Car, Train, and Bus

By Car
You arrive on the E20 highway from Stockholm (495 kilometers/307 miles) and the east or on the E6 coastal highway from the south (Malmö is 290 kilometers/180 miles away.) Markings are excellent, and roads are well sanded and plowed in winter.

By Train
There is a regular service from Stockholm, taking a little over four hours. All trains arrive at the central railway station in Drottningtorget, downtown Göteborg (tel. 031/175000 or 020/757575). Streetcars and buses leave from here for the suburbs.

By Bus All buses arrive in the downtown area. The principal company is **Continentbus/Swebus** (tel. 031/171500).

Getting Around

By Car **Avis** has offices at the airport (tel. 031/946030) and the central railway station (tel. 031/805780). **Hertz** is at Stampgatan 16A (tel. 031/803730).

By Bus and Tram Göteborg has an excellent transit service. The best bet for the tourist is the **Göteborg Card,** which costs SKr120 for 24 hours and gives free use of public transport, various sightseeing trips, and admission to Liseberg and local museums, among other benefits. It is available at Pressbyrån shops, kiosks, and the tourist office.

By Taxi To order a taxi, telephone 031/650000; for advance bookings, call 031/500504.

Guided Tours

Orientation A 90-minute bus tour of the chief points of interest leaves from outside the main tourist office (Kungsportsplatsen 2) every day from early May to mid-August and on Saturdays in September. Call tourist information, tel. 031/100740, for the schedule.

Exploring Göteborg

Highlights for First-Time Visitors

Götaplatsen (*see* Tour 1)
Avenyn (*see* Tour 1)
Elfsborg Fortress (*see* Tour 3)
Harbor (*see* Tour 2)
Liseberg Amusement Park (*see* What to See and Do with Children)

Tour 1: The City Center

Numbers in the margin correspond to points of interest on the Göteborg map.

Start in **Götaplatsen,** a fine, light, modern square dominated by Carl Milles's statue of **Poseidon,** whose shy, downturned gaze and gentle demeanor lend him a distinctly Swedish aura.

❶ Grouped around the square, you will find **Konserthuset** (the Concert Hall), the art museum and the municipal theater, three quite imposing contemporary buildings in which the city celebrates its important contribution to Swedish cultural life. Konserthuset is the home of the highly acclaimed Göteborg Symphony Orchestra (Konserthuset, Götaplatsen, tel. 031/167000).

❷ **Konstmuseet** (the Art Museum), opened in 1925, contains an impressive collection of the works of leading Scandinavian painters and sculptors; it encapsulates some of the moody introspection of the artistic community in this part of the world. Among the artists represented are Swedes such as Carl Milles, Sergel, the Impressionist Anders Zorn, the Victorian idealist Carl Larsson, and Prince Eugen. The small collection of old masters includes Rubens, Rembrandt, and van Dyke. The best

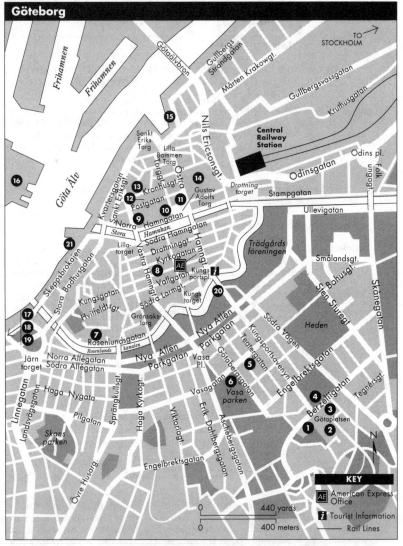

Göteborg

Älvsborgsbron, **18**

Börshuset, **11**

Domkyrkan, **8**

East India Company
Building, **9**

Elfsborgs Fästning
boat, **21**

Feske Körkan, **7**

Fiskhamnen, **17**

Folkhögskolan, **6**

Götaverkan, **16**

Konserthuset, **1**

Konstmuseet, **2**

Kronhusbodarna, **13**

Kronhuset, **12**

Maritima Centret, **15**

Nordstan, **14**

Paddan boats, **20**

Rådhuset, **10**

Röhsska
Konstslöjdsmuseet, **5**

Skarvikshamnen, **19**

Stadsbiblioteket, **4**

Stadsteatern, **3**

collection in Sweden of 19th- and 20th-century French art includes works by Monet, Pissarro, Sisley, Renoir, Cézanne, Gauguin, van Gogh, Rousseau, Matisse, and Picasso. *Götaplatsen, tel. 031/612977. Admission: SKr25. Open weekdays 11–4 (Wed. until 9), weekends 10–5. Closed Mon. Sept.–May.*

❸ **Stadsteatern** (the Municipal Theater) (Götaplatsen, tel. 031/819960), while it has a good reputation in Sweden, remains very much a local phenomenon because the vast majority of its pro-
❹ ductions are in Swedish. Also in Götaplatsen, **Stadsbiblioteket** (the Municipal Library) (Götaplatsen, tel. 031/817–7300), boasts a collection of more than 550,000 books, many in English.

From Götaplatsen, stroll northward past the cafés and restaurants along the **Avenyn** to the intersection with Vasagatan. A short way to the left down Vasagatan, at the junction with
❺ Teatergatan, you can visit the **Röhsska Konstslöjdsmuseet** (Museum of Arts and Crafts), with its fine collections of furniture, books and manuscripts, tapestries, and pottery. *Vasagatan, tel. 031/200605. Admission: SKr25. Open Tues. 11–9, Wed.–Fri. 11–4, weekends 10–5.*

❻ Continue left along Vasagatan to **Folkhögskolan**, Göteborg Universitet (Göteborg University), and, if the weather's good, to relax in neighboring **Vasa Park.** Walk northward along Viktoriagatan, crossing the canal and then making an immedi-
❼ ate left to visit one of the city's most peculiar attractions, **Feske Körkan,** an archaic spelling of *Fisk Kyrkan*, the Fish Church. It resembles a place of worship but is actually an indoor fish market.

Following this you may feel inspired to visit the city's principal
❽ place of worship, **Domkyrkan** (Göteborg Cathedral). To get here from Feske Körkan, follow the canal eastward until you come to Västra Hamngatan, then head north to Kyrkogatan. The cathedral, in neoclassic yellow brick, dates from 1802; while it's not particularly attractive from the outside, the interior is impressive. *Kungsgatan 20. Open weekdays 8–5, Sat. 8–3, Sun. 10–3.*

❾ Continue northward on Västra Hamngatan to the **East India Company Building** (formerly the Museum of Cultural History) at the junction with Norra Hamngatan. This palatial structure, once the warehouse and auction rooms of the East India Company, a major Swedish trading firm founded in 1861, now houses Sweden's largest, but still unnamed, museum-in-progress. When completed in 1995, the new museum will blend what was once three separate museums featuring industrial history, archaeology, and general history into one large museum with an emphasis on thematic rather than departmentalized exhibits. The focus will continue to be on Göteborg, its nautical and trading past, and the Swedish west coast, with exhibits on the Iron Age and on crafts and industries of the more recent past. Sections of the museum remain open to the public, particularly exhibits dealing with the East India Company and the company's ship, the *Göteborg*, which sank just outside Göteborg on a return voyage from China in 1745 while members of the crew's families watched from shore. *Norra Hamngatan, tel. 031/612770. Admission: SKr25. Open Sept.–Apr., Tues.–*

*Fri. 11–4 (Wed. until 9), weekends 10–5; May–Aug., Mon.–
Fri. 11–4, weekends 10–5.*

⑩ Follow Norra Hamngatan eastward to **Gustav Adolfs Torg,** the
city's official center, which is dominated by **Rådhuset** (the City
Hall) (Gustav Adolfs Torg, tel. 031/611000), built in 1699, with
a modern extension by Swedish architect Gunnar Asplund that
caused great controversy when it was completed in 1937. Tours
must be prearranged.

⑪ On the north side of the square is **Börshuset** (the Stock Exchange) (Gustav Adolfs Torg, tel. 031/835900), built in 1849.

⑫ Head northwest from the square along Östra Hamngatan,
turning into Kronhusgatan, to visit **Kronhuset,** the city's oldest
secular building, which dates from 1643. It was once the armory, and in 1660 Sweden's Parliament met here to arrange the
succession for King Karl X Gustav, who died suddenly while
visiting the city. *Postgatan 628, tel. 031/117377. Admission:
SKr25. Open Tues.–Fri. 11–4, weekends 10–5.*

⑬ Close by are the **Kronhusbodarna,** carefully restored turn-of-
the-century shops and handicrafts boutiques. *Kronhusgatan.
Open Mon.–Sat. 10–4, some shops open later in summer.*

The quaintness of Kronhusbodarna as a shopping experience
contrasts sharply with the coldly modern functionalism of
⑭ **Nordstan,** the vast indoor shopping mall a short distance away
off Östra Hamngatan.

Tour 2: The Harbor

Walk across the Götaälvbron (Göta River Bridge) to **Hisingen,**
now the mainly industrial area of the city, on the far bank,
which was the site of earlier settlements before Göteborg was
built. When the city was founded, boats at first anchored in its
canals, but larger vessels had to put in farther west, and as a
consequence, the harbor developed on both banks of the river.

A good starting point for a tour of the docks is **Gasverkskajen**
(Gas Works Quay), just off Gullbergsstrandgatan. Today this is
the headquarters of a local boating association, its brightly colored pleasure craft contrasting with the old-fashioned working
barges either anchored or being repaired at Ringön, just across
the river. Walk back under the Göta River Bridge and head for
⑮ **Maritima Centret** (the Maritime Center) at Lilla Bommen. This
modern development is aimed at revitalizing the inner harbor.
The center contains modern naval vessels, including a destroy-
er, submarines, a lightship, a cargo vessel, and various tug-
boats, that can be visited. *Lilla Bommenshamnen, tel. 031/
101035. Admission: SKr35 adults, SKr20 children 5–12. Open
late May–late Aug., daily; Mar.–Nov., weekends only.*

Continue along the river, down Skeppsbrokajen, for views
⑯ across the river of the **Götaverkan** and **Cityvarvet** shipyards,
which were once the pride of the city but now look distinctly
forlorn. Farther along the riverbank, past Masthuggskajen,
where boats depart for Denmark, you come to **Stigbergskajen,**
where the transatlantic liners once docked. Today most international visitors arrive by air at Göteborg's Landvetter airport
or Arlanda outside Stockholm.

⑰ Just past Stigbergskajen is **Fiskhamnen,** the fishing harbor,
where the day's catch is auctioned weekdays at 7. Continue

walking and you will see signs of changing times all around. An ⓲ excellent view of **Älvsborgsbron,** (the Älvsborg Bridge), the longest suspension bridge in Sweden, is available from Fiskhamnen. Built in 1967, it stretches 3,000 feet across the river and is built so high that ocean liners can pass beneath. The government is considering plans to turn this part of the harbor into a scenic walkway with parks and cafés. Return to the city side of the river across the mighty bridge and from it look to- ⓳ ward the sea to the large container harbors, **Skarvikshamnen, Skandiahamnen** (where boats depart for England), and **Torshamnen,** which bring most of the cargo and passengers to the city today.

Tour 3: Göteborg from the Water

For a view of the city from the water and an expert commentary in English and German on its sights and history, take one of the ⓴ **Paddan** sightseeing boats. *Paddan* means "toad" in Swedish, an apt commentary on the vessels' squat appearance. The boats pass under 20 bridges and take in both the canals and part of the Göta River. *Kungsportbro, tel. 031/133000. Fare: SKr55. Open early May–mid-June and early Aug.–mid-Sept., daily 10–5; mid-June–early Aug., daily 10–9.*

㉑ There also are regular **boat** trips from the quayside close to the city center to the **Elfsborgs Fästning** (Elfsborg Fortress), built in 1670 on a harbor island to protect the city from attack. *Elfsborg båtar, Stenpiren, tel. 031/7752565. Boats leave 6 times daily, mid-May–mid-Sept. Cost: SKr55 adults, SKr37 children round-trip.*

What to See and Do with Children

Here Göteborg comes into its own with **Lisebergs Nöjes Park,** Scandinavia's largest amusement park and one of the best-run, most efficient parks in the world. It not only features a wide selection of carnival rides but also has numerous restaurants and theaters, all set amid beautifully tended gardens. It's only a short walk from the city center. *Södra Vägen, tel. 031/400100. Admission: SKr35. Open mid-Apr.–mid-May and late Aug.– late Sept., weekends; mid-May–late Aug., daily.*

Shopping

Department Stores The local branch of **NK,** Sweden's leading department store, is at Östra Hamngatan 42 (tel. 031/173300), while that of **Åhléns** is in the Nordstan mall (tel. 031/800200).

Specialty Stores **Antikhallarna** (the Antiques Halls) (Västra Hamngatan 6, tel.
Antiques 031/137799) claim to be the largest of their kind in Scandinavia. You'll find Sweden's leading auction house, **Bukowskis,** on Avenyn (Kungsportsavenyn 43, tel. 031/200360).

Handicrafts The most atmospheric settings for the purchase of Swedish handicrafts and glassware are in the various shops in **Kronhusbodarna** (*see* Tour 1, *above*), but excellent examples of local handicrafts can also be bought at **Bohusslöjden** (Kungsportsavenyn 25, tel. 031/160072).

Men's Clothing **Gillblads** (Kungsgatan 42–44, tel. 031/108846) and **Ströms** (Kungsgatan 27–29, tel. 031/177100) have good selections.

Women's Clothing For furs, try **Andreassons** (Södra Hamngatan 49, tel. 031/ 155535), for other fashions, **Gillblads**, **Ströms** (*see* Men's Clothes, *above*), and **Hennes & Mauritz** (Kungsgatan 55–57, tel. 031/110011) all have standard choices.

Sports and Outdoor Activities

Fishing Fishing for mackerel is a popular sport. Among the boats that take expeditions into the archipelago is the M/S *Daisy*, which leaves from Hjuvik on the Hisingen side of the Göta River (tel. 031/963018).

Water Sports Boating, sailing, and windsurfing are all well provided for. Check with the tourist office for details.

Beaches

There are several excellent local beaches. The two most popular (though visitors are unlikely to find them crowded) are **Näset** and **Askim**.

Dining

You can eat well in Göteborg, but you must expect to pay dearly for the privilege. If anything, there is a more casual approach here than in Stockholm, so, unless otherwise indicated, you won't need to dress up. Fish dishes are the best bet here. Check to make sure restaurants are open first, as many close for a month in summer. (For rates, *see* Staying in Sweden in Chapter 1.)

Highly recommended restaurants are indicated by a star ★.

Very Expensive

Belle Avenue. A dramatic tribute to the power of interior decoration, this plush, wood-paneled restaurant entered from the modern lobby of the SAS Park Avenue is another world. The chef at Belle Avenue is expert at utilizing local fishes and creating such gourmet dishes as thin slices of halibut filled with ragout of lobster and artichoke and served with truffles. *Kungsportsavenyn 36–38, tel. 031/176520. Reservations required. Dress: casual but neat. Closed Sat. lunch, Sun., and July. AE, DC, MC, V.*

★ **The Place.** Göteborg's top restaurant, The Place now offers a choice between the restaurant and the less expensive but popular brasserie. Characteristic of both restaurants are the terracotta ceilings, pastel-yellow walls, and white linen tablecloths heightening the warm, intimate atmosphere in which to enjoy the wide selection of contemporary cuisine and quality ingredients. The Place also boasts one of the best wine cellars in Sweden, with Mouton Rothschild wines dating from 1904. *Arkivgatan 7, tel. 031/160333. Reservations advised. Dress: casual but neat. Restaurant closed July. AE, DC, MC, V.*

Expensive

Chablis. Long popular in Göteborg, this excellent fish restaurant is located at *Aschebergsgatan 22, tel. 031/203545. Reservations advised. AE, DC, MC, V.*

Sjömagasinet. The specialty of this seafood restaurant, with its 18th-century atmosphere and pleasant view of the sea, is fillet of sole Walewska. *Klippans Kulturreservat, tel. 031/246510. Reservations required. AE, DC, MC, V.*

Stallgården. This is a high-quality fish restaurant, one of whose specialties is curry-stuffed lobster. *Kyrkogården 33, tel. 031/130316. Reservations required. AE, DC, MC, V.*

Moderate

A Hereford Beefstouw. Probably as close as you come to an American steak house in Sweden, this restaurant has gained popularity in a town dominated by fish restaurants. Diners' beef selections are cooked by chefs at grills in the center of each of the three dining rooms. The rustic atmosphere is heightened by thick wooden tables, pine floors, and landscape paintings. *Linéagatan 5, tel. 031/775–0441. Reservations advised. Dress: casual but neat. AE, DC, MC, V. July dinner only.*

Fiskekrogen. Its name means "Fish Inn," and it has more than 30 fish and seafood dishes to choose from. Lunches are particularly good. *Lilla Torget 1, tel. 031/112184. Reservations advised. AE, DC, MC, V.*

Weise. A centrally located restaurant with a German beer-cellar atmosphere, owned by the same family since 1907, it was once a haunt of local painters and intellectuals and still retains something of that ambience. The tables and chairs date from 1892. It specializes in traditional Swedish home cooking, serving dishes such as pork and brown beans, pea soup, and homemade apple cake. *Drottninggatan 23, tel. 031/131402. Reservations advised. AE, DC, MC, V.*

Inexpensive

Amanda Boman. This little restaurant is in one corner of the market hall and keeps early opening hours, so unless you eat an afternoon dinner, it is primarily a lunch place. It serves Swedish specialties—fish soup, *gravlax* (marinated salmon), and daily hot dishes. *Saluhallen, tel. 031/137676. AE, DC, MC, V. Closed Sun.*

Gabriel. Fresh shellfish and the fish dish of the day draw crowds to this restaurant on a balcony above the fish hall. You can eat lunch and watch all the trading. *Feskekorka, tel. 031/139051. MC, V. Closed dinner and weekends.*

Minus. This restaurant proves that health food doesn't have to be boring. All food is marked with calorie count, but, fortunately, that doesn't affect the taste. *Andra Långgatan 4B, tel. 031/144199. No credit cards. Closed weekends.*

Lodging

In Göteborg, many hotels offer special summer discounts. (For rates, *see* Staying in Sweden in Chapter 1.)

Highly recommended hotels are indicated by a star ★.

Very Expensive

SAS Park Avenue. The lobby of this modern luxury hotel was renovated in 1991, but it still lacks ambience. The well-equipped rooms are decorated in earth tones. Its excellent location on Avenyn and the bright, airy cocktail bar on the top floor are its chief attractions. *Kungsportsavenyn 36–38, S–400 16, tel. 031/176520, fax 031/169568. 318 rooms. Facilities: restaurant, bar, nightclub, sauna, swimming pool, conference room, SAS airline check-in counter. AE, DC, MC, V.*
Sheraton Hotel and Towers. Opened in 1986, the Sheraton Hotel and Towers is Göteborg's most modern and spectacular international-style hotel. It features an atrium lobby. There are several restaurants with varying prices, including a popular Italian café, open at lunchtime, and a more formal restaurant serving international cuisine. *Södra Hamngatan 59–65, S–401 24, tel. 031/806000, fax 031/159888. 340 rooms with bath. Facilities: restaurants, nightclub, health club, 16 rooms for the disabled, swimming pool. AE, DC, MC, V. Closed Christmas.*

Expensive

★ **Europa.** Large and comfortable, this Reso hotel is situated close to the central railway station and the Nordstan mall. *Köpmansgatan 38, S–401 24, tel. 031/801280, fax 031/154755. 475 rooms, 5 suites. Facilities: restaurant, bar, piano bar, nightclub, gift shop, garage, rooms for the disabled. AE, DC, MC, V.*
Opalen. If you are attending an event at the Scandinavium stadium or if you have children and are heading for the Liseberg amusement park, this Reso hotel is ideally located. Completely renovated in 1990, the rooms are bright and modern. *Engelbrektsgatan 73, S–402 23, tel. 031/810300, fax 031/187622. 241 rooms. Facilities: restaurant, bar, swimming pool, sauna, tennis courts, 2 non-smoking floors. AE, DC, MC, V.*
Panorama. Within reach of all downtown attractions, this Best Western hotel nevertheless manages to provide a quiet, relaxing atmosphere. *Eklandagatan 51–53, S–400 22, tel. 031/810880, fax 031/814237. 340 rooms. Facilities: restaurant, nightclub, swimming pool, sauna, Jacuzzi, garage. AE, DC, MC, V.*
Riverton. Convenient for people arriving in the city by ferry, this hotel is close to the European terminals and overlooks the harbor. Built in 1985 and regularly renovated, it has a glossy marble floor and reflective ceiling in the lobby and rooms decorated with abstract-pattern textiles and whimsical prints. *Stora Badhusgatan 26, S–411 21, tel. 031/101200, fax 031/130866. 190 rooms. Facilities: restaurant, bar, swimming pool, sauna, Jacuzzi, garage, conference rooms. AE, DC, MC, V.*

Moderate

★ **Eggers.** Dating from 1859, Sweden Hotels' Eggers has more Old World character than any other hotel in the city. It is located near the train station and was probably the last port of call in Sweden for many emigrants to the United States. The rooms feature antique furnishings. *Drottningtorget, S–401 25, tel. 031/806070, fax 031/154243. 77 rooms with bath. Facilities: restaurant. AE, DC, MC, V. Closed Christmas.*
Foggs Hotel. A little off the beaten path, but still only five min-

utes from the city center by car, the Foggs has large, pastel rooms equipped with desks and sofas in addition to the standard amenities. *Gamla Tingstadsgatan 1, S–402 76, tel. 031/222420, fax 031/512100. 121 rooms. Facilities: restaurant, bar, sauna, indoor pool, squash courts, conference rooms. AE, DC, MC, V.*

Hotel Klang. Renovated in 1986, this family-run modern hotel is situated in a 100-year-old former warehouse. The only evidences of its history are the brick walls on the outside and the high ceilings in all the rooms. *Stora Badhusetgatan 28, tel. 031/174050, fax 031/174058. 50 rooms. Facilities: breakfast room, conference room. AE, DC, MC, V.*

Rubinen. Here's an excellent central location on Avenyn, but this Reso hotel can be noisy during the summer. *Kungsportsavenyn 24, S–400 14, tel. 031/810800, fax 031/167586. 190 rooms. Facilities: restaurant, bar, conference rooms, garage. AE, DC, MC, V.*

Inexpensive

★ **Royal.** Located in the city center near the train station, Göteborg's oldest hotel is small, family-owned, and traditional. It was built in 1852 and refurbished in 1991. The rooms are individually decorated with reproductions of elegant Swedish traditional furniture. *Drottninggatan 67, S–411 21, tel. 031/80610. 86 rooms with bath. Facilities: breakfast room. AE, DC, MC, V. Closed Christmas and New Year's Day.*

Youth Hostels **Oskupan.** Situated in a modern apartment block, this hotel is 5 kilometers (3 miles) from the railway station. *Merjerigatam 2, S–412 76, tel. 031/401050. 220 beds, 6-bed apartments. Facilities: breakfast. No credit cards. Closed Sept.–May.*

Partille. This hostel is in a pleasant old house 15 kilometers (9 miles) outside the city. *Box 201, Landvettersvägen, S–433 24, tel. 031/446163 or 031/446501. 120 beds, 2- to 4-bed rooms. Facilities: meals to order.*

Camping There are campsites at **Delsjö** (tel. 031/252909), **Kärralund** (tel. 031/252761), and **Askim** (tel. 031/286261).

The Arts and Nightlife

Two free publications in English, available in hotels and at the tourist office, list events, shows, and restaurants: *What's On in Gothenburg* is published monthly, *Gothenburg This Week* weekly. The principal morning newspaper, *Göteborgs Posten*, publishes a weekly listings supplement titled "Aveny," which, while it is in Swedish, is reasonably easy to decipher. "Miss Tourist" (tel. 031/117450), a taped telephone service, lists events in English.

Excursions from Göteborg

Bohuslän

This coastal region north of Göteborg, with its indented, rocky coastline, provides a foretaste of Norway's fjords farther north. It was from these rugged shores that the 9th- and 10th-century Vikings sailed southward on their epic voyages. Today small towns and attractive fishing villages nestle among the distinctively rounded granite rocks and the thousands of skerries and islands that form Sweden's western archipelago, best described by Prince Vilhelm, brother of the late King Gustav V, as "an archipelago formed of gneiss and granite and water which eternally stretches foamy arms after life."

Tourist Information The principal tourist office for the region is **Göteborg Turistbyrå** (Kungsportsplatsen 2, 411 10 Göteborg, tel. 031/100740). There are local offices in **Kungälv** (Fästningsholmen, tel. 030/12035), **Kungshamn** (Hamngatan 6, tel. 0523/37150), **Öckerö** (Stranden 2, tel. 031/965080), **Strömstad** (Torget, Norra Hamnen, tel. 0526/13025), and **Uddevalla** (Kampenhof, tel. 0522/11787).

Getting There
By Car The best way to explore Bohuslän is by car. The E6 highway runs the length of the coast from Göteborg north to Strömstad, close to the Norwegian border, and for campers there are numerous extremely well-equipped and uncluttered camping places along the coast's entire length.

By Train There is regular service along the coast between all the major towns of Bohuslän. The trip from Göteborg to Strömstad takes about two hours, and there are several trains each day. SJ (Göteborg, tel. 031/103000 or 020/757575).

By Bus Buses leave from behind the central railway station in Göteborg (bus lines are: Göteborg bus, tel. 031/801235, and Bohustrafiken, tel. 0522/14030). The trip to Strömstad takes two to three hours.

Exploring Bohuslän *Numbers in the margin correspond to points of interest on the Excursions from Göteborg map.*

Ideally you should drift slowly north, taking full advantage of the uncluttered beaches and small, picturesque fishing villages. Painters and sailors haunt the region in summer.

❶ The first stop north of Göteborg is **Kungälv,** strategically placed at the confluence of the two arms of the Göta River and the site of **Bohus Fästning,** a ruined fortress built by the Norwegians in 1308 where many battles between Swedish, Norwegian, and Danish armies took place. Today Kungälv has become something of a bedroom suburb for Göteborg, but it has a white wooden church dating from 1679, with an unusual Baroque interior. (*See also* Exploring the Göta Canal, *below*).

There is excellent deep-sea mackerel fishing from **Skärhamn** on the island of Tjörn, which can be reached by road bridge from Stenungsund.

❷ **Uddevalla,** a former shipbuilding town at the head of a picturesque fjord, is best known for a battle in which heavy rains doused musketeers' matches, effectively ending hostilities.

Lysekil, off the E6 highway on a promontory at the head of the Gullmarn Fjord, has been one of Sweden's most popular summer resorts since the 19th century. It specializes in boat excursions to neighboring islands and deep-sea fishing trips. The best bathing is at Pinnevik Cove.

❸ A little to the north lies the **Sotenäs** peninsula and the attractive island of **Smögen,** which can be reached by road bridge. It is locally renowned for its shrimp.

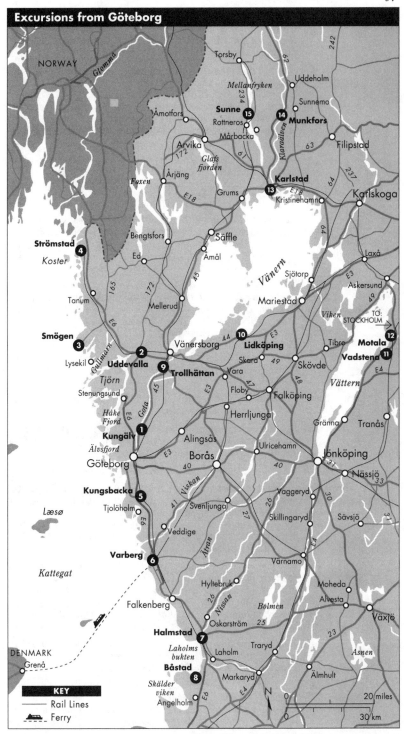

Excursions from Göteborg

Stop at **Tanumshede** to see Europe's largest single collection of Bronze Age rock carvings at **Vitlycke.** They cover 673 square feet of rock and depict battles, hunting, and fishing. The carvings are close to the main road and well marked.

❹ **Strömstad,** a popular Swedish resort, boasts that it has more summer sunshine than any other town north of the Alps. Formerly Norwegian, it has been the site of many battles among warring Danes, Norwegians, and Swedes. A short trip over the Norwegian border takes you to Halden, where Sweden's warrior king, Karl XII, died in 1718.

There are regular ferry boats from Strömstad to the **Koster Islands,** another favorite holiday spot, with uncluttered beaches and trips to catch prawn and lobster.

The Swedish Riviera

The coastal region south of Göteborg is the closest that mainland Sweden comes to having a resort area (locally dubbed the "Swedish Riviera"). Fine beaches abound, and there are plenty of opportunities for many sporting activities. The region stretches down to Båstad in the country's southernmost province, Skåne.

Tourist Information The regional tourist office is VästSvenska Turistråd (West Swedish Tourist Board) (Kungsportsplatsen 2, 411 10 Göteborg, tel. 031/818200). Local offices are in **Båstad** (Stortorget 1, tel. 0431/75045), **Falkenberg** (Stortorget, tel. 0346/17410), **Halmstad** (Lilla Torg, tel. 035/109345), **Kungsbacka** (Storgatan 41, tel. 0300/34284), **Laholm** (Rådhuset, tel. 0430/15216 or 0430/15450), and **Varberg** (Brunnsparken, tel. 0340/88780 and 0340/88770).

Getting There To reach the Swedish Riviera, simply follow the E6 highway
By Car south from Göteborg. It parallels the coast.

By Train Regular service connects the Göteborg central station with all major towns. Contact **SJ** (Göteborg, tel. 031/103000 or 020/757575).

By Bus Buses leave from behind Göteborg's central railway station.

Exploring the Swedish Riviera The first stop heading south from Göteborg is **Kungsbacka,** today fast becoming one of its bedroom suburbs; it holds a market
❺ on the first Thursday of every month. From the top of an Ice Age sand ridge at the nearby village of Fjärås, there is a fine view of the coast, and on the slopes of the ridge are Iron Age and Viking graves.

At **Tjolöholm,** 12 kilometers (7 miles) down the road, you encounter Tjolöholms Slott (Tjolöholm Castle), a manor house built by a Scotsman at the beginning of this century in mock English Tudor style. *S–43033 Fjärås, tel. 0300/44200. Admission: SKr35 adults, SKr10 children 4–14. Open June–Aug., daily; Apr.–May, Sept., weekends.*

Nearby is the tiny 18th-century village of **Äskhult,** the site of an open-air museum. *Tel. 0300/42159 or 0300/34619. Admission: SKr10 adults, SKr2 children. Open June–Aug.*

❻ The next town along the coast is **Varberg,** a busy port with connections to Grenå in Denmark and some good beaches. It is best known for a suit of medieval clothing preserved in the museum in the 13th-century **Varbergs Fästning** (Varberg Fortress). The suit belonged to a man who was murdered and thrown into a peat bog. The peat preserved his body, and his clothes are the only suit of ordinary medieval clothing in existence. The museum also contains a silver bullet said to be the one that killed Karl XII. *Tel. 0340/18520. Admission: SKr10. Open daily 10–7. Guided tours June–Aug., daily; May and Sept., Sun.*

Falkenberg, 29 kilometers (18 miles) farther south, is one of Sweden's most attractive resorts, with fine beaches and salmon fishing in the Ätran River. Falkenberg's Gamla Stan (Old Town) features narrow, cobblestone streets and quaint old wooden houses. Here you'll find Törngren's, a pottery shop, probably the oldest still operating in Scandinavia, owned and run by the seventh generation of the founding family.

7 **Halmstad,** 148 kilometers (92 miles) south of Göteborg, is the largest seaside resort on the west coast, with a population of 50,000. The **Norreport** town gate, all that remains of the town's original fortifications, dates from 1605. The modern Town Hall has interior decorations by the so-called Halmstad Group of painters, formed here in 1929. A 14th-century church in the main square contains fragments of medieval murals and a 17th-century pulpit.

8 By the time you reach **Båstad,** 188 kilometers (117 miles) from Göteborg, you are in Skåne, Sweden's southernmost province. Båstad is the most fashionable resort in Sweden, where ambassadors and local captains of industry have their summer houses. Aside from this, it is best known for its tennis. In addition to the **Båstad Open,** a Grand Prix tournament in late summer, there is the annual **Donald Duck Cup** in July for children ages 11 to 15; it was the very first trophy won by Björn Borg, who later took the Wimbledon men's singles title an unprecedented five times in a row. Spurred on by Borg and other Swedish champions, such as Stefan Edberg and Mats Wilander, thousands of youngsters take part in the Donald Duck Cup each year. For details, contact **Svenska Tennisförbundet** (the Swedish Tennis Association), Lidingövägen 75, Stockholm, tel. 08/6679770).

Time Out   **Norrviken Gardens** (tel. 0431/71070), 3 kilometers (2 miles) northwest of Båstad, are beautifully laid out in different styles, with a restaurant, a shop, and a pottery studio.

The Göta Canal

The **Göta Canal** is actually 614 kilometers (380 miles) of interconnected canals, rivers, lakes, and even a stretch of sea. It links Stockholm with Göteborg and had been a Swedish dream ever since it was first suggested by Bishop Hans Brask of Linköping in the 16th century. In 1718 King Karl XII ordered the canal to be built, but work was abandoned when he was killed in battle the same year. Not until 1810 was the idea again taken up in earnest. The driving force was a Swedish nobleman, Count Baltzar Bogislaus von Platen (1766–1829), and his motive was commercial. Von Platen saw in the canal a way of beating Danish tolls on shipping passing through the Öresund and of enhancing the importance of Göteborg by linking the port with Stockholm on the east coast. At a time when Swedish fortunes were at a low ebb, the canal was also envisaged as a means of reestablishing faith in the future and boosting national morale.

The building of the canal took 22 years and involved a total of 58,000 men. The linking of the various stretches of water required 87 kilometers (54 miles) of man-made cuts through soil and rock, the building of 58 locks, 47 bridges, 27 culverts, and 3 dry docks. Unfortunately, the canal never achieved the financial success hoped for by von Platen. By 1857 the Danes had removed shipping tolls, and in the following decade the linking of Göteborg with Stockholm by rail effectively ended the canal's commercial potential. The canal did come into its own as a 20th-century tourist attraction, however.

Tourist Regional tourist offices are **Bohusturist** (Uddevalla, tel. 0522/
Information 14055), **Västergötlands Turistråd** (Skövde, tel. 0500/18050), and **Turistbolaget AB** (Linköping, tel. 013/125055). Local tourist offices along the route include **Karlsborg** (N. Kanalgatan 2, 0505/12120), **Linköping** (Agatan 39, tel. 013/206835), and **Vadstena** (Rådhustorget, tel. 0143/15125).

Exploring the Drifting lazily down this lovely series of waterways, across the
Göta Canal enormous lakes, Vänern and Vättern, through a microcosm of all that is best about Sweden—abundant fresh air, clear, clean water, pristine nature, well-tended farmland—it is difficult to conceive of the canal's industrial origins.

Traveling the entire length of the canal by passenger boat to Stockholm takes four or six days. For details, contact the **Göta Canal Steamship Company** (Box 272, S–401 24, Göteborg, tel. 031/806315). A bicycle path runs parallel to the canal, offering another way to tour the country. For information on sailing your own boat, contact AB Göta Kanalbolaget (tel. 0141/53510).

The trip from Göteborg takes you first along the Göta Älv (river), a wide waterway that 10,000 years ago, when the ice cap melted, was a great fjord. Some 30 minutes into the voyage the boat passes below a rocky escarpment, topped by the remains of **Bohus Fästning** (Bohus Castle), distinguished by two round towers known as Father's Hat and Mother's Bonnet. It dates from the 14th century and was once the mightiest fortress in western Scandinavia, commanding the confluence of the Göta and Nordre rivers. It was strengthened and enlarged in the 16th century and successfully survived 14 sieges. From 1678 onward, the castle began to lose its strategic and military importance and fell into decay, until 1838, when King Karl XIV passed by on a river journey, admired the old fortress, and ordered its preservation.

The boat passes **Kungälv** (*see also* Exploring Bohuslän, *above*), a pleasant riverside town, then **Lödöse,** once a major trading settlement and a predecessor of Göteborg that is today a quiet village. The countryside becomes wilder, with pines and oaks clustered thickly on either bank between cliffs of lichen-clad granite.

Some five hours after leaving Göteborg the boat arrives in **❾ Trollhättan,** 89 kilometers (55 miles) upriver. This is a pleasant industrial town of around 50,000 inhabitants, where a spectacular waterfall was in 1906 rechanneled to become Sweden's first hydroelectric plant. Most years, on specific days the waters are allowed to follow their natural course, a fall of 106 feet in six torrents. This is a sight that is well worth seeing. The other main point of interest is the area between what were the falls and the series of locks that allowed the canal to bypass them. Here are disused locks from 1800 and 1844 and a strange Ice Age grotto where members of the Swedish royal family have carved their names since the 18th century. Trollhättan also has a fine, wide marketplace and pleasant waterside parks.

Soon after leaving Trollhättan, the boat passes **Hunneberg** and **Halleberg,** two strange, flat-top hills, both more than 500 feet high. The woods surrounding them are extraordinarily rich in elk, legend, and Viking burial mounds. The boat proceeds through **Karls Grav,** the oldest part of the canal. This was begun early in the 17th century, its purpose to bypass the Ronnum Falls on the Göta River, which have been harnessed to a hydroelectric project. Finally the boat reaches **Vänern,** Sweden's largest and Europe's third-largest lake: 3,424 square kilometers (2,123 square miles) of water, 145 kilometers (90 miles) long and 81 kilometers (50 miles) wide at one point. The canal enters the lake at **Vänersborg,** a town of around 30,000 inhabitants that was founded in the mid-17th century. The church and the governor's residence date from the 18th century, but the rest of the town was destroyed by fire in 1834. Vänersborg is distinguished by its fine lakeside park, the trees of which act as a windbreak for the gusts that sweep in from Vänern.

It takes about eight hours to cross Vänern. On an inlet at the southernmost point of its eastern arm lies the town of **⑩ Lidköping,** which received its charter in 1446 and is said to have the largest town square in Sweden. Lying 24 kilometers (15 miles) to the north of it, on an island off the point dividing the eastern arm of Vänern from the western, is **Läckö Slott** (Läckö Castle), one of Sweden's finest 17th-century Renaissance palaces. Its 250 rooms were once the home of Magnus Gabriel de la Gardie, a great favorite of Queen Christina. Only the Royal Palace in Stockholm is larger. In 1681 Karl XI, to curtail the power of the nobility, confiscated it, and in 1830 all its furnishings were auctioned. Many of them have since been restored to the palace.

On a peninsula to the east, the landscape is dominated by the great hill of **Kinnekulle,** towering 900 feet above the lake. The hill is rich in colorful vegetation and wildlife and was a favorite hike for the botanist Linnaeus.

Then, at the lakeside port of **Sjötorp,** the **Göta Canal** proper begins: a cut through earth and granite with a series of locks raising the steamer to Lanthöjden, at 304 feet above sea level the highest point on the canal. The boat next enters the narrow, twisting lakes Viken and Bottensjön and continues to Forsvik though the canal's oldest lock, built in 1813. It then sails out into **Vättern,** Sweden's second-largest lake, nearly 129 kilometers (80 miles) from north to south and 31 kilometers (19 miles) across at its widest point. Its waters are so clear that in some parts the bottom is visible at a depth of 50 feet. The lake is subject to sudden storms that can whip its normally placid waters into a choppy maelstrom.

Some 259 kilometers (161 miles) from Göteborg, the boat finally **⑪** anchors at **Vadstena,** a little-known historic gem of a town. Vadstena grew up around the monastery founded by St.

Birgitta, or Bridget (1303–1373), who wrote in her *Revelationes* that she had a vision of Christ in which he revealed the rules of the religious order she went on to establish. These rules seem to have been a precursor for the Swedish ideal of sexual equality, with both nuns and monks sharing a common church. Her order spread rapidly after her death, and at one time there were 80 Bridgetine monasteries in Europe. Little remains of the Vadstena monastery, however; in 1545 King Gustav Vasa ordered its demolition, and its stones were used to build **Vadstena Slott** (Vadstena Castle), the huge fortress dominating the lake. Swedish royalty held court here until 1715. It then fell into decay and was used as a granary. Today it houses part of the National Archives and is also the site of an annual summer opera festival. *Tel. 0143/15123. Admission: SKr30. Open mid-May–mid-Aug., daily noon–5.*

Vadstena Kyrka is also worth visiting. The triptych altarpiece on the south wall features St. Birgitta presenting her book of revelations to a group of kneeling cardinals. There is also a fine wood carving of the Madonna and Child from 1500.

If you continue down the canal to Stockholm, you sail through **Motala,** where Baltzar von Platen is buried close to the canal. He had envisaged the establishment of four new towns along the waterway, but only Motala fulfilled his dream. He designed the town himself, and his statue is in the main square.

At Borenshult a series of locks takes the boat down to Boren, a lake in the province of Östergötland. On the southern shore of the next lake, Roxen, lies the city of **Linköping,** capital of the province and home of Saab, the aircraft and automotive company. Once out of the lake, you follow a new stretch of canal past the sleepy town of **Söderköping.** A few miles east, at the hamlet of Mem, the canal's last lock lowers the boat into Slätbaken, a Baltic fjord presided over by the ruins of the ancient **Stegeborg** fortress. The boat then steams north along the coastline until it enters Mälaren through the Södertälje Canal and finally anchors in the capital at Riddarholmen.

Lodging
Vadstena
Kungs-Starby Wärdshus. This recently renovated manor house on the outskirts of town, reached on Route 50, is surrounded by a park. The bedrooms are small and functional. *S–59200, tel. 0143/11420. 45 rooms with shower. Facilities: restaurant, sauna, swimming pool, solarium. AE, DC, MC, V. Inexpensive.*
Vadstena Klosterhotel. This hotel is housed in what is Sweden's oldest secular building, parts of which date from the 13th century. *Klosterområdet, off Lasarettsgatan, S–59230, tel. 0143/ 11530, fax 0143/13648. 29 rooms with bath. Facilities: restaurant, satellite TV, rooms for allergy sufferers. AE, DC, MC, V. Inexpensive.*

Värmland

This province, close to the Norwegian border on the north shores of Vänern, is rich in folklore. It was also the home of Alfred Nobel and the birthplace of other famous Swedes, among them the Nobel Prize–winning novelist Selma Lagerlöf, the poet Gustaf Fröding, former Prime Minister Tage Erlander, and present-day opera star Håkan Hagegård. It is a part of the country favored by artists, with a timeless quality to it, a place where Swedes often take their own holidays. Värmland's forested, lake-dotted landscape, along with that of Dalarna, farther north, embodies Sweden as a whole.

Tourist Information The regional tourist office is **Värmlands Turistråd** (Södra Kyrkogatan 10, Karlstad, tel. 054/102160). There are local tourist offices in **Karlstad** (Bibliotek, Västratorggatan 26, tel. 054/195901) and **Sunne** (Sunne Turistcentrum, tel. 0565/13530).

Getting There *By Car* Follow E3 and then E18 west from Stockholm or Route 45 north to E18 from Göteborg.

By Train There is regular service to Karlstad from Stockholm and Göteborg on SJ.

Exploring Värmland **⑬** Värmland's principal city, **Karlstad** (population 74,000), 255 kilometers (158 miles) from Göteborg, is situated on Klaraälven (the Klara River) at the point where it empties into Vänern. Karlstad was founded in 1684, when it was known as Tingvalla. It later changed its name to honor King Karl IX, Karlstad meaning "Karl's Town." It was totally rebuilt after a fire in 1865. In **Stortorget,** the main square, there is a statue of Karl IX by the local sculptor Christian Eriksson. The **Värmlands Museum** has rooms dedicated to both Eriksson and the poet Fröding. *Sandgrun, Box 335, S-65108, tel. 054/111419. Admission: SKr15. Open daily noon–4 (Wed. noon–8).*

The **Marieberg Skogspark** (Marieberg Forest Park) is also worth visiting. A delight for the whole family, the park has restaurants and an outdoor theater. Karlstad is also the site of an **Emigrant Registret** (Emigrant Center, Norra Strandgatan 4, tel. 054/15926) that maintains detailed records of the Swedes' emigration to America. Visitors of Swedish extraction can trace their ancestors at the center's research facility.

Värmland is, above all, a rural experience. You can drive along the Klaräalven, through the beautiful Fryken Valley, to Ransater, where author Erik Gustaf Geijer was born in 1783 and where Erlander, the former prime minister, also grew up. **⑭** The rural idyll ends in **Munkfors,** where some of the best-quality steel in Europe is manufactured, but just past it, you'll find the little village of **Sunnemo,** with its beautiful wooden church. A little farther north, the town of **Uddeholm** on Lake Råda is home of the Uddeholm Corporation, which produces iron and steel, forestry products and chemicals. Continuing north around the lake, you can return to Munkfors and then make a **⑮** diversion west to **Sunne,** from which it is only 55 kilometers (34 miles) to **Mårbacka,** the estate where Nobel Prize winner Selma Lagerlöf was born in 1858. It is preserved as it was when she died in 1940. *Östra Ämtervik, S-68600 Sunne, tel. 0565/31027. Admission: SKr35. Open May–Aug., daily 9–6.*

Turning south and heading back toward Karlstad, you can stop off at **Rottneros Herrgårds Park** (Rottneros Manor), the Ekeby of Lagerlöf's *Gösta Berlings Saga* (The Tale of Gösta Berling). The house is privately owned, but its park can be visited and features a fine collection of Scandinavian sculpture, including works by Carl Milles, Norwegian artist Gustav Vigeland, and Wäinö Aaltonen of Finland. *S-68602 Rottneros, tel. 0565/60295. Admission: SKr45 adults, SKr20 children under 15. Open mid-May–early Sept., daily 9–6.*

Dining *Karlstad* **Inn Alstern.** Overlooking Lake Alstern, this restaurant serves Swedish and Continental cuisine in an elegant atmosphere.

Morgonvägen 4, tel. 054/834900. Reservations advised. Dress: casual but neat. AE, MC, V. Expensive.

Dining and Lodging
Karlstad

Stadshotellet. On the banks of Klarälven (the Klara River), this hotel built in 1870 is steeped in tradition. Completely renovoted in 1991, all the rooms are decorated differently: some in modern Swedish style, others evoking their original look. *Kungsgatan 22, S–651 04, tel. 054/115220, fax 054/188211. 143 rooms. Facilities: 2 restaurants, bar, nightclub, sauna. AE, DC, MC, V. Expensive.*

Gösta Berling. Located in the center of town, this small hotel, named for the hero of the Selma Lagerlöf novel, surrounds guests in genuine Värmland ambience. *Drottninggatan 1, S–652 24, tel. 054/150190, fax 054/154826. 66 rooms. Facilities: restaurant, bar, sauna. AE, DC, MC, V. Moderate.*

5 The South and the Kingdom of Crystal

The southernmost provinces of Sweden—Halland, Skåne, and Blekinge—are different in character from the rest of the country, both in appearance and in the temperament of their inhabitants. This is an extension of the fertile plain of northern Europe, rich farming country, and the people generally are more easygoing than their compatriots farther north. The south is a place of windswept, flat meadows and gently rolling hills, of timber-framed farmhouses in whose yards strut geese being fattened to supply local restaurants with the region's specialty dish. Danish for hundreds of years before being incorporated into Sweden in 1658, the region even today seeks its inspiration from mainland Europe, viewing the rest of Sweden—especially Stockholm—with some disdain. Skåne even has its own independence movement, and the dialect here is so akin to Danish that many Swedes from other parts of the country have trouble understanding it.

While not strictly part of the south, the so-called Kingdom of Crystal, in Småland, is easily reached from here. This is an area of small glassblowing firms, such as Kosta Boda and Orrefors, that are world-renowned for the quality of their products. In addition to visiting these works (and perhaps finding some bargains), the traveler forms an insight into a poorer, harsher way of life that led thousands of peasants to emigrate from Småland to the United States in search of a better life. Those who stayed behind developed a reputation for their inventiveness in setting up small industries to circumvent the region's traditional poverty and are also notorious for being extremely careful—if not downright mean—with money.

Essential Information

Important Addresses and Numbers

Tourist Information Skånes Turistråd, the Skåne Tourist Council, is at Skiffervägen 38, Lund (tel. 046/124350). There are tourist offices in the following towns: **Helsingborg** (Knutpunkten, tel. 042/120310), **Kalmar** (Larmgatan 6, tel. 0480/15350), **Karlskrona** (Stadsbiblioteket, tel. 0455/83490), **Lund** (Kyrkogatan 11, tel. 046/355040), **Malmö** (Skeppsbron 2, tel. 040/300150), **Ronneby** (Kallingevägen 3, tel. 0457/17650), and **Ystad** (S:t Knuts Torg, tel. 0411/77681). For visitors to the Kingdom of Crystal, the **Småland Tourist Office** is at Jönköping (tel. 036/199570) and Växjö (tel. 0470/47575).

Arriving and Departing by Plane

Airport and Airlines Malmö's airport, **Sturup,** was opened in 1972. Sturup is approximately 30 kilometers (19 miles) from Malmö and 25 kilometers (16 miles) from Lund. It has two international destinations, Amsterdam, served by KLM, and Oslo, served by Braathens SAFE. Domestic Swedish airlines—SAS, Transwede Airways AB, and Malmö Aviation—serve the Stockholm airports and use them as hubs for connections with other domestic destinations, especially SAS, which also makes international connections via Stockholm's Arlanda. The airlines represented include: **SAS** (tel. 040/357150 or 020/727000), **KLM** (tel. 040/500530), **Braathens SAFE** (tel. 040/501850), and Malmö Avia-

tion (tel. 040/500330), and **Transwede Airways AB** (tel. 040/
501820).

SAS offers discounts on trips to Malmö. You can buy a round-
trip ticket, Stockholm–Malmö, for the price of a one-way ticket
under the current "Jackpot" discount package (SKr849). The
cost for an additional member of the family is SKr424 and children between 2 and 18 get 50% off the going fare. Hertz car rentals are available for SKr850 for the weekend if you book an
SAS flight. For more information, contact SAS (161 87 Stockholm, tel. 020/910150 or 020/727000).

Between the Buses leave hourly for Malmö and Lund from the Sturup air-
Airport and port. The price of the trip is SKr60 to either destination. For
City Center further information on bus schedules, routes, and fares, call
By Bus 040/501100.

By Taxi A taxi from the airport to Malmö costs about SKr250, and to
Lund approximately SKr200. For SAS limousine service, call
040/501834 or 040/357140.

Arriving and Departing by Car, Train, and Boat

By Car Malmö is 620 kilometers (384 miles) from Stockholm. You take
the E4 freeway to Helsingborg, then the E6 to Malmö and
Lund. From Göteborg, take the E6.

By Train There is regular service from Stockholm to Helsingborg,
Lund, and Malmö. The journey takes around 6½ hours. All
three railway stations are centrally situated.

By Boat The most common form of arrival in southern Sweden is by
boat. Several regular services run from Copenhagen to Malmö,
including Hovercrafts that make the trip in less than an hour,
and a bus/ferry service from Copenhagen Station, which also
goes to Lund. There are also regular ferry connections to Denmark, Germany, and Poland from such ports as Malmö,
Helsingborg, Landskrona, Trelleborg, and Ystad. **Stena Line**
(Kungsgatan 12–14, Stockholm, tel. 08/141475, and Danmarks-
terminalen, Göteborg, tel. 031/858000) is one of the major
Swedish carriers.

Day-trippers can pick up tickets at Malmö Harbor and catch
one of the hourly Copenhagen-bound Hovercrafts operated by
the following ferry lines: **Flybåtarna** (tel. 040/103930), **Pile** (tel.
040/234411), and **Hopping Linje** (040/110099). **Skandlines** (tel.
040/362000) runs the only car-ferry service between Dragör,
Denmark, and Limhamn, a town that adjoins Malmö's southern
edge. For travelers from Denmark who want to rent a car as
soon as they arrive, **Avis** (tel. 040/77830), **Hertz** (tel. 040/74955),
and **InterRent** and **Europcar** (tel. 040/380240), which share an
office, all have locations at Malmö Harbor.

Getting Around

By Car Roads are uncluttered and extremely well marked and main-
tained. Traveling around the coast counterclockwise from
Helsingborg, you take the E6 to Landskrona and then on to
Malmö, then the E66 to Lund, Kristianstad, Solvesborg,
Karlshamn, Ronneby, Karlskrona, and up the coast to Kalmar.

By Train The major towns of the south are all connected by rail. A special
Öresund Runt (Around Öresund) ticket for trains and ferries

to Denmark is available from the Malmö Tourist Office
(Skeppsbron 2, tel. 040/3001507; price: SKr125).

Exploring the South and the Kingdom of Crystal

*Numbers in the margin correspond to points of interest on the
South and the Kingdom of Crystal map.*

Southern Sweden is a world of its own, clearly distinguished
from the rest of the country by its geography, culture, and history. Skåne (pronounced *Skoh*-neh), the southernmost province, is known as the granary of Sweden. It is a comparatively
small province of beautifully fertile plains, sand beaches,
scores of castles and châteaus, thriving farms, medieval
churches, and summer resorts. The two other southern provinces, Blekinge and Halland, are also fertile and rolling and
edged by seashores. Historically, these three provinces are
distinct from the rest of Sweden: they were the last to be incorporated into the country, having been ruled by Denmark until
1658. They retain the influences of the Continental culture in
their architecture, language, and cuisine. Småland, to the
north, is larger than the other provinces, with a harsh countryside of stone and woods. It is noted for its glass industries, as
well as furniture and other wooden products, and for the historic region around Kalmar.

Tour 1: The South

❶ The first town of any importance is **Helsingborg** (still sometimes spelled the old way, Hälsingborg). With a population of
108,000, the town seems to the first-time visitor arriving by
boat little more than a nondescript ferry terminal (it has connections to Denmark, Norway, and Germany). Actually, it has
a rich history, having first been mentioned in 10th-century
sagas and since been the site of many battles between the
Danes and the Swedes. Together with its twin town, Helsing-
ör, across the Öresund (Elsinore in William Shakespeare's
Hamlet), it controlled shipping traffic in and out of the Baltic
for centuries. Helsingborg was officially incorporated into
Sweden in 1658 and totally destroyed in a battle with the Danes
in 1710. It was then rebuilt, and Jean-Baptiste Bernadotte,
founder of the present Swedish royal dynasty, landed here in
1810. The **Stadshuset** (Town Hall) has a small museum featuring
exhibits on the city and the region. *Södra Storgatan 31, tel.
042/105963. Admission: SKr10 adults, SKr5 children 7–16.
Open May–Aug., Tues.–Sun. noon–5; Sept.–Apr., Tues.–
Sun. noon–4.*

All that remains of Helsingborg's castle is **Kärnan** (the Keep).
The surviving center tower, built to provide living quarters
and defend the medieval castle, is the most remarkable relic of
its kind in the north. The interior is divided into several floors,
where there are a chapel, a kitchen, and other medieval fittings. It stands in a park and offers fine views over the Öresund
from the top. *Kärngränden, tel. 042/105991. Admission:
SKr10. Open June–Aug., daily 9–8.*

So, you're getting away from it all.

Just make sure you can get back.

AT&T Access Numbers
Dial the number of the country you're in to reach AT&T.

*ANDORRA	19◊-0011	GERMANY**	0130-0010	*NETHERLANDS	06◊-022-9111
*AUSTRIA	022-903-011	*GREECE	00-800-1311	*NORWAY	050-12011
*BELGIUM	078-11-0010	*HUNGARY	00◊-800-01111	POLAND¹◆²	0◊010-480-0111
BULGARIA	00-1800-0010	*ICELAND	999-001	PORTUGAL¹	05017-1-288
CROATIA¹◆	99-38-0011	IRELAND	1-800-550-000	ROMANIA	01-800-4288
*CYPRUS	080-90010	ISRAEL	177-100-2727	*RUSSIA¹ (MOSCOW)	155-5042
CZECH REPUBLIC	00-420-00101	*ITALY	172-1011	SLOVAKIA	00-420-00101
*DENMARK	8001-0010	KENYA¹	0800-10	SPAIN	900-99-00-11
*EGYPT¹ (CAIRO)	510-0200	*LIECHTENSTEIN	155-00-11	*SWEDEN	020-795-611
*FINLAND	9800-100-10	LITHUANIA◆	8◊196	*SWITZERLAND	155-00-11
FRANCE	19◊-0011	LUXEMBOURG	0-800-0111	*TURKEY	9◊9-8001-2277
*GAMBIA	00111	*MALTA	0800-890-110	UK	0800-89-0011

Countries in bold face permit country-to-country calling in addition to calls to the U.S. *Public phones require deposit of coin or phone card. **Western portion. Includes Berlin and Leipzig. ◊Await second dial tone. ¹May not be available from every phone. ◆ Not available from public phones. ¹Dial "02" first, outside Cairo. ²Dial 010-480-0111 from major Warsaw hotels. ©1993 AT&T.

Here's a travel tip that will make it easy to call back to the States. Dial the access number for the country you're visiting and connect right to AT&T **USADirect®** Service. It's the quick way to get English-speaking operators and can minimize hotel surcharges.

If all the countries you're visiting aren't listed above, call **1 800 241-5555** before you leave for a free wallet card with all AT&T access numbers. International calling made easy—it's all part of **The *i* Plan.**℠

THE *i* PLAN℠

AT&T

All The Best Trips Start with Fodor's

Fodor's Affordables

Titles in the series: Caribbean, Europe, Florida, France, Germany, Great Britain, Italy, London, Paris.

"Travelers with champagne tastes and beer budgets will welcome this series from Fodor's." — *Hartford Courant*

"These books succeed admirably; easy to follow and use, full of cost-related information, practical advice, and recommendations...maps are clear and easy to use." — *Travel Books Worldwide*

Fodor's Bed & Breakfast and Country Inn Guides

Titles in the series: California, Canada, England & Wales, Mid-Atlantic, New England, The Pacific Northwest, The South, The Upper Great Lakes Region, The West Coast.

"In addition to information on each establishment, the books add notes on things to see and do in the vicinity. That alone propels these books to the top of the heap."— *San Diego Union-Tribune*

The Berkeley Guides

Titles in the series: California, Central America, Eastern Europe, France, Germany, Great Britain & Ireland, Mexico, The Pacific Northwest, San Francisco.

The best choice for budget travelers, from the Associated Students at the University of California at Berkeley.

"Berkeley's scribes put the funk back in travel." — *Time*

"Hip, blunt and lively." — *Atlanta Journal Constitution*

"Fresh, funny and funky as well as useful." — *The Boston Globe*

Exploring Guides

Titles in the series: Australia, California, Caribbean, Florida, France, Germany, Great Britain, Ireland, Italy, London, New York City, Paris, Rome, Singapore & Malaysia, Spain, Thailand.

"Authoritatively written and superbly presented, and makes worthy reading before, during or after a trip. " — *The Philadelphia Inquirer*

"A handsome new series of guides, complete with lots of color photos, geared to the independent traveler." — *The Boston Globe*

Visit your local bookstore or call 1-800-533-6478 24 hours a day.

Fodor's The name that means smart travel.

The South and the Kingdom of Crystal

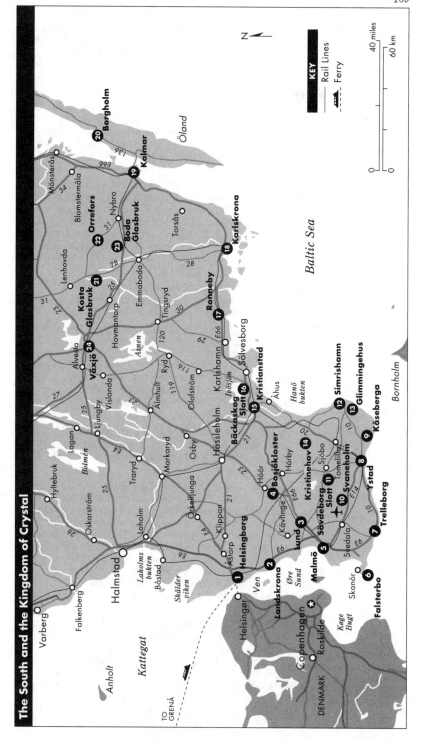

KEY
— Rail Lines
--- Ferry

Baltic Sea

Kattegat

Öland

Öre Sund

Köge Bugt

Laholms bukten

Skälder viken

Hanö bukten

Bornholm

Bolmen

Asnen

Ivösjön

DENMARK

Copenhagen
Roskilde

TO GRENÅ

Helsingør
Ven
Anholt

Varberg
Falkenberg
Halmstad
Hyllebruk
Oskarström
Båstad
Laholm
Traryd
Markaryd
Osby
Örkelljunga
Klippan
Åstorp
Ängelholm

Mönsterås
Blomstermåla
Borgholm
Kalmar
Torsås
Karlskrona
Nybro
Orrefors
Boda Glasbruk
Lenhovda
Emmaboda
Kosta Glasbruk
Alvesta
Växjö
Hovmantorp
Tingsryd
Ronneby
Sölvesborg
Karlshamn
Åhus
Kristianstad
Bäckaskog Slott
Simrishamn
Glimmingehus
Kåseberga
Ystad
Trelleborg
Svaneholm
Kristinehov Slott
Sjöbo
Tomelilla
Hörby
Höör
Bosjökloster
Hässleholm
Almhult
Ryd
Olofström
Vislanda
Ljungby
Lagan
Lenhovda
Falsterbo
Skanör
Malmö
Lund
Sövdeborg Slott
Kävlinge
Skedala
Sjöbo

Helsingborg
Landskrona

40 miles
60 km
N

Sofiero Slott (Sofiero Palace), 5 kilometers (3 miles) outside the town, was once a royal summer residence. Built in 1865 in the Dutch Renaissance style, it has a fine park designed by Crown Princess Margareta. *Solfierovägen (on road to Laröd), tel. 042/ 145259. Admission: SKr20 adults, Skr12 children. Open May– Sept., daily 10–6.*

② The 17th-century Dutch-style fortifications of **Landskrona,** 40 kilometers (25 miles) down the coast, are among the best-preserved of their type in Europe. Though it appears to be just another modern town, Landskrona actually dates from 1413, when it received its charter. Author Selma Lagerlöf worked here at the town's elementary school in 1888 and began her novel *Gösta Berlings Saga.*

Landskrona's **Citadellet** (castle) was built under orders of the Danish King Christian III in 1549 and is all that remains of the original town, which was razed in 1747 on orders of the Swedish Parliament to make way for extended fortifications. The new town was then built on land reclaimed from the sea. Local handicrafts workshops in the castle grounds sell their products during the summer. *Slottsgatan, tel. 0418/16980. Admission: SKr10. Open June–Aug., daily 11–4.*

Three kilometers (2 miles) north of the town lies the **Borstahusen** recreation area, with long stretches of beach, a marina, and a holiday village with 74 summer chalets.

From Landskrona harbor there are regular 25-minute boat trips to the island of **Ven,** where the Danish astronomer Tycho Brahe lived from 1576 to 1597 and conducted his pioneering research. The foundations of his Renaissance castle, **Uranienborg,** can be visited, as can **Stjärneborg,** his reconstructed observatory. The small **Tycho Brahe Museet** is dedicated to Brahe and his work. *Landsvägen, Ven, tel. 0418/72058. Admission: SKr5. Open May–Sept., daily 11–5.*

Ven is also ideal for camping (check with the local tourist office in Landsvägen, tel. 0418/79493), and there are special paths across the island for bicycles (rentals are available at Bäckviken, the small harbor).

③ Head inland now to **Lund,** one of the oldest towns in Europe, founded in 1020 by the legendary King Knud (Canute), monarch of Scandinavia and Britain. In 1103 Lund became the religious capital of Scandinavia and at one time had 27 churches and eight monasteries, before King Christian III of Denmark ordered most of them razed to use their stones for the construction of Malmöhus Castle in Malmö. Lund lost its importance until 1666, when its **university** was established. It is now one of Sweden's two chief university towns and one of the nicest of Swedish towns, having managed to preserve its historic character.

Its monumental gray stone Romanesque **cathedral** is the oldest in Scandinavia, consecrated in 1145. Its crypt features 23 finely carved pillars, but its main attraction is an astrological clock, *Horologum Mirabile Lundense* (the miraculous Lund clock), dating from 1380, which was restored in 1923. It features an amazing pageant of knights jousting on horseback, trumpets blowing a medieval fanfare, and the Magi walking in procession past Virgin and Child as the organ plays *In Dulci Jubilo.* It plays at noon and 3 PM on weekdays and at 1 and 3 PM on Sunday.

Esaias Tegnér, the Swedish poet, lived from 1813 to 1826 in a little house immediately behind the cathedral. Today it is the **Tegnér Museet** in his honor. *Gråbrödersgatan, tel. 046/691319. Admission: SKr10. Open first Sun. each month noon–3.*

On the southern side of the main square is **Drottens Kyrkoruin** (the Church Ruins of Drotten), an "underground" museum of Lund's middle ages located in the cellar of a modern five-story building. The foundations of three Catholic churches are here: the first and oldest was built of wood in approximately AD 1000. It was torn down to make room for one of stone built in about 1100; this was replaced by a second stone church built around 1300. *Kattensund 6, tel. 046/355291. Admission: SKr10. Open weekends 10–2.*

Kulturen (the Museum of Cultural History), is both outdoor and indoor museum, featuring 20 old cottages, farms, and manor houses from southern Sweden plus an excellent collection of ceramics, textiles, weapons, and furniture. *Adelgatan, tel. 046/150480. Admission: SKr30 adults, children under 15 free. Open May–Sept., daily 11–5; Oct.–Apr., daily 12–4.*

One street over and east of the cathedral is the **Botaniska Trädgården** (the Botanical Gardens), which contain 7,500 specimen plants from all over the world—very pleasant on a summer's day. *Ostravalsgatan 20, tel. 046/107320. Admission free. Open daily 6 AM–8 PM; greenhouses open noon–3.*

Time Out Drop by **Storkällaren** (Stortorget 5, tel. 046/115173) in the center of town, a great place to watch and meet locals after a stroll around.

④ About 30 miles (38 kilometers) farther inland off Route 23, north of E66, is **Bosjökloster,** an 11th-century white-painted Gothic castle with lovely grounds on Ringsjö, the second-largest lake in southern Skåne. The castle's original owner donated the estate to the church, which turned it over to the Benedictine order of nuns. They founded a convent school for the daughters of Scanian nobility, no longer in existence, and built the convent church with its tower made of sandstone. The 300-acre castle grounds, with a 1,000-year-old oak tree, a network of pathways, a children's park, a rose garden, and an indoor-outdoor restaurant, are ideal for picnics. *Höör, tel. 0413/250 48. Admission: SKr25 adults, SKr12 children 16 and under. Open May–Oct. Castle grounds open 8–8. Restaurant and exhibition halls open 10–6.*

⑤ **Malmö,** just 31 kilometers (19 miles) to the southwest, is very different from Lund. Capital of the province of Skåne, with a population of about 250,000, this is Sweden's third-largest city.

Visitors can purchase **Malmökortet** (the Malmö Card), which entitles the holder to, among other benefits, free admission or discounts to most museums, concert halls, nightclubs, and theaters, and many shops and restaurants. A one-day card costs SKr110 for adults and SKr55 for children; a two-day card costs SKr200 and SKr100, respectively; and one for three days costs SKr280 and SKr140. The cards are available at most hotels, newspaper kiosks, and tourist offices in Malmö, Lund, and Trelleborg.

The city's castle, **Malmöhus,** completed in 1542, was for many years used as a prison (James Bothwell, husband of Mary,

Queen of Scots, was one of its notable inmates). Today it houses four museums, including an art museum with a collection of Nordic art, a toy museum, a marine museum, and a puppet theater. *Malmöhusvägen, tel. 040/341000. Admission: SKr30. Open Tues.–Sun. noon–4.*

Farther down Malmöhusvägen there's a clutch of tiny red-painted shacks called **Fiskehodderna** (the Fish Shacks) adjoining a dock where the fishing boats come in every morning and unload their catch. The piers, dock, and huts were restored in 1991 and are now a government-protected district.

Nearby is the old town, where the **St. Petri Church,** from the 14th century, is an impressive example of the Baltic Gothic style, with its distinctive stepped gables. Inside there is a fine Renaissance altar.

Rådhuset (the City Hall), dating from 1546, dominates Stortorget, a huge, cobbled market square, and makes an impressive spectacle when illuminated at night. In the center of the square stands an equestrian statue of Karl X, the king who united this part of the country with Sweden in 1658. Off the southeast corner of Stortorget is Lilla Torg, an attractive small cobblestone square surrounded by restored buildings from the 17th and 18th centuries. A sports museum occupies **Baltiska Hallen.** *John Ericssons Väg, tel. 040/342688. Admission free. Open Mon.–Fri. 8–4.*

Also downtown, the **Rooseum,** located in a turn-of-the-century brick building that was once a power plant, is one of Sweden's most outstanding art museums, with exhibitions of contemporary art and a quality selection of Nordic art. *Gasverksgatan 22, tel. 040/121716. Admission: SKr20 adults, children under 16 free. Open Tues.–Fri., noon–7, weekends noon–5. Guided tours weekends at 2.*

On a tiny peninsula 32 kilometers (20 miles) from Mälmö, at the country's southwesternmost corner, are the idyllic towns of
❻ Falsterbo and **Skanör,** both popular summer resorts. Ornithologists gather at Falsterbo every fall to watch the spectacular migration of hundreds of raptors.

Continuing on from Malmö, you can make your way through
❼ ❽ Trelleborg, Sweden's southernmost town, to **Ystad,** a medieval city on the coast, and a smuggling center during the Napoleonic Wars. If you are driving, go by way of **Torup Slott** (Castle), a good example of the square fortified stronghold, built about 1550. Ystad has preserved its medieval character with winding, narrow streets and hundreds of half-timbered houses from four or five different centuries. The principal ancient monument is **St. Maria Kyrka,** begun shortly after 1220 as a basilica in the Romanesque style but with later additions.

Some 24 kilometers (15 miles) east of Ystad, on the coastal road leading to the harbor town of Simrishhamn, is the charming
❾ fishing village of **Kåseberga.** On the hill behind it stand the impressive **Ales stenar** (Ale's stones), an intriguing 76-meter (251-foot) arrangement of 58 Viking rune stones in the shape of a ship. The stones are still something of a puzzle to anthropologists.

Inland, the gentle rolling hills and fields of Skåne are broken every few miles by lovely castles, chronologically and architecturally diverse, which have given this part of Sweden the name

Château Country. Often they are surrounded by beautiful grounds and moats. A significant number of the estates have remained in the hands of the original families and are still inhabited. If you drive back toward Malmö on E14, you'll come to

10 **Svaneholm,** one of Skåne's outstanding Renaissance strongholds. First built in 1530 and rebuilt in 1694, the castle today features a museum occupying four floors with sections on the nobility and the peasants. On the grounds are a noted restaurant, walking paths, and a lake for fishing and rowing. *Skuderup, tel. 0411–40012. Admission: SKr10 adults, SKr2 children. Open May–Sept., Tues.–Sun. 11–5; Sept.–Christmas and Mar.–May, Wed.–Sun. 11–5. Closed Christmas–Mar. 1.*

On your return trip to Ystad on E14, you might want to turn left at Skårby and drive about 56 kilometers (35 miles) north to

11 **Sövdeborg Slott** (Sövdeborg Castle). Built in the 16th century and restored in the mid-1840s, the castle consists of three two-story brick buildings and a four-story-high crenellated corner tower. The Stensal (Stone Hall), with its impressive stuccowork ceiling is the main attraction. *Sjöbo, tel. 0416–16012. Admission: SKr45. Groups by prior arrangement only.*

Time Out If your next stop is Simrishamn, have lunch at **Trydegården** (Tryde 13, Route 19, tel. 0417/137 29), a restaurant in an elegantly renovated farmhouse just west of Tomelilla that combines the best in Skåne haute cuisine with Mediterranean flair; try the wild-boar pâté with elderberry sauce.

12 Follow Route 12 until you reach **Simrishamn** on the coast, a bustling fishing village of 25,000 that swells to many times that number during the summer. Built in the mid-1100s, this picturesque town of cobblestoned streets is lined with tiny brick houses covered with white stucco. The medieval St. Nicolai's Church, which dominates the town's skyline, was once a landmark for local sailors. Inside are models of sailing ships.

13 **Glimmingehus** (Glimminge House), located about 10 kilometers (6 miles) southwest of Simrishhamn off Route 10, is Scandinavia's best-preserved medieval stronghold. Built between 1499 and 1505 to defend the region against invaders, this late-Gothic castle was lived in only briefly. The walls are 2½ meters (8 feet) thick at the base, tapering to 2 meters (6½ feet) at the top of the 26-meter (85-foot)-high building. On the grounds are a small museum and a theater. There are concerts and lectures throughout the summer and a medieval festival at the end of August. *Hammenhög, tel. 0414/30289. Admission: SKr20 adults, SKr5 children under 12. Open Apr., May, Sept. 9–5; June–Aug. 10–6.*

On your way to Kristianstad you might want to stop off at

14 **Kristinehov,** a castle located about 2 kilometers (1 mile) north of Andrarum. Known as the pink castle, Kristinehov was built in 1740 by Countess Christina Piper in the late Caroline style. Open to the public during the summer, the castle has a hunting museum, exhibits, extensive paths, a children's playground, and safari tours in a protected wildlife area with boars and stags. Check the schedule for outdoor summer concerts. *Andrarum, tel. 0417/26110. Admission: SKr15 adults, SKr8 children ages 7–15. Open May 1–June 30 and Aug. 19–Sept.*

30, weekends 11–5 and by arrangement; July 1–Aug. 18, Tues.–Sun. 11–5.

⑮ **Kristianstad** was founded by Danish King Christian IV in 1614 as a fortified town to keep the Swedes at bay. Its former ramparts and moats are today wide, tree-lined boulevards. **Holy Trinity Church,** consecrated in 1628, is an excellent example of so-called Christian IV–style architecture.

About 10 kilometers (6 miles) northeast of Kristianstad is
⑯ **Bäckaskog Slott** (Bäckaskog Castle), located on a strip of land between two lakes. Originally founded as a monastery by a French religious order in the 13th century, it was turned into a fortified castle by Danish noblemen during the 16th century and later appropriated by the Swedish government and used as a residence for the cavalry. The castle was a favorite of the Swedish royalty until 1900. *Fjälkinge, tel. 044/53250. Admission: SKr20 adults, SKr8 children under 12. Open May 15– Aug. 15, daily 10–5; open to groups off-season by prior arrangement.*

⑰ **Ronneby,** a spa town 85 kilometers (53 miles) east of Kristianstad on Route 66, has a picturesque waterfall and rapids called **Djupadal,** where a river runs through a cleft in the rock just 5 feet wide but 50 feet deep. There are boat trips on the river each summer.

⑱ A little farther along the coast is **Karlskrona,** a small city built on the mainland and five nearby islands. It achieved great notoriety in 1981, when a Soviet submarine ran aground a short distance from its naval base. The town was laid out in the Baroque style on the orders of Karl XI in 1679. In 1790 it was severely damaged by fire. Its **Admiralitetskyrkan** (Admiralty Church) is Sweden's oldest wooden church, and two other churches, **Holy Trinity** and **Frederiks,** were designed by the 17th-century architect Nicodemus Tessin. **Arsenal Museet** (the Arsenal Museum), dating from 1732, is the oldest museum in Sweden, detailing the history of the country's navy. *Admiralitetsslatten, tel. 0455/83490. Admission: SKr10. Open daily 9–8.*

⑲ If you follow E66 north for 82 kilometers (51 miles), you'll reach the attractive coastal town of **Kalmar.** Opposite the Baltic island of Öland, the town is dominated by the imposing **Kalmar Slott,** Sweden's best-preserved Rennaissance castle, part of which dates from the 12th century. Here in 1397 Sweden, Norway, and Denmark signed the Kalmar Union, which lasted until 1521, when King Gustav Wasa rebuilt the castle. The living rooms, chapel, and dungeon can be visited. The castle now houses **Kalmar Läns Museum** (Kalmar District Museum), which has good archaeological and ethnographic collections. *Skeppsbrogatan, tel. 0480/15350. Admission: SKr25. Open daily 10–4.*

The **Kronan Museet** in the harbor area features the remains of the royal ship *Kronan,* which sank in 1676. Consisting primarily of cannon, wood sculptures, and old coins, they were raised from the seabed in 1980. *Skeppsbrogatan, tel. 0480/15350. Admission: SKr25. Open daily 10–4.*

The limestone plateau of **Öland,** 139 kilometers (86 miles) long and 37 kilometers (23 miles) at its widest point, was first settled some 4,000 years ago. It is linked to the mainland by one of the longest bridges in Europe (6 kilometers/4 miles). Öland is fringed with fine sandy beaches and is dotted with old wind-mills and such archaeological remains as the massive stone walls of the 6th-century Gråborg Fortress, the 5th-century for-tified village of Eketorp, and the medieval Borgholm Castle. The royal family has a summer home at Solliden, on the out-skirts of **Borgholm,** the principal town. In spring and fall, Öland is a way station for hundreds of species of migrating birds.

Tour 2: The Kingdom of Crystal

An hour or so west of Kalmar off Route 25, scattered among the rocky woodlands of Småland province, are isolated villages whose names are bywords for quality when it comes to fine crystal glassware. In the streets of Kosta, Orrefors, Boda, and Strombergshyttan, red-painted cottages surround the actual factories, which resemble large barns. The region is the home of 16 major glassworks, and visitors may see glass being blown and crystal being etched by skilled craftspeople. *Hyttsil* eve-nings are also arranged, a revival of an old tradition in which Baltic herring (*sil*) is cooked in the glass furnaces of the *hytt* (literally "cabin" but meaning the works). Most glassworks also have shops selling seconds at a discount.

Fifteen kilometers (9 miles) north of Route 25 on Route 28 is **Kosta Glasbruk,** the oldest works, dating from 1742 and named for its founders, Anders *K*oskull and Georg Bogislaus *Sta*el von Holstein, two former generals. Faced with a dearth of talent locally, they initially imported glassblowers from Bohemia. The Kosta works pioneered the production of crystal (to qualify for that label, glass must contain at least 24% lead oxide). *Tel. 0478/50300. Open mid-June–early Aug. Shops and museum, open weekdays 9–6, Sat. 9–3, Sun. 9–4. Demonstrations week-days 9–3:30.*

On Route 31, 17 kilometers (11 miles) north of Route 25 is **Orrefors,** one of the best known of the glass companies. It came on the scene late—in 1898—but set particularly high artistic standards. The skilled workers in Orrefors dance a slow, deli-cate minuet as they carry the pieces of red-hot glass back and forth, passing them from hand to hand, blowing and shaping them. The basic procedures and tools are ancient, and the fin-ished product is the result of unusual teamwork, from designer to craftsman to finisher. One of Orrefors's special attractions is a magnificent display of pieces made during the past century. *Tel. 0481/34000. Open 8–3.*

Boda Glasbruk, part of the Kosta Boda company, is just off Route 25, 42 kilometers (26 miles) west of Kalmar. *Tel. 0481/24030. Open 8–3.*

Farther west on Route 25 is **Växjö,** where the **Småland Museum** has the largest glass collection in northern Europe. *Södra Jarnvägsgatan 2, S–35104, tel. 0470/45145. Admission: SKr10. Open weekdays 9–4, Sat. 11–3, Sun. 1–5. Closed holi-days.*

Växjö is also an important sightseeing destination for some 10,000 American visitors each year, for it was from this area that their Swedish ancestors set sail in the 19th century. The Emigrants' House, located in the town center, tells the story of the migration, during which close to a million Swedes—one quarter of the population—departed for the promised land. The museum exhibits provide a vivid sense of the rigorous journey, and an archive room and research center allow American visitors to trace their ancestry.

What to See and Do with Children

Kulturen (the Museum of Cultural History), is both outdoor and indoor museum, featuring 20 old cottages, farms, and manor houses from southern Sweden plus an excellent collection of ceramics, textiles, weapons, and furniture. *Adelgatan, tel. 046/150480. Admission: SKr30 adults, children under 15 free. Open May–Sept., daily 11–5; Oct.–Apr. 12–4.*

Located on the other side of the park from Malmöhus, **Aq-va-kul** is a swimming-pool complex that offers a wide variety of bathing experiences for children and their parents, from water slides to bubble baths. *Regementsgatan 24, tel. 040/300540. Admission: SKr55 adults, SKr35 children ages 7–15, SKr20 children under 7. Open Mon., Wed. 9–9, Tues., Thurs., Fri. 9–8, weekends 9–5.*

Frasses Music Museum contains an eclectic collection of music oddities, such as self-playing barrel organs, antique accordions, children's gramophones, and the world's most complete collection of Edison phonographs. *Padar Mörksvagen 5, tel. 0414/14520. Admission: SKr10 adults, SKr3.50 children under 12. Open June–Aug., Sun. 2–6.*

About 4 miles (6 kilometers) north of Växjo, a castle ruin called **Kronobergs Slott**, built during the 1300s, lies on the edge of the Helgasjön (Holy Lake). The Småland guerilla fighter, Nils Dacke, used the castle as a base in his attacks against the Danish occupiers during the mid-1500s. You can eat waffles under the shade of birch trees or tour the lake on the toylike *Thor*, Sweden's oldest steamboat. *Tel. 0470/45145. Two boat tours offered: canal trip to Årby (SKr100 adults, SKr50 children) or round-the-lake trip (SKr75 adults, SKr35 children). Boat runs June 25–Aug. 30.*

Off the Beaten Track

On the mainland coast opposite Öland, off E66, numerous picturesque seaside towns dot the coastline, such as Pataholm, with its cobblestoned main square; Timmernabben, which is famous for its caramel factory; and Mönsterås, from which the Borgholm-bound car ferries depart. Miles of clean, attractive, and easily accessible, if windy, beaches line this strip of the coast.

Dining and Lodging

Highly recommended establishments are indicated by a star ★. (For rates, *see* Staying in Sweden in Chapter 1.)

Helsingborg
Dining and Lodging
★

Grand Hotel. In one of Sweden's oldest hotels, the dining room has a long reputation for excellence, with a good selection of wines at reasonable prices. There are special rose-colored rooms for women guests. The hotel is near the railway station and ferry terminals. *Stortorget 8–12, S–251 11, tel. 042/120170,*

*fax 042/118833. 130 rooms. Facilities: restaurant, piano bar.
AE, DC, MC, V. Expensive.*
Villa Thalassa. This youth hostel has fine views over Öresund.
*Dag Hammarskjölds väg, tel. 042/110384. 145 beds, 4- to 6-bed
rooms (in winter 2-bed rooms are also available). Facilities:
conference rooms. No credit cards. Inexpensive.*

Kalmar **Romantik Hotel Slottshotellet.** Situated in a gracious old town
Lodging house on a quiet street, Slottshotellet bears no resemblance to
a hotel from the outside. But inside, it offers a host of modern
facilities. Only breakfast is served. *Slottsvägen 7, tel. 0480/
88260, fax 0480/11993. 36 rooms with shower. AE, DC, MC, V.
Expensive.*
Stadshotellet. Located in the city center, Best Western's
Stadshotellet is a fairly large, Old World hotel. The main building dates from the 19th century. It features a fine restaurant.
*Storgatan 14, tel. 0480/15180, fax 0480/15847. 140 rooms with
bath or shower. Facilities: restaurant, Jacuzzi, disco. AE, DC,
MC, V. Closed Christmas. Expensive.*
Continental. Located about 93 meters (100 yards) from the
train station, the Continental is a fairly basic but comfortable
family hotel. Only breakfast is served. *Larmgatan 10, tel. 0480/
15140. 40 rooms, most with bath or shower. AE, DC, MC, V.
Closed Christmas. Inexpensive.*

Lund **Fiskaregatan.** Chefs Rikart Nilsson and Lars Fogelkous believe
Dining in getting to know their guests and in taking an unconventional
approach to do so. One example is their "gourmet evening"
with nine courses—interrupted by a stroll around the town at
the halfway stage in April and October (no fixed date). A specialty is stuffed breast of pheasant. *Lilla Fiskaregatan 14, tel.
046/151620. Reservations advised. Dress: casual. AE, DC,
MC, V. Moderate.*

Lodging **Grand.** This elegant red-stone Best Western hotel is located
close to the railway station in a pleasant square. *Bantorget 1,
S–221 04, tel. 046/117010, fax 046/147301. 87 rooms. Facilities:
restaurant with vegetarian menu by arrangement, conference
rooms, sauna. AE, DC, MC, V. Very Expensive.*
Concordia. Located in a 100-year-old building in the city center, this Sweden Hotels property was completely renovated recently. *Stålbrogatan 1, S–222 24, tel. 046/135050, fax 046/
137422. 50 rooms. Facilities: rooms for nonsmokers and the
disabled. AE, DC, MC, V. Moderate.*
Djingis Khan. This English-style hotel has a pleasing aspect
and is situated in a quiet part of town. *Margarethevägen 7, S–
222 40, tel. 046/140060, fax 046/143626. 55 rooms. Facilities:
rooms for allergy sufferers and the disabled, conference rooms,
sauna, solarium, gymnasium, bicycles for rent (SKr25). AE,
DC, MC, V. Moderate.*
Hotel Lundia. Only 100 meters (330 feet) from the train station,
Best Western's Hotel Lundia is ideally located for families who
want to be within walking distance of the city center. Built in
1968, the modern four-story square building has transparent
glass walls on the ground floor. *Knut den stores gata 2, Box
1136, S–221 04, tel. 046/124140, fax 046/141995. 97 rooms. Facilities: restaurant, nightclub, garage. AE, DC, MC, V.
Moderate.*
STF Vandrahem Tåget. So named because of its proximity to
the train station (*tåget* means "train"), this youth hostel faces a

park in central Lund. *Bjerredsparken, Vävareg. 14, S–22 37 Lund, tel. 046/142820. 108 beds. No credit cards. Inexpensive.*

Malmö **Årstiderna.** Marie and Wilhelm Pieplow's restaurant (the name
Dining means "The Seasons" in Swedish) has a pleasant, intimate at-
★ mosphere. It is known for large portions and a good medium-
priced wine list. *Grynbodsgatan 9, tel. 040/230910. Reservations advised. Jacket and tie required. AE, DC, MC, V. Expensive.*

Johan P. This extremely popular restaurant specializes in seafood and shellfish prepared in Swedish and Continental styles.
White walls and white tablecloths give it the air of an elegant
French restaurant, which contrasts with the generally casual
dress of the customers. An outdoor section opens during the
summer. *Saluhallen, Lilla Torg, tel. 040/971818. Dress: casual. Reservations advised. AE, DC, MC, V. Expensive.*

Kockska Krogen. Located in the cellar of a 16th-century house,
one of the few in Malmö, this popular restaurant serves internationally influenced Swedish food. Glassware, cutlery, and decor are calculated to re-create a 16th-century atmosphere.
*Stortorget, tel. 040/70320. Reservations advised. Dress: casu-
al. AE, DC, MC, V. Expensive.*

La Mélisse. This friendly little restaurant usually gives extremely good value. The special menu, *Kvartersmenyn,* is an
excellent bet, with four courses for SKr200. *Foreningsgatan
37, tel. 040/116816. Reservations advised. Dress: casual. AE,
DC, MC, V. Expensive.*

Valvet. Centrally located in the St. Jörgen hotel, this restaurant was expanded in late 1992 from the cellar so that it now
also occupies the balcony overlooking the lobby. Although the
wine list has been deemphasized, the restaurant still offers
Swedish cuisine with a French accent and excels at grilled
meats and fish. *Stora Nygatan 35, tel. 040/77300. Reservations
advised. Dress: casual. AE, DC, MC, V. Expensive.*

Anno 1900. Here is a curiosity: a charming little restaurant located in a former working-class area of Malmö. It is a popular
local luncheon place with a cheerful outdoor garden terrace for
summer eating. Try the *dagens rätt* (daily special), which may
be meat or fish. *Norra Bulltoftavägen 7, tel. 040/184747. Reservations required. Dress: casual. AE, MC, V. Moderate.*

B & B. It stands for *Butik och Bar* (Bar Shop) because of its
location in the market hall in central Malmö. There's always
good home cooking, and sometimes even entertainment at the
piano. The restaurant is extremely popular with a young crowd
on weekday nights. *Saluhallen, Lilla Torg, tel. 040/127120.
Reservations advised. Dress: casual. AE, DC, MC, V.
Moderate.*

Dining and Lodging **Mäster Johan Hotel.** The unpretentious exterior of this new
★ Best Western hotel disguises a plush and meticulously crafted
interior. The 1990 top-to-bottom redesign of a 19th-century
building, with the focal point an Italianate atrium breakfast
room, is unusually personal in tone for a chain hotel. The rooms
are impressive, with exposed Dutch brick walls, recessed lighting, oak floors, Oriental carpets, and French cherry-wood furnishings. *Mäster Johansgatan 13, tel. 040–71560, fax 040/
127242. 70 rooms. Facilities: 24-hour room service, breakfast
room, sauna. AE, DC, MC, V. Expensive.*

SAS Royal. This modern luxury hotel has rooms in four styles:
Scandinavian, Oriental, Italian, and Grand. *Östergatan 10, S–*

211 25, tel. 040/239200, fax 040/112840. 221 rooms. Facilities: restaurant. AE, DC, MC, V. Expensive.

Sheraton. Ultramodern, in steel and glass, the Sheraton opened in 1989. *Triangeln 2, S–200 10, tel. 040/74000, fax 040/ 232020. 214 rooms. Facilities: restaurant, bar, fitness center, sauna. AE, DC, MC, V. Expensive.*

★ **Baltzar.** A turn-of-the-century house in central Malmö has been converted into a small, comfortable hotel. *Södergatan 20, tel. 040/72005. 41 rooms. AE, DC, MC, V. Inexpensive.*

Prize Hotel. Centrally located in the newly renovated Malmö Harbor area, this spanking-new hotel features a large front entrance and lobby atrium inventively created out of a narrow strip of empty space between two buildings. The rooms, though small, are comfortable and equipped with cable TV, telephone, and radio. This low-overhead, minimal-service hotel doesn't add a surcharge to the telephone bill. You get exactly what you pay for. *Carlsgatan 10C, tel. 046/40112511. 109 rooms. Facilities: breakfast room. AE, DC, MC, V. Inexpensive.*

Öland
Dining and Lodging

Halltorps Gästgiveri. This manor house from the 17th century has modernized duplex rooms decorated in Swedish landscape tones and an excellent restaurant. *S–38792 Borgholm, tel. 0485/85000, fax 0485/85001. 35 rooms. Facilities: restaurant, sauna, tennis court. AE, DC, MC, V. Moderate.*

Växjö
Lodging

SARA Statt. A conveniently located, traditional hotel, SARA Statt is popular with tour groups. The building dates from the early 19th century, but the rooms themselves are modern, and the hotel has a resident piano bar and an à la carte restaurant. *Kungsgatan 6, tel. 0470/13400, fax 0470/44837. 130 rooms with bath or shower. AE, DC, MC, V. Closed Christmas Eve. Expensive.*

Esplanad. Centrally located, the Esplanad is a small, family hotel offering basic amenities; it has recently been renovated. Only breakfast is served. *Norra Esplanaden 21A, tel. 0470/ 22580, fax 0470/26226. 27 rooms, most with shower. MC, V. Closed Christmas and New Year's Day. Inexpensive.*

6 Dalarna: The Folklore District

Dalarna is considered to be the most typically Swedish of all the country's 24 provinces, a place of forests, mountains, and red-painted wooden farmhouses and cottages by the shores of pristine, sun-dappled lakes. It is the favorite site for Midsummer celebrations, in which Swedes don folk costumes and dance to fiddle and accordion music around maypoles garlanded with wildflowers.

Dalarna played a key role in the history of the nation. It was from here that Gustav Vasa recruited the army that freed the country from Danish domination in the 16th century.

The region is also important artistically, both for its tradition of naïve religious decoration and for producing two of the nation's best-loved painters, Anders Zorn (1860–1920) and Carl Larsson (1853–1915), and one of its favorite poets, the melancholy, mystical Dan Andersson, who sought inspiration in the remote camps of the old charcoal burners deep in the forest.

Essential Information

Important Addresses and Numbers

Tourist Information There are tourist offices in the following towns and villages: **Falun** (Stora Torget, tel. 023/83637), **Leksand** (Norsgatan, tel. 0247/80300), **Ludvika** (Sporthallen, tel. 0240/86050), **Mora e** (Ångbåtskajn, tel. 0250/26550), **Rättvik** (Torget, tel. 0248/10910), and **Sälen** (Sälen Centrum, tel. 0280/20250).

Emergencies For **emergencies,** dial 90000, **Falun Hospital** (tel. 023/82900) or **Mora Hospital** (tel. 0250/25000).

Pharmacies There are no late-night pharmacies in the area, but doctors called to emergencies can supply medicines. **Vasen** pharmacy in Falun (Åsagatan, tel. 023/20000) is open until 7 PM.

Arriving and Departing by Plane

Airports and Airlines Dalarna is served by two airports: **Dala** at **Borlänge** and **Mora** Airport. There are regular daily **Linjeflyg** (tel. 0243/39090) flights from Stockholm to Dala Airport (seven each weekday, two on Saturday, five on Sunday). Mora Airport is served by the problem-plagued private company **Salair** (tel. 0250/30175), with four flights daily from Stockholm.

Between the Airport and Town Dala Airport is 8 kilometers (5 miles) from Borlänge, where there are half-hourly bus connections to Falun, 26 kilometers (17 miles) away. Mora Airport is 10 kilometers (6 miles) from town.

By Bus There are buses every half hour from Dala Airport to Borlänge. The price of the trip is SKr12. From Mora Airport there are buses three times daily into town. The fare is also SKr12.

By Taxi A taxi from Dala Airport to Borlänge costs around SKr90, to Falun approximately SKr200. A taxi to town from Mora Airport costs SKr89. Taxis are best ordered in advance through your travel agent or when you make an airline booking.

Arriving and Departing by Car, Train, and Bus

By Car From Stockholm it is 275 kilometers (170 miles) on Highway 70 leads to Borlänge. From Göteborg the drive is 438 kilometers (272 miles): E3 to Örebro and Route 60 north from there to Borlänge.

By Train There is regular daily train service from Stockholm to both Mora (tel. 0250/11619) and Falun (tel. 023/15830).

By Bus Buses run only on weekends. For information, call **Eurolines** (also known as Continentbus, tel. 08/234810).

Getting Around

By Car **Avis** has offices in **Borlänge** (tel. 0243/87080) and Mora (tel. 0250/16711). **Hertz** has an office at **Dala** Airport (tel. 0243/39807) and agents in **Falun** (tel. 023/18440) and **Mora** (tel. 0250/11760). **InterRent** and **Europcar** have offices in **Borlänge** (tel. 0243/19050) and **Falun** (tel. 023/18850).

Guided Tours

The tourist office in **Falun** can arrange one-day guided coach tours in English of Falun and the region around Lake Siljan. The guide costs around SKr850, the coach, with driver, SKr4,200 (coaches can seat around 50 persons). Other tourist offices can arrange tours or advise on public transport.

Exploring Dalarna

Numbers in the margin correspond to points of interest on the Dalarna map.

❶ **Falun** is the traditional capital of Dalarna, though in recent years the nondescript railway town of Borlänge has been growing in importance. Falun's history has always been very much bound to its copper mine. This has been worked since 1230 by Stora Kopparbergs Bergslags AB (today just *Stora),* which claims to be the oldest limited company in the world. Its greatest period of prosperity was the 17th century, when it financed Sweden's "Age of Greatness," and the country became the dominant Baltic power. In 1650, Stora produced a record 3,067 tons of copper; probably as a result of such rapid extraction, 37 years later its mine shafts caved in. Fortunately, the accident was on Midsummer's Day when most of the miners were off duty, and as a result no one was killed. Today the major part of the mine is an enormous hole in the ground that has become Falun's principal tourist attraction, with its own museum, **Stora Museum.** *Tel. 023/114750. Admission: SKr50, including entry to mining museum; admission to museum alone, SKr5. Open May–Aug., daily 10–4:30. Sept.–Apr., daily 12:30–4:30.*

❷ At **Sundborn,** a small village east of Falun off Route 80, you can visit **Carl Larsson Gården,** the lakeside home of the Swedish artist Carl Larsson, its turn-of-the-century fittings and furnishings carefully preserved. Larsson was an excellent draftsman who painted idyllic scenes from his own family's apparently unceasingly happy and well-adjusted life. His grandchildren and great-grandchildren are on hand to show you the house and a selection of his paintings, which owe much

Dalarna

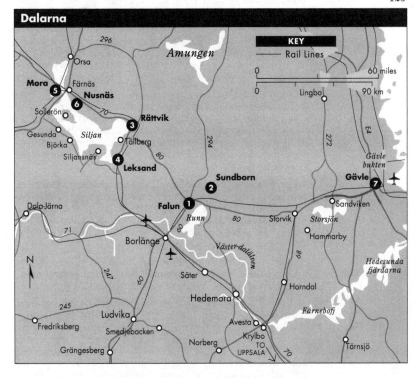

to local folk-art traditions. *Tel. in summer, 023/60053; in winter, 023/60069. Admission: SKr45. Open May 1–Sept. 30, Mon.–Sat. 10–5, Sun. 1–5. Call ahead to arrange for off-season visits.*

The real center of Darlana folklore is the area around **Lake Siljan,** the largest of the 6,000 lakes in the province. From **③** Falun take Route 80 north to **Rättvik,** a pleasant town of timbered houses on the eastern tip of Lake Siljan surrounded by wooded slopes. Rättvik is a center for local folklore, and several shops sell handmade articles and produce from the surrounding region.

Every year hundreds of people wearing traditional costumes arrive in longboats to attend Midsummer services at the town's 14th-century church, **Rättvik Kyrka,** which stands on a promontory stretching into the lake. Its interior contains some fine examples of local naïve religious artwork.

Only a short distance away, the open-air museum **Rättvik Gammalgård** gives the visitor an idea of the peasant lifestyles of bygone days. *Admission free; guided tour: SKr10. Open mid-June–mid-Aug., Mon.–Sat. 11–6, Sun. 12–6.*

④ South of Rättvik on Route 70 is **Leksand,** on which thousands of tourists converge each year for the Midsummer celebrations and, in July, for *Himlaspelet* (The Play of the Way that Leads to Heaven), a traditional musical with an all-local cast, staged in the open near the town's church. It is easy to get seats for this; the local tourist office will have details.

Leksand is also an excellent vantage point from which to watch the "church boat" races on Siljan. These vessels are claimed to be successors to the Viking longboats and were traditionally used to take peasants from outlying regions to church on Sunday. On Midsummer Eve, the longboats, crewed by people in folk costumes, skim the lake. Consult the local tourist office for dates and times.

In the hills around Leksand and elsewhere near Siljan you will find the *fäbodar*, small settlements in the forest where cattle were taken to graze during the summer. Less idyllic memories of bygone days are conjured up by **Käringberget,** a 720-foot-high mountain north of town where alleged witches were burned to death in the 17th century.

After Leksand, take the small road toward Mora along the southern shores of Siljan, passing through the small communities of Siljansnäs and Björka, before stopping at **Gesunda,** a pleasant little village at the foot of a mountain (with a chair lift) from which there are unbeatable views over the lake.

It is also worth paying a quick visit to **Sollerön,** a large island connected to the mainland by bridge, from which there are fine views of the mountains surrounding Siljan and several excellent bathing places. The church here dates from 1775.

⑤ Mora, a pleasant, relaxed lakeside town of 20,000, was the home of Anders Zorn (1860–1920), Sweden's leading Impressionist painter, who lived in Stockholm and Paris before returning to his roots here, painting the local scenes for which he is now famous. His former private residence, a large, sumptuous home designed with great originality and taste by the painter himself, has retained the same exquisite furnishings, paintings, and decor as it had when he lived there with his wife. The garden, also a Zorn creation, is open to the public. Next door, the **Zorn Museet** (Zorn Museum), built 19 years after the painter's death, contains many of his best works. *Vasagatan, tel. 0250/16560. Zorn Home: Admission: SKr20. Open Mon.–Sat. 12:30–5; Sun. 1–5. Museet: Admission: SKr15. Open Mon.– Sat. 10–5, Sun. 1–5.*

South of town, near the lake, you'll find **Zorns Gammalgård,** a fine collection of old wooden houses from local farms, brought here and donated to the town by the artist.

Mora is also the finishing point for the 90-kilometer (53-mile) *Vasalopp,* the world's longest ski race, running from Sälen, a ski resort close to the Norwegian border. The race commemorates a fundamental piece of Swedish history: the successful attempt by Gustav Vasa in 1521 to rally local peasants to the cause of ridding Sweden of Danish occupation. Vasa, only 21 years old, arrived in Mora and described to the locals in graphic detail a bloodbath of Swedish noblemen ordered by the Danish King Christian in Stortorget in Stockholm. Unfortunately, no one believed him and the dispirited Vasa was forced to abandon his attempts at insurrection and take off on either skis or snow shoes for Norway, where he hoped to evade Christian and go into exile. After he left, confirmation reached Mora of the Stockholm bloodbath, and the peasants, already discontented with Danish rule, relented, sending two skiers after Vasa to tell him they would join his cause. The two men caught up with the young nobleman at Sälen. They returned with him to Mora, where an army was recruited. Vasa marched south, defeating

American Express offers Travelers Cheques built for two.

American Express® Cheques *for Two*. The first Travelers Cheques that allow either of you to use them because both of you have signed them. And only one of you needs to be present to purchase them.

Cheques *for Two* are accepted anywhere regular American Express Travelers Cheques are, which is just about everywhere. So stop by your bank, AAA* or any American Express Travel Service Office and ask for Cheques *for Two*.

© 1993 American Express Travel Related Services Company, Inc. *Available at participating clubs.

Rediscover
the most exciting
and exotic country
in the world...
America.

From Fodor's — Comprehensive, literate, and beautifully illustrated guides to the individual cities and states of the United States and Canada, Compass American Guides are unparalleled in their cultural, historical, and informational scope.

"Wickedly stylish writing." — *Chicago Sun-Times*
"Exceptional color photos." — *Atlanta Constitution*

Guides also available to Las Vegas, Los Angeles, New Orleans, Oregon, Utah, and Canada. Available Spring 1994: Maine, South Dakota, Virginia, and Wisconsin

$16.95, at bookstores now, or call 1-800-533-6478 (and please mention #019-01-23)

COMPASS AMERICAN GUIDES
Fodor's

the Danes to become king and the founder of modern Sweden. The race, held on the first Sunday in March, attracts thousands of competitors from all over the world. There is a spectacular mass start at Sälen before the field thins out. The finish is eagerly awaited in Mora, though in recent years the number of spectators has fallen, thanks to the often frigid temperatures and the fact that the race is now usually televised live.

From Mora, take Route 70 back along the eastern shore of Siljan to Rättvik and Falun, leaving it at Färnäs to make an excursion to **Nusnäs,** the lakeside village where the small, brightly red-painted wooden Dala horses are made. These were originally carved by the peasants of Dalarna as toys for their children, but their popularity rapidly spread with the advent of tourism in the 20th century. Mass production of the little horses started at Nusnäs in 1928. In 1939 they achieved international popularity after being shown at the New York World's Fair. Since then they have become a Swedish symbol. Today some of the smaller versions available in Stockholm's tourist shops are even made in East Asia. However, at Nusnäs you can watch the genuine article being made, now with the aid of modern machinery but still painted by hand. Naturally you'll be able to buy some to take home.

Directly east of Falun, on the coast of the Gulf of Bothnia, is the port town of **Gävle,** which achieved dubious renown at the time of the Chernobyl nuclear accident in 1986 by briefly becoming the most radioactive place in Europe. A freak storm dumped extra-large amounts of fallout from the Soviet Union on the town. For a while farmers had to burn newly harvested hay and keep their cattle inside. However, the scare soon passed and today one can visit the town in perfect safety. Gävle is worth visiting for two relatively new museums.

Joe Hill Museet (the Joe Hill Museum), dedicated to the Swedish emigrant who went on to become America's first well-known protest singer and union organizer, is located in Hill's former home in the oldest section of Gävle. Once a poor, working-class district, ironically this is now the most picturesque and highly sought-after residential part of town, and nearby are some art studios and handicrafts workshops. The museum is furnished in the same style as when Hill lived here. Though it contains very few of his possessions, it does display Hill's prison letters. The house itself bears witness to the poor conditions that forced so many Swedes to emigrate to the United States (an estimated 850,000 between 1840 and 1900). When his mother died in 1902, Joe and his brother sold the house and used the money to emigrate to the United States. Hill, whose original Swedish name was Joel Hägglund, became a founder of the International Workers of the World and was executed for the murder of a Salt Lake City grocer in 1914, but he protested his innocence right up to the end. *Nedre Bergsgatan 28, tel. 026/ 613425. Admission: SKr10. Open 10–5.*

Also in Gävle you will find the **Skogsmuseet Silvanum** (Silvanum Forestry Museum). Its name means "The Forest" in Latin, and when it was inaugurated in 1961, it was the first such museum in the world; it remains the largest. The museum provides an in-depth picture of the forestry industry in Sweden, still the backbone of Sweden's industrial wealth. Trees cover more than 50% of the country's surface area. Forest products account for 20% of Swedish exports. Silvanum includes a

forest botanical park and an arboretum that contain examples
of every tree and bush growing in Sweden. *Kungsbäcksvägen
32, tel. 026/614100 or 026/615570. Admission free. Open Tues.–
Sun. 10–4.*

What to See and Do with Children

Near Gesunda, **Tomteland** (Santaland) somewhat unconvinc-
ingly claims to be the home of Santa Claus, or Father Christmas. It features Santa's workshop and kiosks, where you can
buy toys. There are rides in horse-drawn carriages in summer
and sleighs in winter. *Gesundaberget Sollerön, S–79200
Sollerön-Gesunda, tel. 0250/29000. Admission: SKr60. Open
mid-June–mid-Aug. and Dec.*

Shopping

Apart from its little red wooden horses (*see* Nusnäs, *above*),
Dalarna offers knitwear and handicrafts, available in *hemslöjd*
(handicrafts) shops throughout the region.

Sports

All the region's tourist offices can supply details of **skiing** vacations. The principal ski resort is Sälen, starting point for the
Vasalopp. **Canoes** and **kayaks** can also be rented at most of the
lakeside campgrounds.

Dining and Lodging

Do not expect too much in Dalarna. Traditionally, visitors to
the area—many from elsewhere in Scandinavia or from Germany—make use either of the region's many well-equipped campsites or of *stugbyar* (small villages of log cabins, with cooking
facilities), usually set idyllically by lakesides or in forest clear-
ings. (For rates, *see* Staying in Sweden in Chapter 1.)

Highly recommended establishments are indicated by a star★.

Falun
*Dining and
Lodging*

Grand. Now part of the Reso chain, this conventional, modern
hotel has fine light rooms and is close to the town center.
*Trotzgatan 9–11, S–791 71, tel. 023/18700, fax 023/14143. 183
rooms. Facilities: restaurant, bar, rooms for allergy sufferers
and the disabled, conference center, gymnasium, sauna, pool,
solarium. AE, DC, MC, V. Expensive.*

Birgittagården. This small hotel, 8 kilometers (5 miles) out of
town, run by the religious order Stiftelsen Dalarnas Birgitta
Systrar (the Dalarna Sisters of Birgitta), is alcohol-free and set
in a fine park. It is open year-round. *Uddnäs Hosjös S–79146,
tel. 023/32147 fax 023/32471. 25 rooms. Facilities: restaurant,
rooms for the disabled, conference rooms. No credit cards.
Inexpensive.*

Lodging
★

Bergmästaren. This is one of Dalarna's best hotels. Situated in
the middle of town, it is decorated according to local custom and
was completely refurbished in 1985. It is open year-round.
*Bergskolegrand 7, S–791 26, tel. 023/63600, fax 023/22524. 90
rooms. Facilities: breakfast, gymnasium, sauna, solarium,
conference center, parking with engine warmers. AE, DC,
MC, V. Expensive.*

Scandic. This ultramodern, spanking-new Legolike high-rise hotel is located in the expanded Lugnet sports and recreation center outside Falun, where the 1993 World Skiing Championships took place. The comfortable, modern rooms have good views. *Svärdsjögatan 51, 791 31 Falun, tel. 023/221 60, fax 023/ 12845. Facilities: restaurant, snack bar, pub, pool, sauna, exercise room, conference rooms. AE, DC, MC, V. Moderate.*

Falun. Ulf Henriksson and Bernt Brick run this small, friendly but bland-looking hotel just 1,300 feet from the railway station. *Centrumhuset, Trotzgatan 16 S–791 71, tel. 023/29180. 25 rooms, 15 with bath/shower. Facilities: breakfast. AE, DC, MC, V. Inexpensive.*

Mora
Dining and Lodging

Mora. A pleasant little hotel, situated in the center of town, 5 kilometers (3 miles) from the airport, the Mora is part of the Best Western chain. *Strandgatan 12, S–792 01, tel. 0250/11750, fax 0250/18981. 138 rooms. Facilities: restaurant, bar, rooms for nonsmokers, conference rooms, sauna, pool, game room. AE, DC, MC, V. Expensive.*

King's Inn. This modern, reasonably sized hotel is 2 kilometers (1 mile) from the center of town and only 100 meters (330 feet) from the Mora train station. *Kristeneberg, S–792 01, tel. 0250/ 15070, fax 0250/17078. 47 rooms. Facilities: restaurant, rooms for the disabled, conference rooms, gymnasium, sauna, pool, solarium. AE, DC, MC, V. Moderate.*

Moraparken. This modern hotel sits in a park by the banks of the Dala River, not far from the center of town. *Parkgarten 1, S–79201, tel. 0250/17800. 75 rooms. Facilities: restaurant; rooms for the disabled, nonsmokers, and allergy sufferers; conference rooms; sauna; indoor pool; tennis courts; jogging tracks; beach; fishing. AE, DC, MC, V. Inexpensive.*

Siljan. Part of the Sweden Hotel group, this small, modern hotel affords views over the lake. *Moragatan 6, S–79200, tel. 0250/13000, fax 0250/13098. 46 rooms. Facilities: restaurant, rooms for nonsmokers and the disabled, sauna, conference rooms. AE, DC, MC, V. Inexpensive.*

7 Norrland

The north of Sweden, Norrland, is a place of wide-open spaces where you can "listen to the silence." Golden eagles soar above snowcapped crags, huge salmon fight their way up wild, tumbling rivers, rare orchids bloom in Arctic heathland, and wild rhododendrons splash the land with color.

In the summer the sun shines at midnight above the Artic Circle. In the winter it hardly shines at all. The weather changes with bewildering rapidity. A June day can dawn sunny and bright; then the skies may darken and the temperature drop to around zero as a snow squall blows in. Just as suddenly, the sun comes out again and the temperature starts to rise.

Here live the once-nomadic Lapps, or Same, as they prefer to be known, generally smaller and darker than Swedes, with high cheekbones and slightly slanting eyes. They carefully guard what remains of their identity, while doing their best to inform the public about their culture. Many of them still earn their living herding reindeer, but as open space shrinks, the younger generation is turning in greater numbers toward the attractions of the cities. There are 17,000 Same in Sweden. Often the Same exhibit a sad resignation to the gradual disappearance of their way of life as the modern world makes incursions. This is best expressed in one of their folk poems: "Our memory, the memory of us vanishes/We forget and we are forgotten."

Yet there is a growing struggle, especially among younger Same, to maintain their identity and, thanks to their traditional closeness to nature, they are now finding allies in Sweden's Green movement. They refer to the north of Scandinavia as *Sapmi,* their spiritual and physical home, making no allowance for the different countries that now rule it.

Nearly all Swedish Same now live in ordinary houses, having abandoned the *kåta* (Lapp wigwam), and some even herd their reindeer with helicopters. Efforts are now being made to protect and preserve their language, which is totally unlike Swedish and bears much more resemblance to Finnish. The language reflects their closeness to nature. The word *goadnil,* for example, means "a quiet part of the river, free of current, near the bank or beside a rock."

Nowadays many Same depend on the tourist industry for their living, selling their artifacts, such as expertly carved bone-handled knives, wooden cups and bowls, bark bags, silver jewelry, and leather straps embroidered with pewter thread.

The trouble with Norrland, from the traveler's point of view, is its size. It stretches 1,000 kilometers (620 miles) from south to north, makes up more than half of Sweden, and is about the size of Britain. On the west there are mountain ranges, to the east a wild and rocky coastline, and in between boundless forests and moorland. Its towns are often little more than a group of houses along a street, built around a local industry such as mining, forestry, or hydropower utilities. However, thanks to Sweden's excellent transportation infrastructure, Norrland is no longer so inaccessible and even a traveler with a limited time schedule should be able to get at least a taste of it. Its wild spaces are ideal for open-air holidays. Hiking, climbing, canoeing, river rafting, and fishing are all popular in summer; skiing, skating, and dogsledding in winter.

A word of warning: In summer mosquitoes are a constant nuisance, worse even than in other parts of Sweden, so be sure to bring plenty of repellent. Fall is perhaps the best season to visit Norrland. Roads are well maintained, but you should watch out for *guppar* (holes) following thaws. Highways are generally traffic-free, but keep an eye out for the occasional reindeer or two.

Essential Information

Important Addresses and Numbers

Tourist Information
Norrbottens Turistråd covers the whole area (Sandviksgatan 53, Luleå, tel. 0920/94070). There are tourist offices at **Kiruna** (Hjalmar Lundbohmsvägen 42, tel. 0980/18880), **Luleå** (Rådstugatan 9, tel. 0920/93746), and **Jokkmokk** (Stortoget 4, tel. 0971/12140).

Emergencies
For **emergencies** dial 90,000. You can also call **Kiruna Health Center** (Thulegatan 29, tel. 0980/173000), **Luleå district nurse** (emergency tel. 0920/71400), and **Jokkmokk Health Center** (Lappstavägen 9, tel. 0971/11350).

Pharmacies
There are no late-night pharmacies in the area, but doctors called to emergencies can supply medicines. The pharmacy at Kiruna Hospital (Thulegatan 29, tel. 0980/12220) is open until 5 PM.

Arriving and Departing by Plane

There are two non-stop SAS flights a day from Stockholm to **Kiruna Airport** (tel. 0980/12410) and three additional flights via Luleå. Check SAS (tel. 0980/83100) for specific times.

Between the Airport and Town
It is 9 kilometers (6 miles) from the airport to the center of Kiruna. **Buses** connect with the flights from Stockholm. The fare is SKr25. A **taxi** from the airport to the center of Kiruna costs SKr90.

Arriving and Departing by Train

The best and cheapest way to get to Kiruna is to take the 5:40 PM sleeper from Stockholm on a Tuesday or Wednesday, when the fare is reduced to SKr554 single. The regular one-way price is SKr876, double for return. You arrive at 11:26 AM the next day.

Getting Around

By Car
In Kiruna **Avis** has a branch at Industrivägen 10 (tel. 0980/16060). **Hertz** is at Industrivägen 5 (tel. 0980/19000), and **InterRent** and **Europcar** are at Växlaregatan 20 (tel. 0980/14365).

Guided Tours

Numerous guided tours are available through the various tourist offices. For example, a two-hour tour of a local iron mine costs SKr75. A 45-minute flight in a seaplane taking off from a nearby lake costs SKr520. Tours of Same villages and holy places are available. Contact the **Swedish Same Association**

(Brogatan 5, S–902 48, Umeå, tel. 090/141180) or **Sameturism AB** (tel. 0980/83388) for up-to-date information.

Exploring Norrland

Norrland is best discovered from a base in Kiruna, located in the center of the alpine region that has been described as Europe's last wilderness. You can tour south and west to the mountains and national parks, east and south to Sami villages, and farther south still to Baltic coastal settlements.

Tour 1: Kiruna

Numbers in the margin correspond to points of interest on the Norrland map.

● **Kiruna** is the most northerly city in Sweden, spread over a wide area between two mountains largely composed of iron ore, which are its raison d'être. They are called Luossavaara and Kirunavaara. The city, named for the latter, was established in 1890 as a mining town, but true prosperity came only with the building of the railway to the Baltic port of Luleå and the northern Norwegian port of Narvik in 1902. Kiruna has the world's largest underground iron mine, with reserves estimated at 500 million tons. Automated mining technology has largely replaced the traditional miner in the Kirunavaara underground mines, which are some 500 kilometers (310 miles) long.

Kiruna lies at the eastern end of Lake Luossajärvi and with 26,000 inhabitants is one of Norrland's largest cities. It is, at 1,670 feet above sea level, the highest city in Sweden, with an estimated fifth of its population Finnish immigrants who came to work in the mine.

Because the municipality is spread over such a large area, Kiruna is often called "the world's biggest city" (it covers the equivalent of half the area of Switzerland). It is also a city of remarkable contrasts, from the seemingly pitch-black, months-long winter to the summer, when the sun never sets and it is actually possible to play round-the-clock golf for 50 days at a stretch. Here, too, the ancient Same culture exists side by side with the high-tech culture of cutting-edge satellite research. In recent years the city has diversified its economy and now houses the Esrange Space Range, which sends rockets and balloons to probe the upper reaches of the earth's atmosphere, and the Swedish Institute of Space Physics, which has pioneered the investigation of the phenomenon of the northern lights. The city received a boost in 1984 with the opening of *Nordkalottvägen*, a 170-kilometer (105-mile) -long road to Narvik.

One of Kiruna's few buildings of interest is **Kiruna Kyrka** (Kiruna Church), on Gruvvägen, near the center of the city. It was built in 1921, its inspiration a blending of a Sami kåta with a Swedish stave church. The altarpiece is by Prince Eugen (1863–1947), Sweden's painter prince.

Tour 2: Kebnekaise

At 7,000 feet above sea level, **Kebnekaise** is Sweden's highest mountain, but you'll need to be in good physical shape just to

Norrland

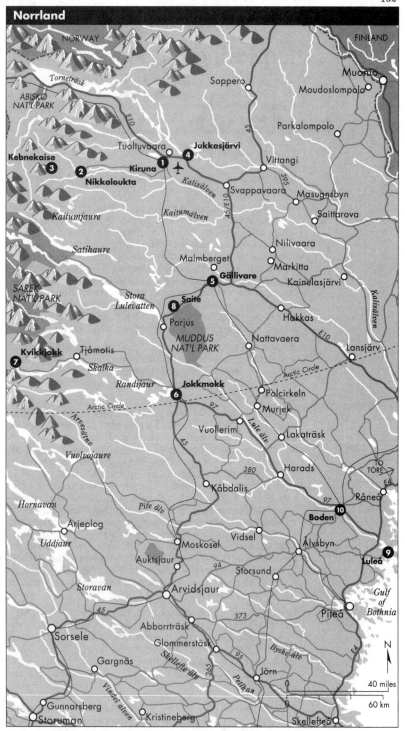

NORWAY

FINLAND

Torneträsk

Muonio

Soppero

Moudoslompolo

ABISKO
NAT'L PARK

Parkalompolo

Tuoltuvaara

Jukkasjärvi ④

E10

Kebnekaise ③

② **Nikkaloukta**

Kiruna ①

Vittangi

Kalixälven

Kaitumjaure

Kaitumälven

Svappavaara

395

Masugnsbyn

Saittarova

Nilivaara

Satihaure

Malmberget

Markitta

⑤ **Gällivare**

Kainulasjärvi

SAREK
NAT'L PARK

*Stora
Lulevatten*

⑧ **Saite**

Porjus

Hakkas

Kvikkjokk ⑦

Tjåmotis

MUDDUS
NAT'L PARK

Nattavaera

E10

Lansjärv

Skalka

Kalixälven

Randijaur

Arctic Circle

Jokkmokk ⑥

Polcirkeln

Arctic Circle

97

Murjek

Arvesjåmo

Vuollerim

Lule älv

Lakaträsk

Vuolvojaure

45

380

Harads

TO
TORE

Hornavan

Kåbdalis

97 ⑩

Råneå

E4

Boden

Arjeplog

Uddjaur

Pite älv

Moskosel

Vidsel

Älvsbyn

⑨ **Luleå**

Auktsjaur

94

Storsund

Storavan

Arvidsjaur

373

Piteå

*Gulf
of
Bothnia*

45

Abborrträsk

Byske älv

N

Sorsele

Glommerstäsk

E4

Gargnäs

365

Jörn

Skellefte älv

85

0 ___ 40 miles

Vivdel älven

0 ___ 60 km

Gunnarsberg

Storuman

Kristineberg

Skellefteå

get to it. From Kiruna you travel about 60 kilometers (37 miles) south, then west to the Same village of **Nikkaloukta**. There are two buses a day from Kiruna in the summer. From Nikkaloukta it is a hike of 21 kilometers (13 miles) to the Fjällstationen (mountain station) at the foot of **Kebnekaise**, though you can take a boat for 7 kilometers (4 miles) across **Lake Ladtjojokk**. Kebnekaise itself is easy to climb in good weather, with no need for mountaineering equipment. If you feel up to more walking, the track continues past the mountain station to become part of what is known as **Kungsleden** (the King's Way), a trail through the mountains and Abisko National Park to Riksgränsen on the Norwegian border.

Tour 3: Jukkasjärvi and Jokkmokk

Jukkasjärvi is just 16 kilometers (10 miles) east of Kiruna and can be reached by bus. The history of this Same village by the shores of the fast-flowing **Torneälven** (Torne River) dates from 1543, when a market was recorded here. There is a wooden **church** from the 17th century and a small **open-air museum** that gives a feeling of Same life in times gone by.

At the peak of winter, this town becomes a popular spot for tourists drawn by the annual construction of the world's largest igloo.

Here, if you are gastronomically adventurous, you may sample one of the most unusual of Same delicacies: a cup of thick black coffee and small lumps of goat cheese. These you marinate in the coffee, fish out with spoons, and consume. Then you drink the coffee. The taste sensation is intriguing, to say the least. Afterward, try riding the rapids of the Torne River in an inflatable boat. In winter Jukkasjärvi also offers dogsled rides.

Follow Route 45/E10 104 kilometers (65 miles) south to **Gällivare**, a mining town with a population of 22,000, then Route 45 106 kilometers (66 miles) farther to **Jokkmokk**, an important center of Same culture. Each February it is the scene of the region's largest market, nowadays an odd event featuring everything from stalls selling frozen reindeer meat to Same handcrafted wooden utensils.

Jokkmokk makes perhaps the best base in Norrland for the outdoor vacationer. The village has three campsites and is surrounded by wilderness. The local tourist office sells fishing permits, which cost SKr25 to SKr40 for 24 hours to SKr200 for the entire year. The office can also supply lists of camping and housekeeping cabins.

Tour 4: Sarek National Park

Sarek is Sweden's largest high mountain area and was molded by the last Ice Age. It totals 197,000 hectares (487,000 acres), a small portion of which is forest, bogland, and waterways. The remainder is bare mountain. The park has 90 peaks some 6,000 feet above sea level. The mountains have been sculpted by glaciers, of which there are around 100 in the park. The Rapaätno River, which drains the park, runs through the lovely, desolate **Rapadalen** (Rapa Valley). There is a surprising variety of landscape, luxuriant green meadows contrasting with the snowy peaks of the mountains. Animals to be found here include elk, bear, wolverine, lynx, ermine, hare, Arctic fox, red fox, and mountain lemmings. Birdlife includes ptarmigan, willow grouse, teal, wigeon, tufted duck, bluethroat, and warbler. Golden eagles, rough-legged buzzards and merlins also have been spotted here.

Visiting Sarek demands a good knowledge of mountains and a familiarity with the outdoors. Sarek can be dangerous in winter because of avalanches and snowstorms. However, in summer, despite its unpredictable, often inhospitable climate, it attracts large numbers of experienced hikers. The best entry point is at **Kvikkjokk,** a village reached by a small road to the east of Jokkmokk (*see* Tour 3, *above*). Hikers can then choose between a trail through the Tarradalen (Tarra Valley), which divides the Sarek from the Padjelanta National Park, located on the northwest side of Sarek, or part of the Kungsleden trail (*see* Tour 2, Kebnekaise, *above*), which crosses the southern end for a distance of about 16 kilometers (10 miles).

Tour 5: Muddus National Park

Established in 1942, this park is less mountainous and spectacular than Sarek, its 49,300 hectares (121,770 acres) comprising mainly virgin coniferous forest, some of whose trees may be up to 600 years old. The park's 1,490 hectares (3,680 acres) of water is composed primarily of two huge lakes at the center of the park and the Muddusjokk River, which tumbles spectacularly through a gorge with 330-foot-high sheer rock walls and includes a 140-foot-high waterfall. Muddus is reached by taking the road southwest of Gällivare to **Saite** en route to the Porjus power station and is well signposted. The highest point of Muddus is **Södra Stuobba** Mountain, 629 meters (2,076 feet) above sea level. Well-marked trails lead through the park, where you can pick cloudberries in the autumn. There are four well-equipped overnight communal rest huts and two tourist cabins. The park contains bears, elk, lynx, wolverines, moose, ermines, weasels, otters, and many bird species.

Tour 6: Luleå and the East Coast

Driving south from Kiruna, continuing along E10 at Gällivare, you pass several small former mining villages before coming into the **Kalixälv** (Kalix River) valley, where the countryside becomes more settled, with small farms and fertile meadows replacing the wilder northern landscape. Follow E4 west from Töre, and some 347 kilometers (215 miles) from Kiruna, you reach **Luleå,** a port at the top of the Gulf of Bothnia, at the mouth of the Luleälv (Lule River). The most northerly major town in Sweden, Luleå was situated some 10 kilometers (6 miles) farther inland when it was first granted its charter in 1621, but by 1649 trade had grown so much that the town was moved closer to the sea. The development of Kiruna and the iron trade is linked, by means of a railway, with the fortunes of Luleå, where a steelworks was set up in the 1940s. Luleå, along with Piteå, Skellefteå, Umeå, and Sundsvall, farther south down the coast road, remains an important northern port. It also boasts a beautiful archipelago of hundreds of islands. Luleå, like most of its fellow ports on the east coast, is a very modern and nondescript city, but it has some reasonable hotels. There is also, at **Norrbottens Museet** (the Norbotten Museum), one of the best collections of Same ethnography in the world. *Hermelinsparken, tel. 0920/93829. Admission: SKr10. Open daily 10–5.*

⑩ From Luleå you can take Route 97 north to **Boden,** the nation's largest garrison town, dating from 1809, when Sweden lost Finland to Russia and feared an invasion of its own territory. **Garnisonsmuseet** (the Garrison Museum), contains exhibits from Swedish military history, with an extensive collection of weapons and uniforms. *Garnisonsmuseet, Boden, tel. 0921/62000. Admission: SKr20. Open daily 10–5.*

You can then return through ever wilder and more desolate countryside to Jokkmokk and Kiruna.

Sports and Outdoor Activities

All the regional tourist offices can supply details of skiing holidays, but never forget the extreme temperatures and weather conditions. For the really adventurous, the Kebnekaise mountain station (*see* Tour 2, *above*) offers combined skiing and climbing weeks at SKr3,475. It also offers week-long combined dogsledding, skiing, and climbing holidays on the mountains, which vary in price from SKr3,995 to SKr4,995. Because of the extreme cold and the danger involved, be sure to have proper equipment. Consult the mountain station well in advance for advice (tel. 0980/55042).

Dining and Lodging

The two are often synonymous at these latitudes. Standards of cuisine and service are, unlike prices, not high, but hotels are usually exceptionally clean and staffs scrupulously honest. (For rates, *see* Staying in Sweden in Chapter 1.)

Highly recommended establishments are indicated by a star ★.

Dining Norrland specialties include *surströmming* (fermented herring), *palt* (a stuffed dumpling), *mandelpotatis* (almond-shaped potatoes), and *tunnbröd* (thin bread made from barley flour) eaten with butter, potatoes, and elk meat, or fermented herring. Trout and salmon are common, as are various cuts of elk and reindeer. But to the foreign palate, the most acceptable of Norrland's culinary specialties is undoubtedly *löjröm*, pinkish caviar from a species of Baltic herring, which is eaten with chopped onions and sour cream, and the various desserts made from the cloudberries that thrive here.

Lodging This is limited, but the various local tourist offices can supply details of bed-and-breakfasts and holiday villages equipped with housekeeping cabins. The area is also rich in campsites, though, with the highly unpredictable climate, this may appeal only to the very hardy.

Jokkmokk **Hotel Jokkmokk.** Although located in the center of town, a
Dining and Lodging modern hotel of this level of luxury seems incongruous in this
★ remote region, but welcome nevertheless. The hotel can arrange helicopter trips to the Sarek and Muddus national parks, and there is excellent fishing nearby. *Solgatan 45, S–96 231,*

tel. 0971/11320, fax 0971/11625. 75 rooms. Facilities: restaurant, pool, solarium, sauna, gymnasium, conference rooms. AE, DC, MC, V. Expensive.

Gästis. This small hotel in central Jokkmokk was opened in 1915. *Herrevägen 1, S–96 231, tel. 0971/10012, fax 0971/10012. 30 rooms. Facilities: restaurant, dancing, sauna. AE, DC, MC, V. Moderate.*

Jokkmokks Turistcenter. This complex is prettily situated in a forest area, near a lake, 3 kilometers (2 miles) from the railway station. *Box 75, S–96 222, tel. 0971/12370, fax 0971/12476. 26 rooms, 84 cabins. Facilities: conference rooms, sauna, solarium, 4 outdoor swimming pools, canoe and bicycle rentals. MC, V. Inexpensive.*

Jukkasjärvi
Dining and Lodging
★

Jukkasjärvi Wärdshus och Hembygdsgård. The restaurant specializes in Norrland cuisine and is the lifework of its manager, Yngve Bergqvist. The hotel has four rooms, and there are 45 cabins around it. *Box 24, S–98021, tel. 0980/21190, fax 0980/21406. 4 rooms, 45 cabins, 30 with bath and kitchen. Facilities: restaurant, rooms for the disabled, conference rooms. AE, DC, MC, V. Inexpensive.*

Kebnekaise
Lodging

Kebnekaise Fjällstation. Recently renovated, this rustic, wooden mountain station consists of seven separate buildings. The rooms accommodate 2 to 4 or groups of up to 15, but none has shower or bath. It is 19 kilometers (12 miles) from Nikkaloukta by footpath or by a combination of boat and hiking, or by helicopter. *S–98 129 Kiruna, tel. 0980/55042, fax 0980/55048. (Contact Abisko tourist office off-season, S–98024, Abisko, tel. 0980/4000). 200 beds. Facilities: restaurant, bar, commissary, sauna, guided mountain tours. AE, V. Closed mid-Aug.–mid-Mar. Inexpensive.*

Kiruna
Dining and Lodging

Ferrum. Part of the Reso Hotels chain, this late-1960s-vintage hotel, renovated in 1991, is situated near the railway station. *Lars Janssonsgatan, S–981 31, tel. 0980/18600, fax 0980/14505. 170 rooms with shower. Facilities: 2 restaurants, bar, sauna, solarium. AE, DC, MC, V. Expensive.*

Kebne och Kaisa. These twin modern hotels are close to the railway station and the airport bus stop. *Konduktörsgatan 7, S–98134, tel. 0980/12380, fax 0980/82111. 54 rooms with shower, 2 rooms with kitchenette. Facilities: breakfast, sauna, solarium. AE, DC, MC, V. Moderate.*

Fyra Vindar. This small hotel, dating from 1903, also has the advantage of being close to the railway station. *Bangårdsvägen 9, S–98134, tel. 0980/12050. 18 rooms, not all with bath. Facilities: breakfast. DC, MC, V. Inexpensive.*

STF Vandrarhem. Formerly a hospital for the aged, this modernized, 1926 building now serves as a youth hostel. It faces a large park near the railway station. *Skytegatan 16A, S–127 84, tel. 0980/17195. 35 2-bed–5-bed rooms. Closed mid-Aug.–mid-June. No credit cards. Inexpensive.*

Luleå
Dining and Lodging

Luleå Stads Hotell. This large, centrally located Best Western hotel has nightly, sometimes rowdy dancing. *Storgatan 15, S–972 32, tel. 0920/67000, fax 0920/67092. 135 rooms, 3 suites. Facilities: restaurant, café, discothèque, rooms for the disabled and allergy sufferers, conference rooms, sauna, solarium. AE, DC, MC, V. Expensive.*

SAS Luleå. As you might expect of an SAS hotel, this one is large, modern, and centrally situated. *Storgatan 17, S–972 32, tel. 0920/94000, fax 0920/88222. 212 rooms. Facilities: restau-*

rant, rooms for the disabled and allergy sufferers, conference rooms, nightclub, sauna, swimming pool, solarium. AE, DC, MC, V. Expensive.

Amber. A particularly fine old building houses this hotel close to the railway station. *Stationsgatan 67, S–972 34, tel. 0920/ 10200. 16 rooms. Facilities: restaurant, rooms for allergy sufferers and nonsmokers. AE, DC, MC, V. Moderate.*

Arctic. Right in the center of town, the Arctic is renowned locally for its restaurant. *Sandviksgatan 80, S–972 34, tel. 0920/ 10980. 95 rooms. Facilities: restaurant, rooms for the disabled, conference rooms, sauna. AE, DC, MC, V. Moderate.*

Aveny. This small hotel is close to the railway station. *Hermelinsgatan 10, tel. 0920/221820. 24 rooms. Facilities: rooms for nonsmokers and allergy sufferers, solarium. AE, DC, MC, V. Moderate.*

Scandic. This hotel, located on Lake Sjö, has an extremely pleasant location but is 2 kilometers (1 mile) from the railway station. *Banvägen 3, S–973 46, tel. 0920/28360, fax 0920/69472. 158 rooms. Facilities: restaurant, rooms for the disabled and allergy sufferers, conference rooms, gymnasium, sauna, indoor pool, solarium. AE, DC, MC, V. Moderate.*

Conversion Tables

Distance

Kilometers/Miles To change kilometers to miles, multiply kilometers by .621.
To change miles to kilometers, multiply miles by 1.61.

Km to Mi	Mi to Km
1 = .62	1 = 1.6
2 = 1.2	2 = 3.2
3 = 1.9	3 = 4.8
4 = 2.5	4 = 6.4
5 = 3.1	5 = 8.1
6 = 3.7	6 = 9.7
7 = 4.3	7 = 11.3
8 = 5.0	8 = 12.9
9 = 5.6	9 = 14.5

Meters/Feet To change meters to feet, multiply meters by 3.28.
To change feet to meters, multiply feet by .305.

Meters to Feet	Feet to Meters
1 = 3.3	1 = .31
2 = 6.6	2 = .61
3 = 9.8	3 = .92
4 = 13.1	4 = 1.2
5 = 16.4	5 = 1.5
6 = 19.7	6 = 1.8
7 = 23.0	7 = 2.1
8 = 26.2	8 = 2.4
9 = 29.5	9 = 2.7

Weight

Kilograms/Pounds To change kilograms to pounds, multiply by 2.20.
To change pounds to kilograms, multiply by .453.

Kilo to Pound	Pound to Kilo
1 = 2.2	1 = .45
2 = 4.4	2 = .91
3 = 6.6	3 = 1.4
4 = 8.8	4 = 1.8
5 = 11.0	5 = 2.3

6 = 13.2	6 = 2.7
7 = 15.4	7 = 3.2
8 = 17.6	8 = 3.6
9 = 19.8	9 = 4.1

Grams/Ounces To change grams to ounces, multiply grams by .035.
To change ounces to grams, multiply ounces by 28.4.

Grams to Ounces	Ounces to Grams
1 = .04	1 = 28
2 = .07	2 = 57
3 = .11	3 = 85
4 = .14	4 = 114
5 = .18	5 = 142
6 = .21	6 = 170
7 = .25	7 = 199
8 = .28	8 = 227
9 = .32	9 = 256

Liquid Volume

Liters/U.S. Gallons To change liters to U.S. gallons, multiply liters by .264.
To change U.S. gallons to liters, multiply gallons by 3.79.

Liters to U.S. Gallons	U.S. Gallons to Liters
1 = .26	1 = 3.8
2 = .53	2 = 7.6
3 = .79	3 = 11.4
4 = 1.1	4 = 15.2
5 = 1.3	5 = 19.0
6 = 1.6	6 = 22.7
7 = 1.8	7 = 26.5
8 = 2.1	8 = 30.3
9 = 2.4	9 = 34.1

Swedish Vocabulary

	English	Swedish	Pronunciation
Basics	Yes/no	Ja/nej	yah/nay
	Please	Var snäll; Var vänlig	vahr snehll vahr **vehn**-leeg
	Thank you very much.	Tack så mycket.	tahk soh **mee**-keh
	You're welcome.	Var så god.	vahr shoh **goo**
	Excuse me. (to get by someone)	Ursäkta.	oor-**shehk**-tah
	(to apologize)	Förlåt.	fur-**loht**
	Hello	God dag	goo **dahg**
	Goodbye	Adjö	ah-**yoo**
	Today	I dag	ee **dahg**
	Tomorrow	I Morgon	ee **mohr**-ron
	Yesterday	I går	ee **gohr**
	Morning	Morgon	**mohr**-ron
	Afternoon	Eftermiddag	**ehf**-ter-meed-dahg
	Night	natt	naht
Numbers	One	en	ehn
	Two	tva	tvoh
	Three	tre	tree
	Four	fyra	**fee**-rah
	Five	fem	fem
	Six	sex	sex
	Seven	sju	shoo
	Eight	åtta	**ot**-tah
	Nine	nio	nee
	Ten	tio	tee
Days of the Week	Monday	Måndag	**mohn**-dahg
	Tuesday	Tisdag	**tees**-dahg
	Wednesday	Onsdag	**ohns**-dahg
	Thursday	Torsdag	**tohrs**-dahg
	Friday	Fredag	**freh**-dahg
	Saturday	Lørdag	**luhr**-dahg
	Sunday	Sondag	**sohn**-dahg

Useful Phrases Do you speak English?	Talar ni engelska?	**tah**-lahr nee **ehng**-ehl-skah
I don't speak . . .	Jag talar inte svenska . . .	yah **tah**-lahr **een**-teh **sven**-skah
I don't understand.	Jag förstår inte.	yah fuhr-**stohr** **een**-teh
I don't know.	Jag vet inte.	yah **veht een**-teh
I am American/ British.	Jag är amerikan/ engelsman.	yah ay ah-mehr-ee-**kahn**/ **ehng**-ehls-mahn
I am sick.	Jag är sjuk.	yah ay **shyook**
Please call a doctor.	Jag vill skicka efter en läkare.	yah veel **shee**-kah **ehf**-tehr ehn **lay**-kah-reh
Do you have a vacant room?	Har Ni något rum ledigt?	hahr nee noh-goht **room** **leh**-deekt
How much does it cost?	Vad kostar det?/ Hur mycket kostar det?	vah **kohs**-tahr deh/hoor **mee**-keh **kohs**-tahr deh
It's too expensive.	Den är for dyr.	dehn ay foor **deer**
Beautiful	Vacker	**vah**-kehr
Help!	Hjälp	yehlp
Stop!	Stopp, stanna	stop, **stahn**-nah
How do I get to . . .	Kan Ni visa mig vägen till	kahn nee **vee**-sah may **vay**-gehn teel
. . . the train station?	stationen	stah-**shoh**-nehn
. . . the post office?	posten	**pohs**-tehn
. . . the tourist office?	en resebyrå	ehn-**reh**-seh-**bee**-roh
. . . the hospital?	sjukhuset	**shyook**-hoo-seht
Does this bus go to . . . ?	Går den här bussen till ?	gohr dehn hehr **boo**-sehn teel
Where is the W.C.?	Var är toilett/ toaletten	vahr ay twah-**leht**
On the left	Till vänster	teel **vehn**-stur
On the right	Till höger	teel **huh**-gur
Straight ahead	Rakt fram	rahkt **frahm**

Dining Out

Please bring me . . .	Var snäll och hamta åt mig	vahr snehl oh **hehm**-tah oht may
menu	matsedeln	**maht**-seh-dehln
fork	en gaffel	ehn **gahf**-fehl
knife	en kniv	ehn **kneev**
spoon	en sked	ehn **shehd**
napkin	en servett	ehn sehr-**veht**
bread	brød	bruh(d)
butter	smør	smuhr
milk	mjølk	myoolk
pepper	peppar	**pehp**-pahr
salt	salt	sahlt
sugar	socker	**soh**-kehr
water	vatten	**vaht**-n
The check, please.	Far jag be om notan?	fohr yah beh ohm **noh**-tahn

Index

Personal Itinerary

Departure *Date*

Time

Transportation

Arrival *Date*   *Time*

Departure *Date*   *Time*

Transportation

Accommodations

Arrival *Date*   *Time*

Departure *Date*   *Time*

Transportation

Accommodations

Arrival *Date*   *Time*

Departure *Date*   *Time*

Transportation

Accommodations

Personal Itinerary

Arrival *Date*   *Time*

Departure *Date*   *Time*

Transportation

Accommodations

Arrival *Date*   *Time*

Departure *Date*   *Time*

Transportation

Accommodations

Arrival *Date*   *Time*

Departure *Date*   *Time*

Transportation

Accommodations

Arrival *Date*   *Time*

Departure *Date*   *Time*

Transportation

Accommodations

Personal Itinerary

Arrival *Date*   *Time*

Departure *Date*   *Time*

Transportation

Accommodations

Arrival *Date*   *Time*

Departure *Date*   *Time*

Transportation

Accommodations

Arrival *Date*   *Time*

Departure *Date*   *Time*

Transportation

Accommodations

Arrival *Date*   *Time*

Departure *Date*   *Time*

Transportation

Accommodations

Personal Itinerary

Arrival *Date*   *Time*

Departure *Date*   *Time*

Transportation

Accommodations

Arrival *Date*   *Time*

Departure *Date*   *Time*

Transportation

Accommodations

Arrival *Date*   *Time*

Departure *Date*   *Time*

Transportation

Accommodations

Arrival *Date*   *Time*

Departure *Date*   *Time*

Transportation

Accommodations

Addresses

Name

Address

Telephone

Name

Address

Telephone

Name

Address

Telephone

Name

Address

Telephone

Name

Address

Telephone

Name

Address

Telephone

Name

Address

Telephone

Name

Address

Telephone

Name

Address

Telephone

Name

Address

Telephone

Name

Address

Telephone

Name

Address

Telephone

Name

Address

Telephone

Name

Address

Telephone

Name

Address

Telephone

Name

Address

Telephone

Addresses

Name	*Name*
Address	*Address*
Telephone	*Telephone*
Name	*Name*
Address	*Address*
Telephone	*Telephone*
Name	*Name*
Address	*Address*
Telephone	*Telephone*
Name	*Name*
Address	*Address*
Telephone	*Telephone*
Name	*Name*
Address	*Address*
Telephone	*Telephone*
Name	*Name*
Address	*Address*
Telephone	*Telephone*
Name	*Name*
Address	*Address*
Telephone	*Telephone*

Fodor's Travel Guides

Available at bookstores everywhere, or call 1–800–533–6478, 24 hours a day.

U.S. Guides

Alaska

Arizona

Boston

California

Cape Cod, Martha's
Vineyard, Nantucket

The Carolinas & the
Georgia Coast

Chicago

Colorado

Florida

Hawaii

Las Vegas, Reno,
Tahoe

Los Angeles

Maine, Vermont,
New Hampshire

Maui

Miami & the Keys

New England

New Orleans

New York City

Pacific North Coast

Philadelphia & the
Pennsylvania Dutch
Country

The Rockies

San Diego

San Francisco

Santa Fe, Taos,
Albuquerque

Seattle & Vancouver

The South

The U.S. & British
Virgin Islands

The Upper Great
Lakes Region

USA

Vacations in New York
State

Vacations on the
Jersey Shore

Virginia & Maryland

Waikiki

Walt Disney World
and the Orlando Area

Washington, D.C.

Foreign Guides

Acapulco, Ixtapa,
Zihuatanejo

Australia & New
Zealand

Austria

The Bahamas

Baja & Mexico's
Pacific Coast Resorts

Barbados

Berlin

Bermuda

Brazil

Brittany & Normandy

Budapest

Canada

Cancun, Cozumel,
Yucatan Peninsula

Caribbean

China

Costa Rica, Belize,
Guatemala

The Czech Republic
& Slovakia

Eastern Europe

Egypt

Euro Disney

Europe

Europe's Great Cities

Florence & Tuscany

France

Germany

Great Britain

Greece

The Himalayan
Countries

Hong Kong

India

Ireland

Israel

Italy

Japan

Kenya & Tanzania

Korea

London

Madrid & Barcelona

Mexico

Montreal &
Quebec City

Morocco

Moscow &
St. Petersburg

The Netherlands,
Belgium &
Luxembourg

New Zealand

Norway

Nova Scotia, Prince
Edward Island &
New Brunswick

Paris

Portugal

Provence & the
Riviera

Rome

Russia & the Baltic
Countries

Scandinavia

Scotland

Singapore

South America

Southeast Asia

Spain

Sweden

Switzerland

Thailand

Tokyo

Toronto

Turkey

Vienna & the Danube
Valley

Yugoslavia

Special Series

Fodor's Affordables

Caribbean

Europe

Florida

France

Germany

Great Britain

London

Italy

Paris

Fodor's Bed & Breakfast and Country Inns Guides

Canada's Great Country Inns

California

Cottages, B&Bs and Country Inns of England and Wales

Mid-Atlantic Region

New England

The Pacific Northwest

The South

The Southwest

The Upper Great Lakes Region

The West Coast

The Berkeley Guides

California

Central America

Eastern Europe

France

Germany

Great Britain & Ireland

Mexico

Pacific Northwest & Alaska

San Francisco

Fodor's Exploring Guides

Australia

Britain

California

The Caribbean

Florida

France

Germany

Ireland

Italy

London

New York City

Paris

Rome

Singapore & Malaysia

Spain

Thailand

Fodor's Flashmaps

New York

Washington, D.C.

Fodor's Pocket Guides

Bahamas

Barbados

Jamaica

London

New York City

Paris

Puerto Rico

San Francisco

Washington, D.C.

Fodor's Sports

Cycling

Hiking

Running

Sailing

The Insider's Guide to the Best Canadian Skiing

Skiing in the USA & Canada

Fodor's Three-In-Ones (guidebook, language cassette, and phrase book)

France

Germany

Italy

Mexico

Spain

Fodor's Special-Interest Guides

Accessible USA

Cruises and Ports of Call

Euro Disney

Halliday's New England Food Explorer

Healthy Escapes

London Companion

Shadow Traffic's New York Shortcuts and Traffic Tips

Sunday in New York

Walt Disney World and the Orlando Area

Walt Disney World for Adults

Fodor's Touring Guides

Touring Europe

Touring USA: Eastern Edition

Fodor's Vacation Planners

Great American Vacations

National Parks of the East

National Parks of the West

The Wall Street Journal Guides to Business Travel

Europe

International Cities

Pacific Rim

USA & Canada

WHEREVER YOU TRAVEL, *H*ELP IS NEVER FAR AWAY.

From planning your trip to providing travel assistance along the way, American Express® Travel Service Offices* are always there to help.

© 1994 American Express Travel Related Services Company, Inc.

*Comprises Travel Service locations of American Express Travel Related Services Company, Inc., its affiliates and Representatives worldwide.

Sweden

GÖTEBORG
American Express Travel Financial Services
Ostra Hamngatan 35
46-31-130712

MALMÖ
Nyman & Schultz
Kattsundsgatan 7
46-40-75200

STOCKHOLM
American Express Travel Service
Birger Jarlsgatan 1
46-8-6795200